# Ways
## in
# Mystery

# Ways in Mystery

## Explorations in Mystical Awareness and Life

### Luther Askeland

WHITE CLOUD PRESS
ASHLAND, OREGON

Printed in the Canada

99 98 97          5 4 3 2 1

Photo credits:
Cover photgraph by J Tove Johansson / Masterfile
Backcover photograph of Luther Askeland by Craig Daniels

Cover design by Impact Graphics

LIBRARY OF CONGRESS CATALOGING-IN-PUBLICATION DATA

Askeland, Luther, 1941-
    Ways in mystery : explorations in mystical awareness and life / by
Luther Askeland.
        p.     cm.
    Includes bibliographical references.
    ISBN 1-883991-16-1
    1. Mysticism.  1. Title.
BL625.A85   1997
291.4'22--DC20                                    96-46096
                                                    CIP

# TABLE OF CONTENTS

# PREFACE

With one exception, the following essays appear in the chronological order of their composition. The later ones proceed from perspectives, experiences, and moments of awareness that earlier essays arrived at and treated in greater detail. This is a possible reason for reading them in sequence.

The Epilogue was written just in connection with the publication of these essays in the form of this book, and just as easily could be called a Preface. But since it is the most recent piece—and so builds just like the other later essays on earlier ones—it appears at the end rather than the beginning.

# ABBREVIATIONS

*AB*    Eckhart, Meister. "Von Abgeschiedenheit." In *Die deutschen Werke*, vol. 5. Edited by J. Quint. Stuttgart: Die Deutsche Forschungsgemeinschaft, 1963.

*CU*    *The Cloud of Unknowing and Other Works* (includes translation of Dionysius' *Mystical Theology*). Hammondsworth, England: Penguin Books, 1961.

*CW*    Saint John of the Cross. *Collected Works of St. John of the Cross*. Washington, DC: ICS Publications, 1979.

*DNS*    Saint John of the Cross. *Dark Night of the Soul*. New York: Image Books, 1959.

*DPT*    Eckhart, Meister. *Deutsche Predigten und Traktate*. Munich: Carl Hanser Verlag, 1963.

# PART I
# THE WAY OF UNKNOWING

# THE WAY OF UNKNOWING

Not *how* the world is, is the mystical, but *that* it is.
—Ludwig Wittgenstein

## PART I: A WAY INTO MYSTERY

"WHY DOES THE WORLD EXIST?" "How am
I to account for the existence of this vast universe and so at least begin to account for my own?" Strangely, we seldom put this question
to ourselves, and even more infrequently, if at all, do we discuss or
even mention it during our times together with one another. Later I
will suggest why this is so. But first I want to point out one important
feature of the question itself. I believe an understanding of it will help
us win a clearer view of one of the mystic's ways into mystery.

Whenever we try to account for the existence of someone or something, we do so by referring to some other being. I would begin to explain my own existence, for example, by referring to my parents. We
account for the snow on the ground in terms of air, humidity, the air's
temperature, and other meteorological phenomena. In general, our
explanations of the existence of any B tend to be of the form A creates
B; A makes B out of C; or A, under certain circumstances, becomes
B. On the other hand, such statements as "B is just there" or "B created itself" seem to us to explain nothing at all.

We note, then, that our explanations of the existence of things involve the prior existence of other things. Since there were other things, however, there clearly must already have been a "world." This means that when we ask for an explanation of the existence of A, we are assuming that the world existed before A did and that certain events within that world led to A's existence. But if we are looking for an explanation of the world's existence, we obviously cannot make that assumption.

It is becoming evident that the question "Why does the world exist?" is radically different from the question "Why does A exist?" The latter question assumes that something that is not A and that existed before A led to A. But what existed before the world? Only "nothingness." The latter question wants to find the something that leads to something else. The former asks how we get from nothing to something. In paradoxical and self-contradictory fashion, it begins to search within non-being for that *something* that will enable us to understand why the world exists. It is looking for something in a place where it is simultaneously assuming there is nothing at all.

It is important to note that if we explain the world's existence by reference to a divine Creator, we are only postponing and complicating the dilemma. For then we can account for why the world exists, but how are we to account for the fact that God does? And if we find it difficult simply to think coherently about the world's existence against the backdrop of nothingness, it will be much more difficult to think about and explain God's. I believe there is only one line of reasoning the intellect can pursue to work its way through this tangle to apparent clarity, and that is to assert that God's existence is necessary. If we could succeed with this argument, known traditionally as the ontological argument, we would then have demonstrated that God *must* exist, and so we could account for God's existence, and consequently the world's.[1] But few today accept any form of the ontological argument—and not many are prepared to assert that the intellect can prove God's existence to be necessary. And if for most of us God's existence is not necessary, how, then, are we going to explain it? We may believe that God exists, and we may even be convinced that the world's

---

1. The argument begins with an analysis of the characteristics a perfect being would have. One of them is existence. It is then said to follow that a perfect being must, therefore, exist.

existence means that there must be a Creator. But none of that is to the point here. The question here is not whether God exists. Rather, even assuming *that* God exists, the question here is how this is possible. How do gods "happen"? How are we to explain the fact that there is an eternal God instead of no eternal God? Further, along what lines might we even try to imagine a *conceivable* answer? If we again postulate a prior being or higher divinity, we are only postponing the dilemma once more. But if we don't posit another being—if we posit nothingness as the alternative—we find ourselves once again hopelessly looking for some kind of explanation or cause within that very nothingness.

By way of summing up what I have suggested so far, let me say that we are faced by a central fact—the existence of the world—and that in our minds this world may or may not include a personal God who has created everything else. It is natural that we should want to understand this fact, but when our intellect attempts to account for it, it is quickly reduced to confusion and soon realizes that it is far beyond its depth. It is not only that our intellect cannot determine the correct answer, as, for instance, it cannot know the last thought that went through Socrates' mind. Rather, our questioning itself soon becomes problematic, for we discover that our question no longer has its usual meaning. Instead, we are now asking how it can be that there is something instead of nothing, or a God instead of no God. The intellect may cast about within nothingness for the hint of an answer, but it cannot say what kind of hint it hopes to find. Apparently we have raised a question that has no possible, plausible, or even conceivable answer. All the intellect can do is repeat the question, "Why does the world exist?" while recognizing that nothing coherent accompanies the sound and that no toehold seems possible anywhere. What we and our intellects have run up against is the absolutely unique, irreducible, impenetrable, astonishing fact of being. The central fact of existence, the wholly unintelligible fact *that* the world is, that, we can now say with Wittgenstein, is "the mystical."

Our intuitions of the mystery of God's being or of the world's being are unpredictable, elusive, and by no means subject to our control. They are not so much awareness as fragmentary premonitions of awareness, premonitions which, if only for a moment, open avenues that recede into the unlimited. In themselves these intuitions are private and, as I said at the beginning of this chapter, they tend to remain private. Generally speaking, they remain on the shadowy fringes even of the individual's private world. Consequently, they tend not to be integrated within the individual's conscious, structured life, not to speak of our shared social and public life. In spite of this, I believe it is possible to detect differing individual responses, or refusals to respond, to the mystical. I shall mention three: those of the philosopher, of "most of us," and of the mystic.

Ludwig Wittgenstein's definition of the mystical, which opens this chapter, is from his *Tractatus Logico-Philosophicus*, which first appeared in 1921. Here are some of his additional comments on the mystical and on the philosophically correct response to questions and assertions about it:

6.522  There is indeed the inexpressible. This *shows* itself; it is the mystical.

6.53  The right method of philosophy would be this. To say nothing except what can be said, i.e., the propositions of natural science, i.e., something that has nothing to do with philosophy: and then always, when someone else wished to say something metaphysical, to demonstrate to him that he had given no meaning to certain signs in his propositions (Wittgenstein 1922, 187-89).

We see here that Wittgenstein (unlike many who were strongly influenced by him) at least allots a place to the mystical. According to him, the mystical "exists" and "shows itself." But he quickly proceeds to draw a line around the mystical so as to prevent any contact between it and philosophy. For Wittgenstein, the task of philosophy is to sort out meaningful from meaningless questions so that we can work on solving the former and waste no time on the latter. "Why does the world exist?" is a "metaphysical" question. The only task the philosopher has in relation to this question is to steer the philosophically naive away from it by showing that it, in fact, makes no sense.

While admitting that the mystical exists, Wittgenstein nevertheless contributes to a demystification of the world by turning our attention from it to the affairs of the intellect, for his approach excludes the mystical from intellectual and philosophical endeavor. When the intellect flounders in the face of mystery, Wittgenstein rescues and then relegitimates the intellect by banishing mystery. His response to the mystical prefigures that of many twentieth-century philosophers and intellectuals. Questions such as this about the world's existence are meaningless, since those who raise them can give no coherent account of what they are seeking. On the other hand, the world is full of questions with real content and verifiable answers, and the various sciences various sciences are the instruments we have for answering those questions.

The philosopher, then, confronts a choice between intellect and mystery and chooses in favor of the intellect. The choice faced by most of us, however, is between mystery and action. Nevertheless, our choice tends to correspond to that of the philosopher, for like the philosopher we prefer to pass quickly by the unanswerable question of existence. Our line of reasoning goes like this: "Obviously, we cannot get anywhere thinking about questions like this, so why do it? I want to get back to my real life, to my job, my family, my recreations, etc."

This response often has an added modulation, one that clearly diverges from the philosopher's response. Since the rest of us do not have the intellectual sophistication of the philosopher, it does not occur to us that we might be able to dissolve the question "Why does the world exist?" as meaningless. Instead, the question strikes us as real and even as important in a disturbing way, but since it interferes with life and action, we experience it primarily as troublesome, an aggravation. The standard solution to this predicament can be seen in the widespread tendency to accept any proposed explanation of the world that has some currency, no matter how superficial that explanation may reveal itself to be upon brief inspection. While the philosopher dissolves the question of existence, the rest of us make believe we have solved it.

Traditionally, God has been accepted as the explanation—even though, as we have seen, that is no explanation at all. An "explanation" often taken seriously today is the so-called *big-bang theory* of the origin of the universe. A moment's reflection reveals that this hypothesis, too, only postpones the dilemma,. If we accept this theory, we then must explain how that very dense mass of "matter" came to be. That moment will reveal, further, that, far from being the origin of the universe, big bangs may be no more than one kind of millions of kinds of infinitely varied happenings within the complete history of things. But most of us circle around past this moment of reflection. We want to act, to "live," and it is much easier to do this if we can believe we have the answers, no matter how superficial those answers may be.

The third response, that of the mystic, initially resembles the philosopher's. Like the philosopher, the mystic notes that there are problems with the question "How can we account for the world's existence, or for God's?" The mystic, too, soon sees that this is not the usual "Why?" question, for the mystic also sees that we are not asking for an A that creates or becomes B, but instead are asking how it is possible to proceed from nothing to something. The mystic agrees that we don't know what a possible answer might be like, so that, consequently, it must be admitted that we don't know what we are asking. We cannot even explain the *question*. But whereas the philosopher then matter-of-factly decides to move on to questions that presumably *do* make sense and have answers, the mystic cannot move; for to the mystic, it seems that something of great significance has just happened and that its ramifications are not at first readily apparent. The mystic cannot simply walk away from this remarkable turn of events, this sudden and complete failure of the intellect in the face of the world's existence. Consequently, the mystic continues to attend to the now even more mysterious fact of existence, even though speechlessness may seem to be the only possible response at first. Having discovered that the intellect is completely out of its depth when faced with the most intimate and basic of all facts, why should we go on calmly cultivating the intellect? To the mystic, it only makes sense to remain at this remarkable scene, even though at first he or she may be entirely at a loss for both words and actions.

We see here the parting of the ways not only between the mystic and the philosopher, but also between the life of contemplation and the life of action. To participate comfortably and energetically in the world of action, most of us are helped by believing that we know what we are doing and why we are doing it. The active life is much easier if we have the world mapped out conceptually and if we can account for ourselves and our actions with words. As we have seen, our mappings and explanations do not have to withstand scrutiny—we don't intend to do much scrutinizing. We just want a rationale; almost any will do, so long as it enables us to go on feigning that we know and can put into words who and where we are and what we are doing.

I mentioned at the beginning that we seldom raise the question "Why does the world exist?" and we have now seen why this is so. It is the kind of question we don't want out on the table. We just want to see it settled, or to pretend that it is settled, because unanswered questions and mystery cloud the life of action. The mystic, on the other hand, does not approach the facts with this demand. The profoundest bent within the mystic is toward awareness and contemplation, not action, and so for the mystic there is no pragmatic requirement that the world be verbally and conceptually mapped and all answers given. Within the mystic there is no need to subscribe to the first somewhat plausible rationale that comes along. This means that the mystic can be more objective about the "Why?" of the world than the rest of us— there are no external requirements inducing the mystic to turn from or conceal the central dilemma. And so, as contrasted with the philosopher and the rest of us, we can define the mystic as seen up to this point as follows. The mystic is someone who recognizes that the central fact or datum—the existence of the world, of God, or of God and world—transcends our intellect. By way of asking why the world exists, the mystic has discovered that we are part of a reality that our intellect cannot grasp or even properly question. The world has revealed itself to be mystery, or God has been revealed as mystery. Hereafter the mystic's attention will remain fixed on that mystery.

That mystery is not just an intellectual mystery, a question mark. If it were, the mystic might well fall into despair. Instead, in the wake of the intellect's dissolution, the mystic is given another sense of things, a new form of awareness. For the mystic now sees (or at least glimpses) a dimension of reality to which he or she had been blind so long as reality was mediated by words and concepts. The experience is like the moment of arrival at the summit of a ridge from which one unexpectedly discovers a vast, unknown landscape, one shining in the sun or shrouded in haze and clouds. It is a new world first seen only after the blindfold of the intellect is removed. It is a discovery of the previously unsuspected depth of the world, or of God, for it is only when the constraints of language are removed that we begin to intuit the infinitude of the world, or of God, realities immeasurable beyond human words and definitions.

I HAVE CALLED THIS ESSAY "A WAY INTO MYSTERY" because what I de-scribe here is only one way out of many. It would be a mistake to take all that I have said here about the philosopher and the rest of us as true of all philosophers and of all of us, and it would be just as erro-neous to suppose that all mystics do or should follow one way. Mys-ticism is the attempt by millions of men and women throughout history to become more intimate with and to stand more fully in the pres-ence of the sacred, whether conceived personally or impersonally. I am not drawing any lines around that attempt. Those who, instead of practicing contemplation, can experience and touch the sacred while coming to the aid of fellow human beings or placing seeds in the ground are certainly on a "mystic way."

The way I describe here belongs more to the way of reflection than to the ways of devotion or action. It is more the way of Meister Eckhart than of St. Teresa or Mother Teresa—or, to take some examples from the religion of India, of Śankara rather than of Rāmānuja or Gandhi. Yet it shares with them and in fact clearly illustrates the underlying direction of all mysticism. Practitioners of the way of mystical reflec-tion share, first of all, a movement in toward what is perceived as the basic, the absolutely fundamental, a movement that then is necessar-ily a turning away from all forms of expansion of the individual self in terms of power or its vicarious expansion by the acquisition of things. The movement is one of the surrender of everything extraneous, the diminution of the self to that center which is also the center of all things. What is sought is intimacy, direct knowledge, the sense of an imme-diate presence of the sacred which seizes the whole person. Whether known to the mystic as God, the One, *nirvāna*, Vishnu, the signless, mystery, or the God beyond God, the mystic finds in that center a fullness and sustenance he or she cannot find anywhere else.

What I describe here, then, is just one way out of many. It is, more-over, only the beginning of that way, nothing more than a few steps. Even though in this respect, too, I have described just one part and not the whole, these few steps can reveal much to us about the entire path. On the analogy with life conceived as a progress or an accumu-lation, we may suppose that the mystic quickly incorporates what I have described here and then moves farther along the mystic way. In fact, however, the mystic now has arrived at the limits of our capac-ity, the farthest inner frontier. Instead of "advancing," it is much more likely that the mystic will lose the mystical and then return to it again

by retracing the steps described here. As the cycle of loss and rediscovery repeats itself, the mystic does not move beyond mystery, but
what is possible is that a deepening will take place, a growth that comes
from dwelling in this one place. The movement then is in one respect
a mirror of the entire way, for that way is not one of linear progress,
but of repetition, abiding and deepening.

I prefaced this chapter with a quote from Ludwig Wittgenstein,
and much of what I have said here could be described as an elabora-
tion of his tersely oracular utterance. This is because there is a critical point at which the philosopher's path and the path I have described
merge. That point of union is the discovery that the world's existence
is unintelligible, a mystery we cannot penetrate.

As we have seen, the two paths quickly separate. Wittgenstein immediately draws a line between the activities of the philosopher and
those of the mystic. He and those who have followed him seek to cure
us of "metaphysics," including the impulse to inquire into the mystical, so that we can get on with something that makes sense: the pursuit of natural science. For must of us this "something that makes sense"
is much less cerebral. The reason we bracket the mystical is so that we
can get on with the jobs, relationships, amusements, and acquisitions
that we make the center of our lives.

From the point of view of the philosopher and of the rest of us,
then, there is something irrational, backward, and wayward about the
mystic. From the philosopher's point of view, the mystic is someone
who has strayed into a life of preoccupation with senseless questions,
one who therefore resembles, to use an image from another of Wittgenstein's works, a fly buzzing about in a bottle. From the point of view
of the rest of us, busy as we are getting on with our lives, the mystic is
stuck back there at the mystical; for though there may be talk of ways
and paths, the mystic, as we have seen, remains enthralled by and never
will get beyond the mystical. Corresponding to the philosopher's ideal
of progress in knowledge, we have an ideal of the individual's progress
through time in the world of action, one that involves the successful
"making" of a life of rounded wholeness. In our society that ideal revolves around career, family life, and reputation, together with the social
connections, possessions, and experiences that are required in order
to live this life in the proper style. The creation of such a life for ourselves, and of the completed and satisfied self that we hope will emerge
from it, is a matter of great urgency to us, the main business of life.

As a result, it is impossible for us to understand why the mystic continues to linger back there at the mystical with no apparent intention of achieving anything else.

The mystic sees things differently, of course, though he or she certainly shares our sense of urgency. As much as anyone else, in fact, the mystic is inclined to stress the critical importance of this life, a life that absolutely must not be trivialized. It is for precisely this reason, in fact, that the mystic finds the behavior of the rest of us so puzzling, for to the mystic we seem to stroll past the mystical so casually and inattentively. So puzzling is this, in fact, that it occurs to the mystic that some of our easy serenity might be feigned. For what could be more significant than the discovery that the reality of the world or the reality of God is entirely beyond our grasp, something impervious to our questioning. And once this has been discovered, how can we avoid circling round and coming back to this central mystery? On the other hand, what could be more paradoxical than the unseeing, unquestioning complacency with which most of us pass through existence, an existence we do not comprehend? What is more peculiar than the pretense that surprise would be in order only if there were no world at all, or one entirely different from this one? What is more inexplicable than the impression we give, glancing matter-of-factly out at the world from our daily rounds, that it is all, in fact, clear and self-evident, precisely what one would expect?

Such considerations suggest that the mystic is in fact more rational than the philosopher and more in touch with reality than the rest of us. The philosopher aspires to an ordered system of human knowledge, and the rest of us pursue the ideal of a full and complete human life. To the mystic these ideals are naïve, the play of children, for to the mystic a human life is a few moments within mystery, an infinity we cannot begin to grasp, much less organize. The philosopher sides with the intellect, and the rest of us hold to our conviction that "we know where we are." But the intellect fails when confronted by the most basic fact of all, the one fact that makes possible all other facts. How can it make sense, then, to turn away from mystery and return to the intellect? As for our routinized sense of the world's familiarity, it is only a state of mind that facilitates action. The daily round of choice, planning, and activity depends on the self-evident world that our words and intellect create. Our sense that we know where we are is an adaptation, an illusion life requires. The mystic in all of us occasionally glimpses a world beyond that illusion.

## Part II: A Form of Mystical Life

IN THE COURSE OF THE MYSTIC'S DISCOVERY of mystery, his or her intellect yields to a new form of awareness, one that dwells wordlessly on the mystical. This discovery of new, unlimited territory restores to the mystic the child's joyful knowledge that reality is inexhaustible and so begins to suggest a fullness of future endeavor and possibility. What has happened has been a kind of rebirth. For the moment, at least, the mystic has died to the finite, defined world of words and concepts and been reborn in the unlimited. Here, then, is a new world and new life for the mystic to explore, an Infinitude, in fact, to which one life cannot begin to do justice. The discovery of a way into this Infinitude, one that will extend and deepen the awareness already won, becomes the central aim of the mystic's life.

Just how is this deepening achieved? And what is the nature and content of this new form of life? How, moreover, can we observe these phenomena in the various mystical traditions that have been passed down to us? For what I have attempted to suggest so far—the discovery of the mystical—is an elusive inner movement that is alien to words and public life. What I will describe now, on the other hand, exists at the point where the mystical life emerges into the observable world and into history. I call this particular form of mystical life (which, I repeat, is only one way of many) the way of unknowing.

In trying to understand this way it is important to note, first, that the mystic always will remain a novice, a fledgling pioneer on the fringes of this new land. Traditions of saints, holy men, and enlightened masters can be inspiring as ideals, but they also can be misleading and destructive if they are perceived as realistic models for immediate imitation. Inevitably there is an element of wishful thinking in many accounts of mystical lives and heroes—their relation to the actuality of mystical life is like that of love poetry and college catalogs to marital and academic life. The authentic personal documents of saints and masters that we do have tend to convey a different and much more complex awareness of the writer's own humanness and of the frailty and limitations that necessarily inhere in that humanness. Only as they are seen by others, and especially as they recede into the past, do piety and aspiration transform these same figures into perfect saints and fully enlightened masters.

The various traditions also hand down images of an orderly linear progression toward perfection: for example the ascent of Mt. Carmel in St. John of the Cross, or the Ten Oxherding Pictures in Zen. These show us the "logic" of mystical development, a progression from the initial setting out on the path to its hypothetical completion. As twentieth-century Westerners, we are especially prone to misinterpret these images, for whatever we may set out to master or change in ourselves, we assume that it can certainly be achieved within one lifetime, and perhaps within months or even weeks. We must be careful, then, not to deceive ourselves, for those "maps" which chart a steady progress to personal completion do not mirror the mystic's actual experience in time. Much of what I say in the rest of this essay will bear this out. For now, I would like to suggest a more accurate picture of actual contemplative experience by referring to a universal characteristic of all traditions and a specific image from one.

The universal characteristic is the constant return in the literature of contemplation to the most basic admonitions on character and conduct: Do not be arrogant, envious, idle, or lustful; do not seek wealth, fame, or even a good name; pay no heed to the desires of the finite self. This unending stream of exhortation reveals that human beings never entirely overcome these impulses. There will be no magical transformation into "someone else," no exotic disappearance in the distances of the new world. Instead, the mystical life will always have as one of its central elements the perfectly ordinary struggle with selfishness, idleness, hatred, and desire.

The specific image, the Indian conception of reincarnation, pictures for us very graphically a path full of reversals and detours that promises at best a painfully slow progress toward liberation. Christians have often expected an imminent, radical transformation of the entire world, the Kingdom; where this belief is missing there usually remains a private version of it, an expectation of achieving individual perfection not long after the end of this one brief life, at the latest. We should balance this optimistic expectation, one of complete transformation in the not-very-distant future, with the picture of the soul's progress as seen from the Indian vantage point. From that perspective, the path to perfection is all but endless, embracing countless existences over a span of time that will include the creation and destruction of successive universes without number. Within this vastly different framework of time and personal history, it is brought home to us that, from one short lifetime, itself only a minuscule segment of the series to which it belongs, a few halting steps toward the goal would be a realistic aspiration. The dream of a sudden, dramatic change from our present condition, on the other hand, is manifestly out of place, a naïve expectation that has yet to see the scope and awesome difficulty of the task.

Born into this "present life" as a human being, the mystic remains just such a human being throughout this life. And though I distinguished earlier between the mystic, the philosopher, and the rest of us, it is important to remember that we are all more alike than different. The mystic is and always will be, then, more human than enlightened—a human being who has only glimpsed the mystical, a novice in the place of mystery. This perpetual beginner status has important implications for what happens following the collapse of the intellect and the resulting commitment to mystery. For it soon becomes clear that the general limitations I have described apply with full force to the relationship between mystic and intellect. Initially the mystic may expect to leave the intellect behind and disappear quickly into the beckoning far reaches of the wordless, but the intellect does not concede or accept abandonment readily. For just as it is impossible to rid oneself overnight of envy, arrogance, and so on, it is equally impossible to quickly pass beyond the intellect. The mystic, who for a moment is ecstatically out of the human condition, soon returns to it. Included therein is a return to the intellect, which now seeks to reassert its legitimacy. The mystical side of the mystic now has good reason, however, to question that legitimacy. This tension between the mystic and the intellect, a tension that never will be resolved, produces those developments that further determine the form of mystical life on the way of unknowing. Let us first consider two of them: 1) the apparent further spread of the intellect's failure, and 2) the continuing and inescapable presence, nevertheless, of the intellect.

The mystic and the philosopher, as represented by Wittgenstein, already have agreed that the fact *that* the world is, is mystical. Wittgenstein contrasts the *that* of the world with the *how* of the world, by which he means how the constituent elements interrelate, and this *how* is then to be described by the physical sciences. But, we might ask, aren't we leaving out the *what* of the world? Just where are we? What is the nature of this place in which we find ourselves? Do we have a conception of *what* the world is?

We can approach a preliminary answer by noting that the intellect characteristically seeks to understand the nature or *whatness* of things in terms of duality and contrast. We delimit and consequently comprehend the categories of the animal, vegetable, and mineral by means of their reciprocal differences. Without the word *light, darkness* would have no meaning. Of the twin concepts of the personal and the impersonal, it is possible to have *both* or *neither*, but it is *not* possible to have just one. Our understanding of the whatness of things is based, then, on duality, but the world has no contrasting opposite. The world—which we may conceive as including no god, one god, or many gods—is simply "all that exists," and, as we have already seen, that word *exists* contains nothing but mystery. The fact that we say the word *world* so easily suggests to us that we know what the world is. It helps create that illusion of familiarity, the conviction that we know where we are. It enables us to avoid the perception that to contemplate the vastness of place and time is to contemplate the incomparable. For an immediate awareness of this mysteriously existent world is also an awareness of absolute singularity; this in turn suggests that we can no more define the world than we can explain its existence.

The philosopher recognizes the mystical, but then attempts to confine it within a clearly demarcated area outside the philosopher's area of interest and activity. The mystic, on the other hand, contemplates with delight the spread of mystery through all of being. Within the various traditions; the nature of the world or of God has been just as much a place of mystery as their existence. For example, a central movement of thought within Christian mysticism begins with reflection on the orthodox concept of God as a perfect being. It notes that all the terms we can use to illustrate or explain God's perfection originate in our very imperfect senses and understanding. Surely God's knowledge and goodness, for instance, are infinitely beyond and so wholly different from what we can imagine of knowledge and goodness. Consequently, it is not illuminating but actually misleading to describe God as good, all-powerful, all-knowing, or even as a perfect being. The intellect has cancelled itself out once again, this time in relation to whatness, for it now appears that the nature of God, as well as God's existence, transcends human understanding.

The historical development of Buddhism reveals a similar movement of thought on a grand scale, one applied not specifically to God's nature but to the nature of the entire world. Within early, or Hīnayāna, Buddhism, everything in the world, all "conditioned things," can be described in terms of three basic qualities: These three "marks" are impermanence, involvement with pain, and absence of a self. Here is a world, then, the nature of which can be understood or stated. But with the emergence of Mahāyāna Buddhism, all knowledge about the whatness of the world disintegrates. The world (*samsāra*) and all things (*dharmas*) within it can only be seen as "empty." The three marks no longer apply; in fact, there are no longer any "marks" or "signs" that apply. The leading Mahāyāna texts assert that nothing can be said concerning either the existence or the nature of the world, not even that it exists or that it is the world.

The mystic's ongoing reflection on the intellect results in a growing sense of the intellect's failure, its incapacity to reveal to us the nature of the world or to explain its existence. Simultaneously, however, the mystic is discovering that the intellect cannot be swept aside easily, if at all. To recognize in reflection the inadequacy of the intellect and its words and dualities is one thing. To live without making use of this discredited faculty is a different matter altogether.

The reasons why this is so derive from the continuing humanness of the mystic, the fact that the mystic will not and cannot simply vanish into mystery's signless and inhuman landscape. For with its complex structure of words, concepts, and categories, the intellect is an integral part of the mystic's humanness. Just how deeply rooted the intellect is becomes apparent when we observe the powerful, largely unconscious ways in which it shapes our perceptions of the world. Creatures of language that we are, we automatically assume, for instance, that we have learned something essential about people or things when we have learned only their names. Equally unconscious and powerful is the assumption that all our linguistic opposites mirror objective dichotomies. Just as we ordinarily regard colors as inhering in things, so we assume, for example, that the world resolves itself unproblematically into the personal and the impersonal, and that our own experience divides itself just as unproblematically into the clear, distinct categories of reality and dream.

It is not only a question of powerful unconscious influences, however. There are terms and categories the mystic may be reluctant to give up or even to question, notions that seem profoundly human in the best sense of the word. In Luke 14:26, Christ asserts that someone who wishes to be his disciple must hate father and mother, wife and children. The mystic on the way of unknowing is asked to give up these very terms, to abandon the concepts of these elemental human bonds. Who but an inhuman fanatic would want to deny the world of fathers and mothers, of husbands, wives, and children? We note, finally, that the mystic remains a human being living in the shared physical world of people and things, and it is utterly impossible to make one's way through this world without using the words, distinctions, and categories of the intellect. Walking over to the neighbors, preparing a meal, dressing ourselves—reflection reveals that we could do none of these things, or any of hundreds of other things we do in our daily rounds, without being and having been creatures of language.

Since we observed the initial collapse of the intellect and the discovery of the mystical *thatness* of the world, the mystic's situation has been invaded by complexity and tension. On one hand, the sense of the intellect's impotence has persisted and even spread to the whatness of God or world. Increasingly it seems that the intellect poisons the contemplative meeting between self and reality and so must be eliminated. On the other hand, it appears that both human nature and the circumstances of human life make it inevitable that the mystic will continue to employ the maps drawn by the intellect. There have been moments of vision, passing intuitions of the great splendor of the unlimited, but now the mystic is experiencing once again the contradictions that inhere in human life.

For this dilemma in the mystic's relations with the intellect there is a philosophical "solution." In varying ways the traditions distinguish between absolute and relative truth, just as they distinguish between the world of the absolute and the world of appearances or between being and flux. This distinction makes it possible to say that the intellect has a legitimate function within, and only within, the world of appearances. Of the absolute itself, nothing can be said, so absolute truth is beyond the intellect with its words and dualistic concepts. On the other hand, the intellect is useful and even indispensable to the extent that we must function within the world of appearances. It establishes categories, identities, and relations and helps us distinguish genuine perceptions from mirages, sound reasonings from inconsistent ones. Within this conditioned world of becoming, the intellect is our guide to relative truth. Consequently, the mystic must learn only to distinguish the appropriate uses of words and concepts from those that are not.

It is possible to raise philosophical questions about this Wittgensteinian solution. After all, as the Mahāyāna Buddhists have long insisted, isn't the distinction between the absolute and the world of appearances just one more pernicious intellectual duality we should see through and then transcend? Even if we were to grant the distinction philosophical legitimacy, it is much too abstract, too one-dimensional to be integrated within the subtle and complex life of our inner worlds, the locale of both linguistic awareness and the mystical life. If the distinction were viable, it would be easy for the mystic to assign the intellect to its proper sphere of activity and then move on to other matters. But language cannot be manhandled in this way. It creates a world to which the entire person—intellect, emotions, and will—responds, and the mystic cannot simply order all or part of this world to vanish or to present itself in a new way.

The most persuasive evidence on this point is given by the various traditions themselves, for they make it clear that the struggle with the intellect remains a central element in the mystical life. The emerging tension between mystic and intellect that I have described is not dissolved by philosophy or by anything else. Instead, the exploration of the intellect's subtle and tenacious hold and the search for ways to loosen that hold become central, enduring preoccupations. We will never get beyond our arrogance, our self-centeredness, our concern for what others may think. Similarly, we will never get beyond words, which inhere in our nature and in the basic circumstances of our lives. For the mystic on the way of unknowing, this difficult and unending struggle with the intellect becomes the decisive factor shaping this particular form of mystical life.

This ongoing struggle with the intellect, which is a strong current within most major traditions, is known in Christianity as the *negative way*. Within the Christian tradition God, not the world, is the central fact; so the goal, the promised land of the Christian mystic, is a life in the full and immediate presence of God. As we have already seen, however, the Christian mystic will soon begin to sense that the intellect, with its words and concepts, limits God. God is greatness beyond measure, speech, and conception. At best we are able to catch nothing more than fragmentary hints of God's mystery and depths. As the Christian mystic contemplates God, it becomes clear that the God of the intellect is but a feeble imitation, a parody of God, and so it suggests itself that words must be eliminated before a life in God's presence can be achieved. The negative way, which seeks to cancel out all assertions, words, and images concerning the nature and existence of God, is this process, this "work" of elimination.

The classic statement of this method is found in the writings of Dionysius the Areopagite (sixth century C.E.). We find important later versions in the work of Meister Eckhart, in the anonymous *The Cloud of Unknowing*, in St. John of the Cross, and in other writings. For all these contemplatives, there are also important emotional and volitional elements in the mystic's way, such as the demand that one cast out one's own will so that God's will can take its place. But for all of them, the dismantling of the intellect is of central importance, as suggested by Eckhart's emphasis on achieving "unknowing" and by the metaphors of the cloud of unknowing and the obscure night. From the beginning, moreover, the Christian negative way is formulated with a systematic thoroughness which holds nothing back. For Dionysius, all statements and concepts concerning God, whether relating to God's existence or to God's nature, must be nullified. God is not truth, wisdom, goodness, or unity. God is not God, nor can we say that God exists. For Dionysius, we must neither affirm nor deny anything whatsoever of God, for, as he strains language to say, "this surpassing nonunderstandability is 'ununderstandably' above every affirmation and denial" (*CU*, 218).

We can define the negative way as a twofold process. First, the mystic tries to become consciously aware of the various ways in which the intellect presumes to approach God: all the statements, concepts, words, and images that may be thought to enable one to know something about God. The mystic then attempts to deny and pass beyond all these devices of the intellect. We note the logic of this enterprise as well as the enormity of the task. Let us also observe that the logic of the negative way inevitably leads the mystic toward a denial of the most fundamental teachings and concepts of the very tradition to which the mystic belongs. In fact, it is precisely these teachings and concepts that form the heart of the mystic's particular "misconception" of God: They are the subtlest and also the most deceptive layer of the blindfold. For this reason, Dionysius and Eckhart single out the most basic orthodox conceptions of God—God's existence, unity, wisdom, and goodness—for the most explicit and vehement denial.

Processes similar to Christianity's negative way, processes that aim at the systematic dismantling of the intellect, have flourished in the Eastern mystical traditions. As early as the sixth century B.C.E., the

*Tao Te Ching* taught that "the Tao that can be spoken is not the Tao itself." At about the same time in India, the Upanishads revealed that the ultimate power in the universe is *neti neti*, "neither this nor this." The Upanishads speak further of two ultimate powers, the *Brahman-of-sounds* and the highest *Brahman*, who/which is beyond name and form. This sense that movement toward the center of things is movement wholly beyond speech was an important stimulus in the emergence of numerous forms of meditational and yogic techniques that originated in the East, especially in India. More systematically and consciously than is the case with the Christian negative way's lists of verbal denials, these techniques have been developed as methods by which not only the will and the emotions but also the intellect can be "burned out" and so gone beyond.

Of all the traditions, I believe Buddhism has pursued the questions I am raising more exhaustively than any other, for one of the central threads of its history is an intense, collective millennia-long struggle arising from the unending tension between mystery and intellect. We can regard the second-century writings of the great philosopher-mystic Nāgārjuna as the Buddhist equivalent of Dionysius' achievement, though it is important to note that Nāgārjuna's version of the negative way does not relate specifically to God but, rather, to all of reality. Nāgārjuna takes the negative way to its limits, asserting that we cannot affirm or deny anything of anything whatsoever. There are, for instance, four possibilities as to the existence of any A: 1) A exists, 2) A doesn't exist, 3) A both exists and doesn't exist, and 4) A neither exists nor doesn't exist. In all cases, Nāgārjuna denies all four.

I have already suggested how this line of thought leads to Nāgārjuna's famous teaching on Emptiness. It also leads, as Nāgārjuna himself saw, to an awareness of the "emptiness" of Buddhism itself—for, after recognizing that nothing can be said about the Buddha, *nirvāna*, ignorance, or enlightenment, we must further admit that the very concepts are empty of content, meaningless. The complete dissolution of Buddhism as an intellectual and verbal reality—a dissolution that is one crucial aspect of the negative way's dismantling of the intellect—subsequently became a characteristic feature of Buddhism. Two of the most influential sutras, the *Diamond Sutra* and the *Heart Sutra*, are perfectly straightforward, systematic, total denials of all the basic teachings and concepts of Buddhism, not so as to arrive at some other conceptual truth but in order to go beyond words and concepts altogether. These two sutras have been of great importance for Zen, which, with its contradictions and irrationality, represents a further development in the traditional Buddhist effort to neutralize and transcend the intellect.

This brief historical survey of the negative way suggests to us its great importance in giving form to the way of unknowing. The mystic sets out on this particular way in a moment in which the intellect fails, allowing the mystic to hover if only briefly in the bottomless mystery of God or world. Three factors are subsequently decisive in shaping the path the mystic will follow. They are the mystic's desire to recover and deepen the experience of the mystical; a widening sense of the intellect's incapacity to grasp God or the world; and a growing awareness of the intellect's subtle pervasiveness and of its inescapable inherence in human nature and life. Out of the interplay of these factors, which reflect the perpetual, unresolvable tension between mystic and intellect, emerge the various versions of the negative way.

These three factors also enable us to understand more fully the place, as well as the form, of mystical life on the way of unknowing. I said earlier that the mystic always remains a novice in the new land, and we can see now more clearly why this is so. Though aware that the newly discovered landscape extends infinitely out into mystery, the mystic will, in reality, remain largely confined to the border area between the territories of the intellect and the mystical. Permanent occupation of the new land is out of the question, for the way of life of the mystic is, at best, one of "raids on the unspeakable." The gift of knowledge which is not knowledge will always be fragmentary and fleeting. Each moment of time tends to bring the mystic back to the landscape of the intellect, a place where everything has the deceptive appearance of familiarity and form.

To cross the boundary, passing into the formlessness of God or Being, is also to move into silence, a place without concepts or words. This is, for the mystic, the highest goal, the end of the contemplative life. As we have seen, language cannot be brought along on this wandering, for this is territory the intellect cannot map. Words cannot give an accurate picture of what the mystic sees and hears there, nor can they describe for us what the mystic touches or is seized by or what nourishment he or she takes in. We know, however, that the mystic will not simply disappear into immensity, for a return to the shared human world and its maps is inevitable. And if we attend to the mystic's movements, and also to his or her conduct and words once back on this side of the boundary, we discover that it is not only necessity that draws the mystic back. It often happens that the mystic returns to the world of the rest of us even before necessity would have required it. Why is this, and how might this affect our understanding of the form of mystical life?

As for why this happens, let us note, first, that the other side of words is not to be equated with paradise. It can manifest itself as paradise, but also as something very close to hell, and the mystic cannot control which it will be. The place of infinite, wordless depths can seem alien and threatening. At other times it may appear to be no more than a monotonous uniformity without end, a desert waste that holds only a miserable death for anything alive that mistakenly strays into it. Weariness and boredom were familiar to medieval contemplation, and St. John of the Cross has described in painstaking detail the "aridities" and afflictions that torment the soul journeying through the dark night. Biographical accounts of Zen masters usually include at least one intense emotional crisis, the "Zen sickness," which often becomes the prelude to an even more profound experience of enlightenment. Clearly there will be times, then, when the mystic, motivated by fear, dread, or boredom, will come back to this side for the warm creature comforts of words and human companionship.[2]

Secondly, the mystic may return to this side not to seek temporary refuge but because of a strong desire to communicate to us something about the wonders experienced "over there." As with all things human, an infinitely variable mix of motives is possible. The roles of explorer and prophet are appealing to our pride, our insecurity, and our ambition. It also may happen that the mystic is more inwardly attuned to words about the mystical and to attempts to verbalize it than to direct experience of mystery itself. In such cases, times spent on the other side are best seen as brief sorties into the boundless from which the mystic returns with fresh "material." Instead of or in addition to these factors, the mystic may be motivated by the instinctive human urge to talk about what moves us deeply, or the desire to share with others something of great value we have found. If, then, we ob-

---

2. To the non-mystic, the mystical characteristically manifests itself as the monstrous or as vacancy. Existentialism represents the Western intellect's closest approach to the absolute emptiness and "meaninglessness" described,

serve the mystic voluntarily returning to our side in order to "talk," the reasons for this will be human and therefore complex, as suggested by what we know of such individuals as Eckhart, St. Teresa, St. John of the Cross, and, from our own particularly complex time, Thomas Merton.

We have already seen that the negative way, the deliberate struggle *against* words and concepts, constitutes one crucial element in the mystic's relationship with the intellect and in the mystical form of life I call the way of unknowing. The mystic's voluntary return in order to talk about mystery reveals to us the second. Mystical literature is full of attempts to communicate the incommunicable, to convey at least some sense of the landscape revealed to intuition when the intellect's blindfold is removed. Having devoted great efforts to neutralizing and going beyond the intellect, the mystic now opts to employ it. Certainly not all mystics on the way of unknowing return to our side in order to speak to us of the mystical, but this paradoxical speech is so characteristic of the various traditions, filling as it does thousands upon thousands of mystical texts, that it deserves to be placed alongside the negative way as a central component of this form of mystical life.

In addition to the existence and sheer volume of these accounts, I would like to mention one other feature. As we have seen, the practice of the negative way aims at the removal of the intellect from the encounter with mystery. Since mystics on the way of unknowing tend to be mystics of the reflective kind, they are in the greatest danger of being beguiled by sophisticated, abstract language, the language of reflection. Consequently, the dismantling efforts of the negative way tend to concentrate on abstract theological and philosophical concepts, the intellect's most refined graspings. The success of these clearing away efforts can be seen in the much more concrete language, the language of sense experience and the emotions, which mystics use in their attempts to communicate the mystical. This suggests to us that mystical experience is not reflective or abstract, but instead has the intimacy and immediacy we associate with the world of the senses. We know the world and we know mystery by direct "knowing." Our first sensings

---

for instance, by Nāgārjuna. Its rationalistic background and expectations limit its experience of mystery, however, to one of dread and nausea, and the mystical is reduced to the "absurd."

of mystery mirror our species' silent awareness in the distant past of the physical world, and so the creation of mystical speech attempts a second creation of speech out of the urgent, mute pressure of the immediately known.

Within the same traditional texts we can often detect the sharply contrasting alternation between the assault on abstract language and the use of concrete, physical imagery. In explaining to us the negative way, Meister Eckhart speaks of knowing, willing, goodness, being, etc., and the need to transcend them. He portrays the experience itself, however, as the birth of Christ in the soul, or as resembling the disappearance of a drop of water in the sea. In one of his poems, John of the Cross describes the negative way forcefully, though abstractly:

> In order to arrive at knowing everything, you must seek to know nothing. . . .
> In order to arrive at that which you do not know, you must go by a way you do not know (Brenan 1973, 134).

In other poems, however, he, like St. Teresa, uses vivid imagery of love and marriage to convey metaphorically the soul's relationship to God. Śaṅkara teaches that *Brahman* is indefinable, beyond the range of mind and speech. Resorting to metaphor, he nevertheless writes that the presence of *Brahman* in all things is like the presence of one and the same substance, clay, in all clay pots. In our ignorance, we see the pots as distinct, but in fact they are all the same thing. Enlightenment resembles the experience of someone who at first "sees" a snake, but then realizes it is a rope. With greater immediacy Śaṅkara urges us to "drink the joy" and to "taste the sweetness" of *Brahman*. In Zen, finally, the attempt to communicate the powerful immediacy of mystical experience breaks out of language and finds direct expression within the physical world. In Rinzai Zen, a loud shout or a physical blow is perceived as more fully expressive of enlightenment than any words might be. And in Sōtō Zen, the very *act* of sitting in meditation is strikingly equated with enlightenment itself.

Though the widespread use of images relating to light and vision indicates that the mystic has experienced a new form of awareness, other imagery makes it clear that the experience is by no means theoretical or narrowly intellectual. Unlike the austere, systematic, scholastic language of the negative way, the language used to suggest the mystical itself is elemental in a way that precedes the abstract division of the person into the intellect, emotion, and will. The entire person has been seized, as when the full recollection of a vivid scene or experience unexpectedly courses through us. Unlike recollection, however, it is an awareness directed out into reality, the reality of the present moment. What has seized the entire person is the experience of the world's dissolution into the unknown, the disappearance of God into God.

It is evident, then, that the simultaneous discoveries of the intellect's failure and of mystery have not reduced the mystic to stalemate. Instead, a new and complex form of mystical life, one of several that would have been possible, has begun to take shape. This life actualizes itself in the area on both sides of the boundary between language and mystery, between beings and nothingness. A detailed examination of the various movements and practices within Islam, Judaism, Christianity, Buddhism, Hinduism, Taoism, and other religious traditions would reveal the manifold versions and sometimes unexpected turnings of this form of life. A primary occurrence within them all, however, is the evolution of new relationships with words and concepts, a development guided by what happens in silence on the other side. Practice of the negative way helps bring the mystic closer to mystery, and the mystic returns later from the boundless and tries to convey by words what has been seen, heard, and felt there. At all times, however, the mystic's presence at and within mystery remains the forming but itself formless vital center, the soul of this form of mystical life.

## PART III: A WAY YOU DO NOT KNOW

IN PART II, I OUTLINED THE FORM of mystical life that can emerge from the encounter with mystery. I observed that the mystic on this "way of unknowing," while struggling unceasingly with the intellect, travels the negative way into the wordless and then may return in an ambiguous attempt to render the wordless into human speech. That life is a complex life, the paradoxical life of a creature of words and intellect whose life seeks its center on the other side of language. My cursory description of this form of life was constructed of words and concepts. It must in fact be seen as a typical product of the intellect, one based on categories, concepts, dualities, affirmations, and denials. If we take seriously the mystic's growing sense that the human intellect cannot grasp reality, we can only regard what I have said about this mystical form of life with suspicion. How can we or the mystic comprehend what the mystic is doing? How can we describe or even name it? Does it make sense to assert that nameless mystery pervades the basic reality of God or world, and then paradoxically assume that we human beings know full well just what we and others are doing, and why we are doing it?

"You must go by a way that you do not know." I quoted this line from a poem by John of the Cross earlier, and I refer to it now because it states concisely a remarkable aspect of the way of unknowing, the fact that it is the nature of this way to dissolve itself as something knowable and namable. The negative way calls into question the intellect's rendition of everything, including even the intellect's rendition of the negative way. Initially it is likely that the mystic on the way of unknowing will concentrate primarily on dissolving the intellect's God or world so as to experience them as unknowable and unsayable. Typically, in other words, we are most likely to discover mystery as it encompasses us (I described one form this discovery can take in Part I). But once upon the negative way, the mystic eventually will have to face its reflexive nature, the fact that it also dissolves itself and the wayfarer upon it in mystery. *The way of unknowing, negative way, enlightenment, mystic,* and *I* are all words. They are as much products of the intellect as are *God, world,* and *reality,* and consequently the situation would seem to demand that the mystic on the way of unknowing must transcend them as well.

In Part I, I contrasted the mystic's desire to remain in the place of mystery with the eagerness of the rest of us to return to the world of action. I also pointed out the importance for that life of action of rationales, mappings of the world that name, explain, and justify our actions and goals. In Part II, I showed the mystic on the way of unknowing becoming committed to a form of action: the mystical action called the negative way which aims at enlightenment, union, or a more profound experience of mystery. Let me now point out that this particular mystical form of life appears to deny all rationales, including those that may be offered in its own behalf. Those whose lives are centered on accumulation, consumption, or status, on the commitments, struggles, and joys of family life, on social-political action, or on a life of active love can rest and reaffirm themselves in verbal affirmations of what they are doing and why they are doing it. The mystic on the way of unknowing cannot. For the mystic must apply the method of the negative way to the negative way itself. All attempts the mystic may make to name, describe, explain, or justify his or her commitment and form of life are performances of the intellect. They are all just "words," and the mystic on the way of unknowing is committed to no longer depending on words.

To be engaged in a form of life that rejects all rationales does not only distinguish the mystic on the negative way from the other broadly defined groups I just listed. Historically, it also separates those Christians, Buddhists, Hindus, and others who are on the negative way from those who are not. Rightly or wrongly, we tend to see the traditional religious individual as living a life firmly grounded in a clear set of beliefs. But this straightforward verbal clarity cannot exist for the contemplative who no longer finds words to be the way to approach the reality of God or world. Such a contemplative has entered into or been invaded by a radically different reality, a reality that cannot be grasped or spoken. It is in this new reality that the mystic will seek to be somehow grounded, not in the old world of words and of the dogmas and precepts that can be formulated with them—that in the mystic's best moments have been left behind.

It appears, then, that on the way of unknowing the way itself dissolves into the unknown, and so the mystic finds that all words explaining and justifying such a life are untenable. For a human being this is a great deprivation. I have already suggested how important rationales are for action by noting how these rationales create for us a comprehensible world, one in which our lives and actions make sense. As I indicated in Part I, these rationales may be nothing more than stereotyped formulas or superficial, hastily-thrown-together legitimations of action. They can be used to justify our more or less accidental wants or to legitimate the many forms of insecurity, fear, and despair that threaten us. On a more profound level, however, the need for a rationale also reflects the fundamental human need to be able to say, "This is who I am, and this is what I am about." Our sense of responsibility as mature human beings to others and to ourselves, our awareness of death and of this one short life that is ours, our fear of nothingness, our desire that our lives will have been "something" all enter into our longing to be able to render an account of ourselves and our lives, an account that will explain and justify us both for others and ourselves. Here what is humanly best in us also is present in the urgent need we feel to put ourselves into words.

It is the nature of the negative way, however, to deny this need, and this means that we have arrived at the second possible stalemate or impasse on the way of unknowing. I described the first in Part I as the dissolution of the world into the unintelligible. This possible stalemate was overcome as the unintelligible became mystery and so something more than the merely absurd or meaningless. Now what the mystic is and does have themselves been dissolved by the negative way into the unintelligible. The threat of meaninglessness has moved closer to home, from external reality to the mystic's own life and activity. The mystic on the way of unknowing is being asked not just to contemplate what cannot be put into words but to live a life that cannot be put into words and so cannot be justified, explained, or even named. Is such a life unsupported by words and accountings humanly possible? This will be one of my primary concerns throughout the remainder of this essay. In this chapter let us consider, first, how the traditions have portrayed this conceptual self-dissolution of the negative way and, second, how they have responded to the serious questions concerning action that this dissolution seems to raise.

Within Christian mystical traditions, explicit and detailed articulations of the negative way's conceptual self-dissolution are uncommon. The fact that Christian mysticism dwells with such pointed intensity on God—as opposed to reality, the world, or human action within it—is undoubtedly the primary reason for this. It is possible to claim, in fact, that the negative way is properly applied only to God, and this in fact appears to be the view of *The Cloud of Unknowing*. Through the grace of God we are able, says the author, to know "fully" about all other matters, "yet of God himself no man can think" (*CU*, 67). For the author of the *Cloud* it appears that the mystic on the way of unknowing can confidently assume even full self-knowledge and so does not face possible questions of the negative way's self-dissolution. In the works of St. John of the Cross and Meister Eckhart, on the other hand, there are clear formulations, sometimes stated in considerable detail, involving the dissolution of the negative way as an action we can name and describe. The line I quoted from the poem by St. John of the Cross says that the way of unknowing is itself unknown. In the *Dark Night of the Soul*, St. John of the Cross states that the soul must be "at rest from all knowledge and thought" (*DNS*, 71). The faculties, including the intellect, must be "perfectly annihilated" (ibid., 99). In contrast with the author of *The Cloud of Unknowing*, St. John of the Cross asserts that this annihilation of the intellect, or darkening of our natural light, applies "both to things above and things below" (ibid., 116). He advocates, in other words, the application of the negative way to all the workings and formulations of the human intellect. Consequently, as he repeats in the *Dark Night of the Soul*, the way itself dissolves into the unknown. The soul, he says, "is going by a way which it knows not and wherein it finds no enjoyment" (ibid., 154). Further,

> . . . this road whereby the soul journeys to God is as secret and as hidden from the sense of the soul as the way of one that walks on the sea, whose paths and footprints are not known, is hidden from the sense of the body (ibid., 163).

On all these points Meister Eckhart is in agreement with St. John of the Cross. The soul, he says, must outgrow or grow away from "all light and all knowledge" (*DPT*, 414, my translation). More specifically, the goal is to "know nothing either of God, of created things, or of oneself" (ibid., 306). This clearly implies that the person on the way of unknowing will no longer have words for describing or naming this process, and in his sermon on being poor in spirit Eckhart asserts this view. As do both the author of *The Cloud* and St. John of the Cross, Eckhart typically describes the process of the way as one of God working in us. We can only begin to empty ourselves of our intellect and our will, and God must work in us to complete the process. In this sermon, however, Eckhart applies the negative way to this fundamental Christian conceptualization of the process. The person who seeks to be poor in spirit "will not know or recognize that God is active within him" (ibid.). He will seek to be free of the thought that God is living and working within him. By abandoning this and all other verbal, conceptual, and metaphorical forms, the mystic gains that freedom from all "knowledge" which was his "when he still was not" (ibid., 305-306).

In both St. John of the Cross and Meister Eckhart we have found clear basic statements that apply the negative way to itself and so leave the mystic on the way of unknowing with no words for his or her own life and actions. When we turn to Eastern forms of the negative way, we find similar formulations, presented more frequently and systematically, and often in more detail. Eastern ways of knowing, and hence their corresponding negative ways of unknowing, do not focus intensely on one God, as do Western monotheisms, but on more general views of "reality" and of the paths available to humanity for liberation from or within that reality. We have seen that St. John of the Cross attends to the fact that the way of unknowing is itself unknowable, but at the same time it is clear from every page of his writings that, for him, the absolute center of experience is the encounter with the awesome and bottomless depths of the divine. The Easterner, on the other hand, tends to be less of a "specialist" and so more interested in the way *all* phenomena, including one's own actions, transcend the intellect.

To take one example, most of the Upanishads teach that *Brahman*, the ultimate principle beyond all distinctions, is the innermost reality in all things and so the real actor in all events. The path to liberation, therefore, is the process of coming to a total recognition of the fact that we are, in our innermost essence, that *Brahman* and not the isolated, transient individuals we have mistakenly taken ourselves to be. We are being asked, in other words, to reflect not only on *Brahman*, but also on all things, ourselves, and the path; and if we should begin to follow the negative way in this context, it will be natural to apply it to all four. It is also possible that a more systematic epistemological reflection, especially on the part of the Buddhists, has contributed to this more thorough application of the negative way. Specifically, their writings often show a clear awareness of the intellect's dependence on duality, the fact that the intellect evolves a complex world by developing pairs of opposites such as being and non-being, good and bad, personal and impersonal. Consequently, they are much more likely to recognize such dichotomies as knowledge and ignorance, bondage and liberation as the work of the intellect they have come to distrust.

Within Hinduism it is especially in the writings of the Vedanta that we find formulations of the way of unknowing that dissolve the way of unknowing itself. For the Vedanta, as for so much of the Hindu tradition, the world of time and individual phenomena is *māyā*, a kind of illusory play, and this illusory quality consequently also characterizes all those actions that we view as the movements of individuals toward liberation. We as individuals, and so all of our actions as individuals, are enmeshed in *māyā*. We can free ourselves from *māyā* and gain the realization that we are *Brahman* by negating the countless pairs of opposites which constitute the world of *māyā*. The author of the *Avadhūta Gītā* writes,

> I am the all-pure divine essence (*brahman*), devoid of all differentiating, limiting, and mutually conflicting qualities (*guna*). Then how should there be in me anything like bondage or release? (quoted in *PI*, 448).

The *Aṣṭāvakra Samhitā* provides an enormous list of questions, a version of the negative way put in the form of the question, "Where is?"; and the way itself figures prominently in that list:

> Where is death; where is life; where are the worlds; or where is the realm of earthly entanglements and obligations? Where is the dissolution, the absorption, the melting away; or where is supreme absorption—for me who abide in my own glorious greatness? . . .
>     Where is the concentrating of my consciousness to one-pointedness; where is the awakening to transcendental reality or where the state of being an unenlightened fool; where is exultation, where dejection—for me who am forever inactive? . . .
>     Where is instruction; where is the sacred textbook based on revelation; where is the pupil, where the teacher; where is the highest goal of man—for me who am without distinguishing characteristics and full of bliss? (ibid., 453-55)

The great Śaṅkara writes,

> Only the one who has abandoned the notion that he has realized Brahman is a knower of the self; and no one else (ibid., 456-457).

Finally, perhaps more concisely and completely than elsewhere, we read in Gaudapāda's commentary to the *Māṇḍūkya Upaniṣad*:

> There is no dissolution, no beginning, no bondage, and no aspirant; there is neither anyone avid for liberation nor a liberated soul. This is the final truth (ibid., 456).

Especially in the first two of these quotations there is an interest-ing reversal of *The Cloud of Unknowing,* for the Indian texts use at least some positive terms, such as "forever inactive" and "full of bliss," about our ultimate identity, while applying the negative way most energeti-cally to *this* world, the world of *māyā* and distinctions. In the lines from Śaṅkara, we see the negative way extended to include the comple-tion of the path, but we also observe the intellect's tendency to return with ever new formulations, here the phrase "knower of the Self." These are issues to which I shall return. In these quotations, Gaudapāda ap-pears to be the most thoroughgoing in his application of the negative way—though, again, one might ask what he means by "the final truth."

The compression, bluntness, and completeness that characterize the quotation from Gaudapāda are reminiscent of certain Buddhist texts, and such influences on Gaudapāda are quite possible. I said in Part II that the most systematic and thorough dismantling of the in-tellect as it relates both to the world in general and to one's own tra-dition in particular can be found in the great texts of Mahāyāna Buddhism. It is here, too, that we will find the most explicit formula-tions of the self-dissolving quality of the negative way. This impres-sive critique of all verbalizing occurs somewhat paradoxically at a time in the development of Buddhism in which action, especially action directed out into the world toward other beings, begins to receive much more emphasis. This is the time of the emergence of the radically new ideal of the Bodhisattva, who postpones entry into nirvana until all other beings have been saved and whose compassion for others is as great as his wisdom. Mahāyāna texts contrast the Bodhisattva with Hīnayāna's *arhat,* whose mystical action is largely internal and whose aim is limited to the *arhat*'s own liberation. Of course, internal and external actions are equally subject to the self-dissolving aspect of the negative way. What is striking about the Bodhisattva ideal is that the Bodhisattva undertakes an action that is virtually infinite in its scope, but one that at the same time cannot be thought, said, or explained—an action, in other words, that has no connection whatever with words or the intellect. The Bodhisattva "acts" to save all beings, but with a wisdom that has gone beyond the very notion of action.

This ideal emerges because the Mahāyāna, while increasing the range of action and the importance of action in the world, at the same time removes all verbal and intellectual supports or rationales for action. A central component of Nāgārjuna's demonstration that all words and concepts are "empty" is the application of this claim to all the key words that have been used to name and describe the way itself. For Nāgārjuna it is delusion to speak or think of such things as *nirvana*, oneself, liberation, or the way. We err when we make such distinctions as truth and error, enlightenment and ignorance, and liberation and bondage. Nāgārjuna refuses to allow any verbal formulations of mystical action or the mystical form of life, and many important sutras such as the *Heart Sutra* and the *Diamond Sutra*, continue to emphasize this point. We read, for instance, in the *Heart Sutra*:

> There is no suffering, no origination [of suffering], no stopping, no path. There is no cognition, no attainment, and no non-attainment (Conze 1972, 89).

In just a few words the entire verbal and intellectual edifice of Buddhist thought and practice has been razed to the ground, leaving the follower of the way with no form of rationale whatsoever.

The authors of these Mahāyāna texts do not apply the negative way only to traditional formulations of the way but to their own new formulations as well. They create the wisdom and way of the Bodhisattva only to dissolve them. The Bodhisattva has vowed to save all beings, but at the same time a Bodhisattva will not be deluded into thinking that there are beings. The Bodhisattva is full of compassion, yet that compassion has no real object, for there is no one to be led to *nirvana*, which itself is a term empty of meaning. If one person gives a gift to another, there is no giver, no gift, no recipient of the gift. In fact, of course, we are deluded when we speak of Bodhisattvas. The term *Buddha*, like all terms, is empty; so we should not rely on it or "settle down" within the illusory security and support it offers.

The single-mindedness with which Mahāyāna texts hunt out and then deny all verbal/conceptual forms can take on the appearance of empty intellectualism unless we remain aware of the decisive fact that the source of this energy is something in us that is beyond the intellect and that responds to mystery. Let us recall that Nāgārjuna and the others are not simply saying, "There is no self, no path, no enlightenment." Rather, they are pursuing that refinement of the negative way which they call the "middle way." Recognizing that negation or denial is itself a form of verbal statement, they are not opting for any of the four affirming and denying statements that might be made about them. They are not using words to deny reality. Instead, they are denying *words* so as to find a viable way to come into reality's word-transcending presence.

There is nothing unusual about their basic philosophical assessment of what we usually term "human knowledge." Such a dominant philosopher as Kant held that the intellect cannot know reality as it is "in itself," but only as perceived through our specifically human forms of understanding. In the form of relativity and the uncertainty principle, this view is now a commonplace in our physical sciences. Where Kant, as an orthodox modern Westerner, and Nāgārjuna differ is in their subsequent response to the basic perception that the intellect cannot know reality as in itself. Kant chooses to focus on and dwell within the world that the human intellect fashions. Nāgārjuna's response is the exact opposite: to continue to honor and to seek a way to exist in the presence of reality as it is in itself. Our characteristically Western way is to wrap ourselves exclusively in the human, and in so doing to isolate ourselves from the larger reality. The Mahāyānist, on the other hand, continues to seek a way to dwell within the boundless totality in which we find ourselves. As we have seen, the negative way, which we might call the sacrifice of the human intellect, becomes the primary means to this goal. Emptied of all words and concepts, all forms of understanding, we may then coexist in our own "suchness" with the pure suchness of things.

My immediate concern is the consistent application of the negative way not only to external reality but to mystical action itself, to what I am and what I am doing if I am one who is on the way of unknowing. Since we and our acts are also part of reality, it would seem to follow that Kant's and the Mahāyāna's views on our inability to know reality as it is in itself would apply here, too. This would mean that my own ultimate reality eludes all my words, concepts, and images, that my intellect cannot grasp my own "reality" as it is in itself. Here, too, the Mahāyānist negative way, with its refusal of all affirmations and denials about ourselves, offers itself as an alternative approach to the intellect-transcending mystery that we, our acts, and our lives are.

As we have seen, Western philosophies such as Kant's and contemporary science can prepare us to accept the Mahāyāna's assessment of our knowledge of external reality and consequently to begin to practice that aspect of the negative way. It is then all the more striking that they do not similarly prepare us to accept the Mahāyāna's analogous assessment of our verbal and conceptual self-knowledge. It is as if, having isolated ourselves from the infinite reality of which we are part, we cling all the more tenaciously to that verbally negotiable self-knowledge, which is all that remains. Kant, for example, finds it perfectly possible to be skeptical about the most fundamental aspects of our perception of the world: He grants that space and time, far from being objective or absolute, are simply subjective forms of human perception. Turning inward, however, Kant remarkably finds solid bedrock in his internal awareness of duty's requirements, requirements that Kant is persuaded he can spell out in precise verbal formulations. By the same token, there have been no Einsteins or Heisenbergs in our social or human sciences emphasizing to us that their findings are by their very nature relative and indeterminate.[3] It is as if the physical scientists, knowing that they had clearly achieved *something*, could consequently regard the place of their work in the context of totality with considerable dispassion. Social scientists, on the other hand, sensing that their position is much more tenuous, have compensated with their more intense rhetoric and convictions.

We begin, of course, with a naïve faith in the validity of the words and concepts with which we pretend to grasp both external and internal reality, and although our inner-directed perceptions of who we are, what we are doing, and what we should be and do seem less secure than our external perceptions, we have seen that for many reasons the prospect of losing them disturbs us greatly. We long to be defined, and we suppose that commitments to action and achievements will give us that definition. When we are in the midst of the world of activity, and especially when basic harmony exists between us and what we are doing, it can easily seem clear to us that we know just who and where we are and what we are doing. These clarities can begin to dissolve, however, if circumstances or choice lead us to withdraw from activity and to reflect on ourselves in a contemplative way. I note then, for instance, that an infinite time preceded my birth. Another infinite time will follow my death. I am just one of some billions of human beings, and those billions of us now living are a small minority ranged against those who have been and will be. For almost all of this seem-

---

3. There have been "relativists," of course, but they usually have been relativists about values while at the same time dogmatically supporting some particular version of the facts, usually behaviorism.

ingly endless time, it is my nature not to be. When I reflect in this way on my transience and creatureliness, on what I take to be the basic "facts," my sense that "I know" begins to weaken and I become more open to that dissolution of my self-understanding that the negative way entails.

In a more limited way reflection on our human sciences can re-enact this process. These sciences, like activity itself, are a seemingly limitless sea. Our natural tendency is to jump into that sea and to take up the cause of one of the many competing points of view within one of the many competing fields. Within the very small world with which we are then at close quarters, an aura of plausibility and rationality reigns. For example, a well-written, well-thought-out work of history, biology, or psychology conveys a strong impression of plausibility. The various debates going on within any one field at any one time seem interrelated and meaningful. Our sense must change, however, if we contemplate the totality. A single good book has an aura of plausibility. Does a collection of several thousand books arguing persuasively for several thousand competing and conflicting points of view have the same aura of plausibility? Do we get a sense of reasonableness if we stand back and attempt to contemplate the totality of all the competing, conflicting mass of human self-knowledge which, not to speak of either past or future, is being offered *today* in biology, neurology, psychology, sociology, anthropology, history, economics, linguistics, literary criticism, theology, and philosophy? This totality, in fact, is the antithesis of the plausible and rational. It cannot offer us a verbal, conceptual sense of who we are and what we are doing because it offers us hundreds or thousands of rival versions, only a few of which we can actually begin to digest. This dizzying, seemingly limitless number of increasingly complex, increasingly variegated, mutually competing accounts of our human reality stands in a curiously inverse supporting relationship to the negative way, for it is a self-destructing *positive* way, one that has reached such a degree of bizarre fecundity and self-contradiction that it cancels itself out as a way for the intellect to discover and reveal who we are.

The human sciences' incessant production of endlessly varied human self-knowledge gives us no fundamental self-knowledge. In this respect they only offer us a more complex and extreme version of the incoherent picture created by humanity's equally varied, though simpler, self-understandings throughout history and around the globe. We are

flesh; no, we are spirit. We should live for this world; we should live
for the next. Let us do our duty; let us enjoy life as much as we can.
You are responsible first of all to yourself, to your family, to your clan,
to your community, to the nation; do not limit yourself and discrimi-
nate, but recognize that your real responsibility is to humanity as a
whole, or perhaps to something still greater. Our condition is one of
decline, of steady progress of awaiting or seeking to create some dras-
tic change. There must be some purpose, but what purpose could there
possibly be? It is imperative to at least try to do something; let us not
do, but *be*. Somewhere, sometime things will be better for us. We are
in a tragedy, a comedy. As things are now, so they will always be.

Most of us naturally seek and with more or less difficulty eventually find and live with "answers" to these issues, views that give us pictures of ourselves and our acts. To the mystic on the way of unknowing,
however, these answers are more a covering up than a disclosure of
who we are. To that mystic, our concepts, words, and images fail to
touch our underlying reality, and so all our verbal and conceptual pictures are not reality, but myth. We usually associate myth with the past,
with accounts of the exotic deeds of the gods. But as seen from the
negative way, the words we use to create pictures of ourselves are also
myth, myth that alienates us from ourselves, never allowing us to be
more than mythological beings to ourselves. That aspect of the way
of unknowing which concerns our self-understanding is, from this point
of view, an attempted demythologization of ourselves, one designed
to bring us into contact with the mystery we are.

The negative way, which offers self-knowledge through the canceling of all self-knowledge, is an alternative to the ungraspable, infinitely expanding chaos of our human sciences' positive way. But the
question of action remains, for the canceling of all self-knowledge
includes the denial of my perception that my own primary action is
pursuit of the negative way. Is it possible to act without the terms,
descriptions, and justifications ordinarily provided by the intellect?
Can one act, having abandoned the very idea of action? Since the
negative way involves a sacrifice of the intellect and its words, it is clear
that the mystic on the negative way can continue to act only if there
is a form of action which bypasses the intellect. Since the intellect is
to play no role, options and choices of actions cannot be formulated
verbally. Consequently, there is no place for the "will," for it operates
by choosing and willing verbally formulated alternatives of action. We

require, then, a form of action without dependence on the human intellect or will. Have the traditions suggested any such forms, or at the end of the way of unknowing is there perhaps no action?

Versions of the negative way within Hinduism clearly are attracted to the latter alternative. As we saw above, one of the few self-descriptions that the author of the *Aṣṭāvakra Samhitā* allows himself is "forever inactive," a technical term which Zimmer renders as "beyond all activities" (Zimmer 1969, 459). The supreme state of the Vedanta is often characterized as the non-active condition of Being-Consciousness-Bliss, and it is clear that from the Vedantic point of view there is no connection between this supreme state and the accidental specificity of individual action, for how can any one action express or relate to the supreme truth more effectively than any other?

For the Vedantin, there is no connection between absolute awareness and the phenomena that occur in this world of *māyā*. Nevertheless, the Vedanta recognizes that even the one who has won through to reality will continue to act for as long as that individual is alive, and the Vedanta suggests how this happens without any dependence on intellect or will. One who has complete the way is *jīvan-mukta*, one "released while living." Though the *jīvan-mukta*, as we have seen, is beyond all activity, those karmic seeds that already have "germinated" must continue and finish their growth, and this is what constitutes the remainder of the *jīvan-mukta*'s life. The *jīvan-mukta* is inactive, having become Being-Consciousness-Bliss. But these seeds create a life, a biography, for him or her. Since these seeds are, on the whole, good seeds, they tend to create virtues, for "Such virtues as non-hatred arise and abide of themselves with one in whom the Awakening of the Self has come to pass." (*Naiṣkarmya-siddhi* 4.69, quoted in ibid., 445.) But to all this the *jīvan-mukta* is indifferent. In Zimmer's phrase,

> He observes his own insubstantial history as a witness unconcerned with what is going on in the phenomenal personality—as one might let one's hair blow in the wind (ibid.).

Certainly it would be a gross oversimplification to regard all the various strands within Hinduism as antagonistic to action. In Tantrism the One and this world of particularity are intimately bound up with one another, so that the Tantric adept can use both psychological and physical actions as paths to transcendent reality. In the Bhagavad Gita, action in the form of doing one's duty and playing one's assigned role in daily life is often praised as a way preferable to asceticism and ritualism. The key to action is non-attachment to the fruits of action, for "in performing action disinterestedly a man attains the highest" (*Bhagavad Gita*, 1964,160). But there are powerful trends within Hinduism, including those most inclined toward the negative way, which clearly manifest an underlying indifference toward action.

Within Buddhism, on the other hand, preoccupation with the negative way has been associated with a deepened interest in the question of action. I have already suggested one important reason for this: the emergence of the Bodhisattva ideal, with its commitment to work for the liberation of all beings. But there is another important reason, one inherent in the "logic" of the negative way itself. Though claiming to follow the negative way, the Hindus often leave intact the intellect's distinction between the real transcendent One, the reality of which is Being-Consciousness-Bliss, and the illusory world of particulars, change, and action. As we have seen, Mahāyāna Buddhists persist on the negative way and break down such distinctions, consequently identifying form with emptiness, *samsara* with *nirvana*, being with becoming. For the Mahāyāna and Zen Buddhist, the characteristic Hindu dream of a state beyond all activity must itself be transcended, for it rests on the false discrimination between a world of unreal activity and another world of pure being and awareness.

As an example of Hindu non-action, we can turn to the life of Anandamayi Ma, a Hindu saint who died in 1982. Anandamayi Ma taught that "God alone is," and she was so merged with God that her body essentially disappeared from her thoughts. Oblivious to her body, she required the constant physical care of others. Her hands would not grasp food, so she had to be fed. Anandamayi Ma said that she could not distinguish fire and water and that "this body" would be quickly destroyed unless taken care of by others (Marlin 1987, 5-6). That perfect awareness and saintliness should be reflected in complete physical "incompetence" is an exact reflection of the indifference to action we have seen in some Hinduism. As a manifestation of enlightenment, this incompetence is, as we shall see, the polar opposite of Buddhism's, and especially Zen's, ideal.

Hindu versions of the negative way have not created their own responses to the question of action—the picture of the *jīvan-mukta* who is beyond activity, but for whom a kind of phantom life is created by his past karma, is simply taken over from the general Hindu tradition. In Buddhism, on the other hand, the new emphasis on action, together with the fundamental questions about action which the negative way raises, have led to a new interpretation of action that is as significant within Buddhism as the Bhagavad Gita's new vision of action. Duty and non-attachment to its results are central to the Bhagavad Gita's new vision of action. For Buddhism the new ideal revolves around what can perhaps be called "spontaneity," and the primary reason for this has already become quite clear. Since the negative way dissolves the intellect, and since the will depends on the intellect to picture alternatives, the action of one who pursues the negative way will need to be independent of both intellect and will. Somehow it will have to take care of itself. Let us call it, then, the ideal of "spontaneous mystical action."

Within the Mahāyāna, we find spontaneous mystical action associated with Bodhisattvas, those beings of perfect wisdom and compassion. The *Lankāvatāra Sutra* says of a Bodhisattva's actions that he "works without effort like the moon, the sun, a wishing jewel or the four primary elements" (Conze 1967, 237). The *Dasabhūmikā* illustrates this effortlessness at greater length, comparing it to a great seafaring boat:

> When the boat is not yet at sea, much labor is needed to make it move forward, but as soon as it reaches the ocean, no human power is required; let it alone and the wind will take care of it. One day's navigation thus left to itself in the high seas will surely be more than equal to one hundred years of human laboring while still in the shallows. When the Bodhisattva accumulating the great stock of good deeds sails out on to the great ocean of Bodhisattvahood, one moment of effortless activity will indefinitely surpass deeds of conscious striving (ibid.).

In this passage the contrast between the intellectual and volitional requirements of ordinary action and the effortlessness of spontaneous mystical action, which is carried out by "the wind," is clearly drawn. Exactly how this relates to a human practitioner of the way of unknowing is not clear, however, for in these passages the ideal of spontaneous mystical action is projected on the figure of the Bodhisattva, a perfected enlightenment-being who has already completed the path.

Spontaneous mystical action is presented as an ideal, a dream of the perfect action that will be ours when we achieve that remote perfection of Bodhisattvahood, but the Mahāyāna does not touch on its possible present reality. In its pursuit of the way of unknowing, the central achievement of the Mahāyāna is its relentless dismantling work, its dissolution of all verbal and conceptual constructs relating to the world, to Buddhism, and to the way itself. The self-canceling nature of the negative way is carried through more thoroughly here than anywhere else, leaving us bereft of all intellectual support in a reality of pure suchness. As we have just seen, the Mahāyāna then hints at a radically new form of action in this void of pure suchness, but that is all.

Within Mahāyāna Buddhism spontaneous mystical action remains an occasional suggestion, a secondary characteristic of the Bodhisattva ideal. It is only with the rise of Zen, which represents a further development of Mahāyāna Buddhism primarily in China and Japan, that the question of action on the way of unknowing becomes a primary concern. More than other mystical traditions, Zen emphasizes action, especially action in the world, as an immediate expression of basic insight. Its special contribution is its remarkable attempt to find a way to live and act in the world without dependence on words, concepts, and rationales. Within the world of Zen it is understood that no solution to the dilemma of action can be spelled out in words. Instead, the stories and koans that are so central in Zen attempt with great subtlety, imaginativeness, and energy to show us a way that does not involve the intellect or will, but in which action is effortless, simple, and spontaneous. Let us consider three of these anecdotes.

A monk once asked Chao-chou, "Master, I am still a novice. Show me the way!" Chao-chou said, "Have you finished your breakfast?" "I have," replied the monk. "Then go wash your bowl!" Thereupon the monk was enlightened (Dumoulin, 1969, 37).

When the monk puts his question to Chao-chou, it is the intellect that is speaking. In his response, however, Chao-chou refuses to meet the intellect on its own terms or even to acknowledge it. Chao-chou does not attempt to satisfy the monk's intellect, but vigorously asserts the primacy of another realm, that of action. Instead of persuading, Chao-chou simply ignores the intellect and responds in a way designed to jar the monk into a radically different way of being.

The general assertion of the primacy of action over intellection is certainly a familiar Western theme as well, Goethe's rewording of Genesis—"In the beginning was the deed"—being one of its most concise formulations. We can become aware of its force not by arguing over whether action or intellect ought to have primacy, but by observing that, in fact, action takes precedence over intellect much more often than we ordinarily suppose. One aspect of getting to know ourselves is learning to what a great extent "we" consist of physiological and psychological processes of which we normally are not aware. Alternatively, by looking back over our own lives and those of others we can see that the conscious intellect is much less of a factor in shaping critical decisions than we believe at the time those decisions are made. In retrospect it is easier for us to see that the intellect tends to be the servant or at best the often harried mediator between countless internal and external forces, and consciousness is the disorderly and overcrowded clearing house in which it tries to operate. Subsequently the intellect may also be called upon to legitimate the decisions and actions that emerge from this confused interplay.

When Chao-chou urges the monk to become centered in action and not in the intellect, we can perhaps say that his goal is to restore him to his natural "home" (that is, to action), but this does not necessarily mean that he is urging him to follow the mystic's path. To the extent that Zen only asserts the primacy of action over intellect, it is much more general and can be turned to uses that have nothing to do with Buddhism or the negative way. During its first centuries in Japan, Zen was in fact militarized, widely used as a technique for attaining intellect-free spontaneity in physical combat. In our anecdote, however, Chao-chou does not urge the monk to take up a sword but delimits the range of action by ordering him to wash his bowl, one of the routine acts of the monastic life. A second anecdote will enable us to see more clearly how action is to express itself within the bounds of this specifically religious or mystical form of life:

Tanzan and Ekido were once traveling together down a muddy road. A heavy rain was still falling.

Coming around a bend, they met a lovely girl in a silk kimono and sash, unable to cross the intersection.

"Come on, girl," said Tanzan at once. Lifting her in his arms, he carried her over the mud.

Ekido did not speak again until that night when they reached a lodging temple. "We monks don't go near females," he told Tanzan, "especially not young and lovely ones. It is dangerous. Why did you do that?"

"I left the girl there," said Tanzan. "Are you still carrying her?" (quoted in Reps 1957, 18).

This story takes us beyond the first one in several ways. Let us note, first, that the scene of action is now transferred from the monastery to the world, a movement from a degree of exclusiveness and possible distinctions to an all-embracing sense of the unity of the absolute and the conditioned, the sacred and the profane, the other world and this one. On this level Tanzan's action is reminiscent of the message of the Bhagavad Gita reconciling spirituality and action in the world. As suggested above, that message is: "Do your worldly duty, but do not be attached to the results of your action; live in the world, but without attachment or desire." Tanzan appears to fulfill perfectly the Gita's injunction, but we can see that he also embodies the Mahāyāna ideal of effortless action. Unlike the monk in the first story, Tanzan does not need to be told what he should do. Just like a Bodhisattva, he does what is to be done effortlessly and spontaneously, without any intellectual confusion, conflicting impulses, or an effort of will. For Ekido, the life of the celibate Zen monk clearly includes elements of tension, conflict, and struggle, but somehow Tanzan is beyond this. He spontaneously lifts the girl up to help her and then just as spontaneously puts her back down, proceeding on his way without further thoughts or complications. Here the sketchy Mahāyāna ideal of spontaneous mystical action seems to be perfectly realized. Let us consider a third text, which helps us understand how this is possible:

> Before you study Zen, mountains are mountains and rivers are rivers. While you study Zen, mountains are no longer mountains and rivers are no longer rivers. When you have attained enlightenment, mountains again are mountains and rivers again rivers (Schumann 1974, 168).

This brief narrative suggests to us the process of transformation Tanzan has undergone. To begin with, one lives in the world of the intellect and its words, the world of mountains, trees, animals, and

persons, and one responds to this world with the full range of emotions and desires. Then, with the dismantling of the intellect on the
way of unknowing, all these "things" vanish. Our reference now is not
the Bhagavad Gita, but the negative way pursued so tenaciously by
Nāgārjuna and other authors of Mahāyāna texts. At the end of the
negative way is the experience of absolute emptiness. There is no self,
no path, no Buddha, no mountain or river, no girl or rain. All these
terms are empty, but just as empty is "emptiness" itself. Hence we must
not fall into the error of distinguishing the absolute from the conditioned, *nirvana* from *samsara*, or emptiness from form. The *Heart Sutra*
asserts "Form is emptiness and the very emptiness is form" (Conze
1972, 81), and here in abstract terminology is the seed of that return
to the world and to action which is such a striking feature of Zen. The
worlds of emptiness and form coalesce. The mountains and rivers
reappear, but at the same time they are now pervaded by the emptiness, which is also the "fullness" of the unconditioned. Now one can
live and act in the world while moving with perfect ease through its
emptiness. Tanzan is in the world and he does what is to be done with
perfect spontaneity and effortlessness, for his action is an expression
of perfect insight, that spontaneous mystical action which emerges as
the negative way itself dissolves.

Earlier in this essay I described the shouts, blows, and eccentric
actions of the Rinzai Zen masters as manifestations of enlightenment
in actions instead of words. I mentioned as well Sōtō Zen's equation
of enlightenment with the act of *zazen*. With those references, and the
stories just considered, I have only scratched the surface, but they at
least suggest to us Zen's great importance as the one tradition that has
concentrated on dealing with the self-canceling logic of the negative
way as it relates to action and on discovering forms of action that do
not depend on words, rationales, and accounts. On the other hand,
as we have seen, Hindu followers of the negative way have shown less
interest in the question of action. How does the Christian negative way
relate to these two alternatives?

In general we can note first that Christian followers of the way of
unknowing, like both Hindus and Buddhists, advocate the emptying
of the human intellect and will. They teach that we can set out on the
way, aided by grace, but that at a certain point the human intellect and
will must yield, turning all over to God and so allowing God to continue the process to completion. Our work, says the author of *The Cloud*

*of Unknowing,* is limited to the "stamping out all remembrance of God's creation," while the other work, the "urgent movement of love is wholly God's work" (*Cloud,* 94). Similarly, St. John of the Cross teaches that the dark night itself is God's work, a process of purgation in which God annihilates the intellect, will, memory, and imagination so that God can replace them with something entirely new and humanly incomprehensible: Divine Wisdom and Love. As St. John of the Cross writes, "God is freeing thee from thyself and taking the matter from thy hands" (*DNS,* 154).

These suggestions of an entirely new form of activity which invades us after our intellect and will have been annihilated are analogous to the Mahāyāna-Zen ideal, with God taking on the role of the winds in the Mahāyāna passage quoted. In other important respects, however, these two Christian mystics seem more akin to the Hindus concerning action. Let us note first that St. John of the Cross and the author of *The Cloud,* like the Hindus and unlike the more thoroughgoing Buddhists, tend to retain their most fundamental positive concepts. For the Hindus these are Being-Consciousness-Bliss. For the Christians it is God and the basic terms associated with God. I will discuss this question later. I only note now that the quotations from *The Cloud* and *Dark Night* above are inconsistent with the negative way since they are, in fact, positive theology, that is—they are verbal and conceptual accounts of a process of transformation the soul undergoes.

In their retention of certain fundamental terms and assertions, the two Christian mystics show a closer resemblance to Hindu than to Buddhist "unknowers." *All* suggest that the human intellect and will are superseded, but the Hindus and these Christians offer an intellect-based account of the process of transformation and the actors involved. An additional bond between the Christian and Hindu mystics is the tendency to retain a fundamental dualism, one that leads to a relative lack of interest in the world of particulars and action within it. The Hindus oppose the unified luminescence of Being-Consciousness-Bliss to the illusory world of individuals, while the Christians oppose God to the world. As we just saw, the author of *The Cloud* urges us to "stamp out all remembrance of God's creation." Similar injunctions, which manifest a fundamental dualism the Buddhists attempt to overcome, abound in St. John of the Cross. For one who has living hope in God:

... all things of the world seem to (him) to be, as in truth they
are, dry and faded and dead and nothing worth (*DNS*, 177).

In the saint's description of the "hiding place of unitive contemplation" we are forcefully reminded of the Vedantin's blissful withdrawal
from the world of action to another place that alone is real, another
"world" all but entirely severed from this one:

> When it comes to pass that those favours are granted to the soul
> in concealment (that is, as we have said, in spirit only), the soul
> is wont, during some of them, and without knowing how this
> comes to pass, to see itself so far withdrawn and separated accord-
> ing to the higher and spiritual part, from the sensual and lower
> portion, that it recognizes in itself two parts so distinct from each
> other that it believes that the one has naught to do with the other,
> but that the one is very remote and far withdrawn from the other.
> And in reality, in a certain way, this is so; for the operation is now
> wholly spiritual, and the soul receives no communication in its
> sensual part. In this way the soul gradually becomes wholly spiri-
> tual; (ibid., 189-190).

Concerning action, then, *The Cloud* and *Dark Night* appear to represent trends within the Christian negative that show important resemblances to Hindu versions. Meister Eckhart, on the other hand,
moves in an atmosphere closer to that of Mahāyāna and Zen. In general Eckhart writes more positively of action in the world than do the
other Christian mystics considered here. At the same time, he tends
to pursue the negative way more thoroughly than do his Christian
colleagues. Consequently, Eckhart is led toward an ideal of spontaneous mystical action like that of the Buddhists.

I suggested above that its new emphasis on action, combined with
its relentless dissolution of all our verbal and conceptual accounts of
action, led the Mahāyāna to a dramatically new sense of action, one I
call spontaneous mystical action. In Eckhart, too, the emphasis on
action is strong. Though many passages in his sermons seem to suggest that withdrawn contemplative union with the imageless, nameless God should be our goal, there are also numerous passages asserting
that this experience is best found and expressed in action in the world.
In his sermon on Mary and Martha, for example, Eckhart reverses the

import of the Biblical account by portraying the active life as higher than the contemplative life, or rather as its culmination. Our goal at the end of the way is not to pass beyond all activity, but to realize the virtues in action for the first time (*DPT*, 289). For Eckhart action means primarily tending to the material and especially the spiritual needs of others. We must not, he asserts, love our own blessedness or salvation more than that of others (ibid., 359). And in a passage reminiscent of the Bodhisattva's vow to save all beings, Eckhart says, "I alone make all creatures ready again for God" (ibid., 272).

While stressing in this way the importance of action, Eckhart goes further than other Christian mystics in his dissolution of all verbal accounts and rationales of action. As we have seen, God is the primary actor in mystical transformation as conceived in the Christian tradition, yet Eckhart often dissolves "God," suggesting, for instance, that we must become "free of God" and "rid of God" (ibid., 305 and 308). Consequently, Eckhart turns the way of unknowing upon itself, suggesting that we surrender all accounts of this process together with all other knowledge. It is of great significance, finally, that Eckhart, like Mahāyāna Buddhism and Zen, is inclined to dissolve the intellect's fundamental distinction between God and world, or the real and the apparent, which we have seen to remain untouched in most Hindu and Christian texts. Endeavoring to bring us into the presence of the real, the Mahāyāna Buddhists dissolve the intellect-based duality of form and emptiness, *samsara* and *nirvana*. Analogously, Eckhart says we must seek to be in a place where "the highest angels and the fly and the soul are the same" (ibid., 305). In the state of breakthrough, he writes, "I am free of my own will and the will of God, and of all his works and of God himself; then I am over all created things and am neither 'God' nor creature (ibid., 308).

Like the Buddhists, Meister Eckhart retains a commitment to action while dissolving both the negative way itself and that underlying dualism which, in Hinduism and other Christian writings, often remains the untouched and conceptual context for the negative way. As we have seen, countless Mahāyāna and Zen Buddhists shared a centuries-long effort to realize these goals and to evolve a new approach to action consistent with them. Eckhart's sermons suggest to us a similar, but more isolated and so much more difficult, struggle. This becomes apparent as we read his sermon on Mary and Martha. Here he takes on directly the question of action, wishing both to affirm action as the culmination of the way and to point the way toward that radically new form of action that the way of unknowing clearly requires. Instead of a perfectly coherent and finished presentation, we encounter in this sermon a number of attempts, some groping and unclear, to convey this new sense of action. Eckhart speaks suggestively, for instance, of the identity of one's light—that is, one's mystical enlightenment—with one's work (ibid., 283). Making a distinction that is applicable to Tanzan, Eckhart says of Martha that she is "with *things*," but that things are not "within *her*" and so are not "hindrances" for her (ibid.). He says there are three ways to God. The first is to seek God in all creatures. The second is a "pathless path" where, free from all will and all images, one is removed to a place above oneself and all things. The third, and best, is a "being at home," an identity of way, truth, and life, a path that is "beyond everything that can be grasped in words" (ibid., 284-85). Much here is obscure, but Eckhart's conception is certainly reminiscent of Zen's threefold relation with mountains and rivers described above (see page 44).

What may be Eckhart's most successful formulation of the new form of action, and the one closest to that of the Buddhists, is found in two other sermons. To suggest the crucial point that mystical action, like all other phenomena, transcends the intellect's words and concepts, Eckhart describes it simply as action *ohne Warum* (that is, without a "why" or a "because"). In one of these sermons he says, for instance, that all our actions should arise out of our innermost ground, that site of the divine spark, which for him is entirely beyond speech, and he adds further that we should perform these actions "without a why." A few lines later he returns to this theme:

> Ask life for a thousand years, "Why do you live?" It would answer nothing other than "I live because I live." The reason is that life lives out of its own ground and flows out of itself. So it lives without a why in that it lives for itself. Ask a true person who acts out of his own ground, "Why do you do what you do?" He would rightly answer nothing other than "I act because I act" (ibid., 180).

In the other sermon, which deals with Eckhart's central vision of the just, he describes them in part as follows:

> The just love neither this nor that about God. If God gave them

all his wisdom and everything besides himself he could offer, they wouldn't heed or savor it. For they do not will or seek anything, since they know no "because" for the sake of which they would do anything. So the just act without a why in exactly the same way as God, who acts without a why and knows no why (ibid., 371).

In these passages Meister Eckhart paradoxically addresses us from that place beyond speech in which there are no words for God or external reality, and also no words for ourselves and our acts. It is a place of pure being without explanations, of simple act without a why or because, a place in which the "I am that I am" of the Old Testament becomes the "I act that I act" of spontaneous action in mystery. In his pursuit of the way of unknowing, Eckhart has moved farther away from his tradition's fundamental words and concepts than do St. John of the Cross or the author of *The Cloud of Unknowing*. Three and a half centuries after Eckhart, however, we find striking reminiscences of his work in the poems of the German mystic Angelus Silesius. In numerous poems Silesius follows the negative way with Eckhart's thoroughness, as when he admonishes himself in one poem to pass "beyond God into a desert." (Angelus Silesius, 1960, I, 7, 30, my translation.) In the following poem, which I render literally, we are strongly reminded of Eckhart's words on actions without a why.

### Without a Why

The rose is without a why; it blooms because it blooms. It pays no attention to itself, and doesn't wonder if it is seen (ibid., I,:289, 57).

It is appropriate that Angelus Silesius takes his image from the vegetative world, a world of intellect-free growth and action. No explanation can be given for the purely spontaneous blossoming of the rose. It is a spontaneity free, moreover, of all the complications of will, intellect, and self-regard with which we are all too familiar. The rose's own self isn't involved, for it is not a self-seeking action or, for that matter, an act "for the sake of" anything at all. There is no complex dialectic of moral judgment, no weighing of my own wants against others' wants and opinions. The poem gives us a Western version of the *Dasabhumikā*'s Bodhisattva, who sails effortlessly out into the great ocean of Bodhisattvahood in that evasive and eternal moment of spontaneity in which Silesius' rose blooms.

## PART IV: THE DREAM OF SPONTANEOUS MYSTICAL ACTION

IN PART III, I BEGAN TO EXPLORE the self-dissolving quality of the negative way, the fact that the mystic who travels it will eventually reach the point at which he or she is asked to surrender all words and concepts relating to the way itself. To the theoretical intellect, the discovery of this seemingly necessary surrender constitutes a *reductio ad absurdum* of the way of unknowing itself. The mystic, however, will not automatically embrace this perspective, for the mystic has already once overcome the absurd in relation to the inexplicable existence of the world, or God, and has learned that the discovery of the absurd may be only the beginning of "wisdom." But at the same time the mystic remains in part, and even primarily, a human being living in the realm of the intellect and its words, and consequently cannot simply ignore the way's apparent dissolution. The effect of that dissolution, which by our usual human standards could be expected to be powerful indeed, is twofold. First, the mystic is allowed no account, description, or even name for his or her own actions and way of life, for the self-dissolution of the way of unknowing means that there is no way of unknowing and also that all distinctions between unknowing, knowing, and "worldly" action are empty. Second, there can be no verbal justification or vindication of a life devoted to that "fiction" called the way of unknowing, for all rankings and explanations are simply out of the question. The mystic on the way of unknowing is now being asked to live and act without being able to render an account of his or her own basic commitment, without map, rationale, or justification; we might well ask how this can be possible for a human being.

In the remaining pages of this essay, I will explore this question and some further thoughts to which it gives rise. In Part III I outlined what the traditions offer us in this regard. We have seen that texts from the different traditions formulate the negative way's self-dissolution with varying degrees of thoroughness. We have also seen that these variations have given rise to two very different versions of the nature of mystical action on the way of unknowing. One, associated with Hinduism and some Christian mystics, takes the form of a withdrawal from all relations with the world of particulars. The other, traced here in Buddhism and Meister Eckhart, cancels out the duality of this world and the ultimate and goes on to emphasize an ideal of spontaneous mystical action in this world. What is offered here is not withdrawal but a perfectly harmonious reintegration with the "non-dual" reality of this world. This reintegration is presented as something spontaneous, "without a why," an event that does not depend on our intellect or will and so renders accounts and rationales superfluous. In the final analysis, both withdrawal and spontaneous mystical action are, of course, "actions." One is an inward movement away from the many to the one while the other moves back into a world which is both many and one.

Are these forms of action we can put into practice? Do they successfully overcome the problems created by the negative way's self-dissolution, and should we therefore adopt one of them if we wish to follow the way of unknowing? In this section I will explore this complex of questions, attending to some problems in traditional versions of the way of unknowing and to others in our characteristic response to the tradition. Many of these problems are rooted in a phenomenon to which I have already alluded, the fact of the intellect's powerful hold over us, the fact that we are and always will be creatures of words and the intellect. I suggested in Part I that we quickly accept explanations of the world's existence that quite obviously explain nothing at all, which in fact only compound the mystery. Analogously, practitioners of the negative way easily overlook their continued dependence on and use of the intellect and its words. It is possible for us to believe we are following the way of unknowing when, in fact, we have abandoned it and returned to what is quite clearly a "positive" way.

This confusing return to the intellect, words, and affirmative claims is a characteristic feature of ways of unknowing that culminate in withdrawal from the world of particulars. For Meister Eckhart and for Zen, mystical action is, as we have seen, indescribable, without a why. But their Christian and Hindu counterparts often describe the mystical process in positive terms that clearly indicate that it can, in fact, be named and described. For St. John of the Cross, God enters the soul and becomes the real actor in the mystical process. In the Vedanta, the karmic seeds produce action in the illusory world of phenomena, while one's true self, *Atman-Brahman*, dwells in pure consciousness. We note, further, that in these texts theories of salvation or liberation also are still operative, theories that name and describe a process culminating in absolute purity. For St. John of the Cross this process, which he describes in detail, can only be completed in the next life, while it culminates for the Vedantin only at the end of countless existences.

Finally, both St. John of the Cross and the Vedantic negative way retain their respective traditions' basic "positive" picture of the world. In spite of all negation, the Vedantin retains the triad Being-Consciousness-Bliss as well as the basic dualistic contrast between the real world of changeless Being and this illusory world of Becoming. Similarly, St. John of the Cross and the author of *The Cloud of Unknowing* retain the key terms *God* and *soul*, and also the basic dichotomy between God and the world, the sacred and the profane.

It is remarkable that these Christian and Vedantic authors display no awareness of the contradiction between their espousal of the negative way and the intellect-based pictures of the world to which they so constantly return, a contradiction that suggests the subtlety of the intellect's pervasive hold. They urge us to surrender our feeble intellect and its words, but at the most crucial points they seem to retain complete trust in certain key names and theories. Of the mystical process St. John of the Cross says that it is "so secret that the soul cannot speak of it and give it a name" (*DNS*, 159). Further,

> . . . even though the soul might have a great desire to express it and might find many ways in which to describe it, it would still be secret and remain undescribed (ibid.).

A few pages later, however, he is naming and describing this process with great precision:

> . . . the principal characteristic of contemplation, on account of which it is here called a ladder, is that it is the science of love. This, as we have said, is an infused and loving knowledge of God, which enlightens the soul and at the same time enkindles it with love, until it is raised up step by step, even unto God its Creator. For it is love alone that unites the soul with God (ibid., 166).

This ladder, moreover, has ten steps, all of which are described in some detail.

St. John of the Cross writes movingly and powerfully of a process that cannot even be named, let alone described or explained. He then names, analyzes, and explains it. Puzzled by this contradiction and still more so by the saint's apparent obliviousness to it, the reader can only wonder about the underlying direction of this particular way. Does it lead finally to a silence beyond all speech, or does it culminate in "God"? Are we to take the statements about God, love, wisdom, and the soul as groping and provisional attempts to put into words what cannot be put into words, or are the utterances about ineffability and surrendering the intellect both rhetorical and exaggerated? Untroubled by this question, St. John of the Cross alternates negative and positive ways without seeming to notice it. Vedantic texts also illustrate this tendency to espouse the negative way only to return to categorical verbal affirmations. As I have already indicated, the triad Being-Consciousness-Bliss tends to be "immune" from unknowing. We note that the author of the *Aṣṭāvakra Samhitā* rejects the duality of exaltation and dejection but retains the distinction between activity and non-activity. He claims to be without any distinguishing characteristics, yet in the same breath he tells us that he is "full of bliss" (see above, p. 31).

My object in this essay is to explore where we are led if we become followers of the negative way. My more immediate focus concerns what we are to make of the tradition's response to the negative way's apparent self-dissolution. In this particular connection the authors I have considered cannot help us, for at this critical point they tend to abandon the negative way, returning, as we have seen, to the intellect, words, and positive ways. In the final analysis they have not understood the full implications of the negative way, nor have they fully grasped the great difficulty, if not impossibility, of truly going beyond the intellect and its words. They do not confront the negative way's self-dissolution in a way that belongs to the negative way, but by abandoning it for positive ways.

Here we can turn with some hope to the Mahāyāna and Zen Buddhists. Unlike the traditions just described, they have made it a point to analyze with relentless energy the intellect's pervasive and subtle hold, and to explore deliberately the full implications of the decision no longer to rely on the intellect and its words. Specifically, the Buddhists have exposed the important word-based dualities that remain operative in forms of mystical action that involve withdrawal from the world of particulars so as to dwell exclusively in the presence of some other reality. As we have seen, St. John of the Cross retains a metaphysical dualism between God and world, the Vedantins a duality of evanescent phenomena and pure Being-Consciousness-Bliss. The Buddhists, asserting the non-difference of *samsara* and suchness, go beyond this duality. By abolishing the polarity of the sacred and the profane, the Buddhists attempt to overcome the intellect's bifurcation of reality into two parts, only one of which is mystically significant. By bringing to light these fundamental dualities, and such additional ones as being/becoming, right views/wrong views, activity/non-activity, and speech/silence, the Buddhists expose withdrawal and all other possible accounts or rationales of mystical action as grounded in the intellect and so incompatible with the negative way.[4]

This exhaustive rooting out of the intellect, which is a massive collective effort in Buddhism and a great personal effort for Meister Eckhart, leads naturally to the ideal of spontaneous mystical action, which consequently must be seen as the tradition's greatest attempt to deal with the way of unknowing's self-dissolving nature in a manner that remains true to the way of unknowing itself. Having attempted to transcend all positive claims and all dualities, including those of activity/non-activity and of speech/silence, the ideal becomes one of a pure spontaneity without a why which is entirely at home in this non-dual world, a spontaneity which, moreover, does not distinguish among speech, silence, and act, and which therefore is equally at home in and the "master" of all three. Such a life of spontaneous action does not provide conceptual answers to the disturbing questions to which the negative way's self-dissolution gives rise. It does, however, nullify all their disturbing qualities and make the questions themselves irrelevant, just as "Wash your bowl!" renders the monk's question irrelevant.

---

4. It is interesting to ask why, of the traditions I am considering, only the Buddhists have made a collective and systematic attempt to explore the hold over us of "the word" so as to come into the presence of mystery, the *suchness* or *thatness* which transcends words. We can note that the Buddhists, unlike Hindus or Christians, have no central sacred texts corresponding in power to the Bible, God's word, or the Veda, a divine texts that enjoys eternal existence. Thus Christian and Vedantic practitioners of the way of unknowing must come into conflict, perhaps both consciously and unconsciously, with their traditions' common claim that the truth has been definitively and divinely uttered in verbal form. The Buddha's teachings, though revered, do not have this status. Secondly, the preeminent social and political status of the Catholic hierarchy and the Brahmin caste have been tied closely to notions of orthodoxy and to claims of possessing accurate, detailed systems of verbally formulated "truth." The status of Buddhist monks generally has been lower and also less dependent on claims of verbal authority.

The tradition offers us the ideal of spontaneous mystical action as the one form of life truly compatible with the way of unknowing. But if we then ask whether such a form of life is actually possible for us, we quickly discover that the tradition itself is divided and often ambiguous or noncommittal on this point. Texts often dwell on this form of action at great length, but with no apparent interest in considering whether we can expect to achieve it in this life or whether we should even dream of such achievement. We have seen that the ideal of spontaneous mystical action appears first in Buddhist traditions as an attribute of Bodhisattvas. The career of a Bodhisattva spans an almost infinite number of existences, beginning with the first "thought of enlightenment" and completing itself in perfect Buddhahood. Having had the thought of enlightenment and having vowed to postpone complete liberation until all beings have achieved it, the practicing Buddhist could be said to be in a beginning phase of Bodhisattvahood. But it is the more advanced Bodhisattvas on whom the Mahāyāna sutras constantly dwell, and these "celestial" Bodhisattvas, who have completed seven or more of the ten stages, are remote from human reality. And it is only at this point that they, having passed beyond intellectual activity (*abhisamskāra*) and effort (*ābhoga*), attain the level of spontaneous action (*BT*, 234-237). Though the sutras do not state it explicitly, they imply that spontaneous mystical action can be for us, at best, an ideal. Clearly it is not a form of action we can hope to achieve in this "body" or life.

The Mahāyāna sutras imply that spontaneous mystical action, which "solves" the problem of the negative way's self-dissolution, cannot, however, be a solution for us. When we turn from Mahāyāna Buddhism to Zen, the situation becomes more complex. In Zen, as we have seen, action and the ideal of mystical spontaneity become primary concerns. In Zen, too, a powerful current questions the vast temporal perspectives brought from India and appears to suggest that complete enlightenment is a real possibility in this life. I am referring to the notion of instant enlightenment, an idea associated with the name of Hui-nêng, the famous sixth Patriarch, and often referred to as a distinguishing feature of Zen. If complete enlightenment is possible in this life, it would seem that the ideal of spontaneous mystical action, the form of action most appropriate to enlightenment on the way of unknowing, also is a real possibility, as these lines from Hui-nêng suggest:

... He who realizes the Essence of Mind may dispense with such doctrines as Bodhi, Nirvana, and "Knowledge of Emancipation" ... It makes no difference to those who have realized the Essence of Mind whether they formulate all systems of Law or dispense with them. They are at liberty to "come" or to "go". ... They are free from obstacles or impediments. They take appropriate actions as circumstances require. They give suitable answers according to the temperament of the enquirer (Hui Neng 1969, 87).

Although I will not try to do so here, it would be interesting to explore in detail the extent to which various Zen masters and schools actually taught that complete enlightenment, and the spontaneous, harmonious action which flows from it, are realistic goals for this life. "Instant enlightenment" became the rallying cry of the Southern school of Chinese Zen in its successful efforts to overcome the Northern school and its doctrine of gradual enlightenment. As such, it was a strong unifying force; but as a view in its own right, it was one that even the Southern school found necessary to modify if not abandon. In Chinese Zen texts we find many passages that clearly support it. Of Nan-Ch'üan, for instance, it is said that he "achieved sudden enlightenment. He immediately freed himself from what he had previously learned and attained the joy of *samādhi*" (*OT*, 153). And of the Kuei-shan we read:

The Master propagated the teachings of Ch'an for more than forty years. Numerous followers achieved self-realization, and forty-one disciples penetrated to the final profundity of his teaching (ibid., 208).

On the other hand, Yang-shan offers us a quite different perspective:

To attain sudden enlightenment is very difficult. If a student of Ch'an is a man of great capacity and profoundly intuitive, he may grasp a thousand things in a moment and thus become totally enlightened. However, a man of such capacity is hard to find. Therefore the ancient sages said that those of lesser talents should content themselves with their meditations and be pure in thought, for if they aimed at sudden enlightenment they would be entirely lost (ibid., 217).

And as a reminder that the path will not be easy and harmonious, we have these lines from *Yün-mên*:

> Don't say I didn't tell you that you still have blood flowing in your
> veins and that you will suffer wherever you go (ibid., 292).

It is evident that in Zen, especially in its early development, the possibility of perfect enlightenment in this very life looms as an important issue. This phenomenon within Zen mirrors the more widespread tendency at this point in Buddhist history to make liberation "easier." Buddhist Tantrism was concerned with finding ways to win Buddhahood "in this very body," and the Pure Land school was teaching that the mere utterance of the Buddha Amitābha's name assures rebirth in his celestial land. In these movements, which suggest the possibility of imminent salvation, Buddhism approaches Christianity and Islam. But in the long run the notion of instant enlightenment has receded into the background and even been abandoned. To give one example, Dōgen, the founder of the Sōtō sect in Japan, rejects the *Hui-nêng Sutra* as apocryphal (Dumoulin, p. 173) and offers the following "gradualist" point of view:

> The traditional way of comprehending the teachings of Zen consists
> in gradually improving the things one has grasped and thought
> in one's heart by ever greater conformity to the instructions of
> the master (ibid., p. 172).

On this matter contemporary Zen Buddhism is probably even less optimistic. According to Robert Aitken Roshi, writing in *The Middle Way*, it is commonly said of enlightenment in Buddhist monasteries that Sākyamuni Buddha himself is "only half-way there, and is still practicing zazen in the Tuṣita heaven" (Aitken 1987, 215).

Among the Christian writers associated with the ideal of spontaneous mystical action, I am not aware of any statements that suggest that it is an ideal we can actually hope to achieve in this life. Indeed it is striking—and I shall return to this point later—that Meister Eckhart and Angelus Silesius, like the authors of the Mahāyāna Sutras, display little interest in this question. It is as if it is enough for them to have imagined and communicated the ideal, so that the question of actually living it is strangely irrelevant. Consequently, it is only by implication that their writings bear on this question, and the implications we can find do not encourage us to expect that action "without a why" is a genuine possibility for us. Certainly the basic attitude of Christian mystics toward any ideal of perfection is that it would be arrogant and futile to aspire to wholeness in this life. In their accounts, moreover, Meister Eckhart and Angelus Silesius present spontaneous mystical action more as a vision of perfection than as actual reality. Eckhart describes action without a why as characteristic of the "true" and the "just," Platonic ideals of humanity contrasting with the complex realities we are. Just as tellingly, Angelus Silesius goes outside humanity to find in the concrete world an image of simple and untroubled spontaneity. He finds it in the blossoming of the rose, just as the Mahāyāna texts I quoted find it in the non-human simplicity of the moon or in a boat guided by the wind.

I have suggested that the ideal of spontaneous mystical action is the traditional way of unknowing's specific "solution" to the problem of action and of rationales created by the negative way's self-dissolution. We have now noted the striking fact that though the tradition presents spontaneous mystical action as this solution, it does not (except for Zen's passing interest in instant enlightenment) present it as a solution *for us*. It is the solution only for the vastly transformed beings we may someday be, an ideal to which we can only remotely aspire, a "solution" that can be perhaps humanly imagined but not humanly realized. If we then turn to consider the actual historical realities, as opposed to the writings, of mystics and mystical movements, we will only be strengthened in the surmise that spontaneous mystical action is not a reality operative in this world and this life. The various traditions characteristically attempt to comprehend the reality of mystical life by placing it in the context of an overall development culminating in a more or less remote perfection. St. John of the Cross structures his account as a graduated movement through the dark night to final union with the divine. The Bodhisattvas pass through their ten stages, finally becoming perfected Buddhas. Similarly, the traditional biographies and autobiographies of Zen masters portray a movement through periods of great doubt and anguish, the Zen sickness, culminating in progressively more profound experiences of enlightenment. But there is no reason to suppose that these simple diagrammatic pictures accurately represent the reality of mystical life within the traditions themselves. Their optimism naturally seems most unwarranted when it is supposed that we can complete the entire path in this life. But even when perfection is postponed to a near or even remote future, the underlying assumption of progress toward an eventual perfect realization has no evident justification and tends to conceal or undervalue the ambiguities, the complexity, and especially the tragic element within real spiritual life.

I mention this not with the intention of devaluing the great mystical traditions of the past, but simply to make the point that there is no reason to suppose that human beings ever attain the level of spontaneous mystical action. I believe Zen marks one of the summits in humanity's mysterious encounter with "reality"; but, at the same time, it has always been a movement of human beings and so never free from naïveté, confusion, and all-too-human motivations. I have already pointed out that during its first centuries on Japanese soil, its "classic" period there, Zen spontaneity was applied extensively to political and martial ends. If we look below the surface of this period's fine "art" of swordsmanship, we find Zen leaders and temples dependent on and intertwined with competing aristocrats, warlords, and samurai; and we find monasteries turned into military fortifications on a war footing with one another. This unedifying spectacle—the struggle for power and the killing of monk by monk—hardly encourages the view that the principle of spontaneous mystical action should be thought operative within Zen.

A similar though less violent picture emerges of the original schism between the Northern and Southern Chinese Zen schools. To a considerable extent, the Southern school owed its victory to the successful ideological attacks of its leader, Shen-hui, on the Northerners. In such battles it is both sadly and humorously clear that the way of unknowing has been forgotten, for though the masters are invariably portrayed as entirely beyond dualities of truth and falsehood or enlightenment and ignorance, the sects denoune one another for their "false" views on enlighten-ment's "true nature" (see Dumoulin 1976, 84). This ambiguous picture of mystical groups—ambiguous because the groups are made up of human beings—is, of course, universal. The first large-scale contemplative movement in Christian history was that of the Desert Fathers, who from the fourth to the sixth centuries left the cities and towns of the Near East to practice asceticism and contemplation. Though this group certainly did not emphasize the way of unknowing, it is relevant to note that for many of these contemplatives their quest issued in despair, aberration, and even madness. The human vulnerability of contemplatives is sadly manifest in India today. Tens of thousands of Tibetans, many monks among them, have fled Tibet and subsequently faced great difficulties as exiles in India. Among these monks suicide and insanity are widespread (ibid., 138).

Though we may hope that mystical groups display somewhat more harmony, inner strength, and love than do other groups, there is no reason to think that a principle of spontaneous mystical action is operative in their varied and complex histories. This is equally true of individual mystics. Admirable as certain mystics of the way of un-knowing may be, we need not think that at some point in their lives they achieved that mode of effortless, spontaneous, purely harmoni-ous action which they associate in their writings with "the just," ce-lestial Bodhisattvas, and Zen masters of bygone days, for the manifold world the intellect creates and the complexity of the human heart will always be with us. When he was not composing mystical verses, the pro-Catholic Angelus Silesius was engaged in rough-and-tumble po-lemics against Protestantism, from which he converted, publishing, for instance, in 1674, two years before his death, his most violent at-tack, *Exposé of the Blaspheming Hound of Hell and Close Friend of the Reformation Who Calls Himself Aegidius Strauchius.*

Eckhart's end is more complex, perhaps tragic. We have no direct knowledge of Eckhart's inner life during those final years, which were dominated by his attempt to defend himself against the Inquisition's investigation of him. We know that he actively defended himself, even traveling to Avignon to that end. He defended himself in public and before ecclesiastical commissions, but in vain. The papal bull which condemned him asserts that Eckhart acknowledged and recanted his "heresies" before his death. We can only speculate on the thoughts and emotions of Eckhart's inner world during those final years in which the massive institution which had nourished him, and which he had served, turned its power against him. But in those speculations we will not do full justice to Meister Eckhart the human being if we assume that, having passed beyond will and intellect, he had transcended his humanness and acted from within an entirely harmonious sphere of mystical action "without a why." (See this book's concluding essay "Avignon.")

Personal confession is not, of course, characteristic of those in-dividuals from earlier centuries we associate with the way of unknowing.

Eckhart's sermons focus entirely on their spiritual content, equally of use to all. Zen autobiographies are stylized to conform to a traditional pattern, so that only the details are individual while the basic structure remains standardized. The individual who reveals himself most intimately is probably St. John of the Cross. And as we consider both his prose works and his poetry in relation to his life, we are struck, not by the fact that at some point the saint goes "beyond," but by the intensity of his spiritual experience throughout his life and by its great emotional range, from utter desolation to radiant joy. On the whole, however, we can only speculate about the complex inner lives of these mystics of the past. This situation changes if we turn to our own time, with its greater interest in individual experience.

Though not exclusively, Thomas Merton is associated with the way of unknowing. His early work, *The Seven Storey Mountain*, is the confident account of someone who, at the end of a long struggle, found his home in the monastic, contemplative way of life. The underlying structure of *The Seven Storey Mountain* mirrors the temporal development we would wish for ourselves, that of movement, within this one life, to resolution, inner peace, perhaps even spontaneous mystical action. But such optimistic pictures greatly oversimplify the mystical life, and the confidence of *The Seven Storey Mountain* would not endure. Decades later, at the end of a life that had taken turns unanticipated in his early work, Merton stood again at a crossroads and was even considering leaving monastic life. For Merton, in other words, the all-too-human realities of struggle, inner conflict, and uncertainty were not to be transcended.

That all the complexity and ambiguity of our lives won't be resolved at some point into the simplicity of which we dream also is suggested in Dag Hammarskjöld's *Markings*. His book tells of the at least momentary resolution of self-surrender or of the touch of "the Unknown." But at the same time it reveals to its very end an almost unbearable inner tension and lonely suffering. There are few suggestions of harmony or effortlessness in this book.

Finally, a sense of the vagaries of lived mystical life, a life that may fall even comically short of the perfection to which we aspire, is suggested by these remarks of a contemporary Ch'an master, Hsüan Hua, at the close of a week of intense group meditation:

Now we have finished. Everyone stand and we will bow to the

Buddha three times to thank him. We thank him, because even if
we did not have a great enlightenment, we had a small enlightenment. If we did not have a small enlightenment, at least we didn't
sick. If we got sick, at least we didn't die. So let's thank the Buddha (Hyers 1973, 185).

I am concerned here with the relationship between the ideal of
spontaneous mystical action and reality, and specifically with the
question of whether this ideal is one we might hope to realize. Though
there are important exceptions, we have seen that the traditions do
not portray this ideal as a genuine possibility *for us*. I also have suggested that the notion of spontaneous mystical action is of no use in
our efforts to understand the personal and historical reality of mystical experience on the way of unknowing. If we turn from these historical considerations to direct reflection on the question itself, another
important point emerges: To interpret spontaneous mystical action
as a genuine possibility for human beings is to come into conflict with
the way of unknowing itself. To say that we can achieve this ideal involves a departure from the path. To the extent that it is put forward
as an actual "solution" to the problems created by the negative way's
self-dissolution, the ideal of spontaneous mystical action, like that of
withdrawal, finally represents a return to the intellect and to positive
ways.

Let us note, first, that the ideal of spontaneous mystical action
remains dependent on intellect-based dualities, subtle and appealing
though those dualities may be. The duality it creates is the contrast
between two radically different forms of human existence, the life of
spontaneous mystical action and the complex, conflict-ridden life of
"imperfect" action. Generally, the contrast is one between the mystic's
acts and all other acts. But more precisely and importantly, it juxta-
poses the mystic's present reality and an imagined alternative mystical life free of conflict, anxiety, and pain. This thoroughgoing duality
involves both our inner and outer lives, the totality of our experience.
Inwardly, a life in which doubt, emotional conflict, conflict between
desire and morality, and tension between the intellect and the way of
unknowing are always more or less present is opposed to a life free of
complexity and conflict. Outwardly, a life of weighing options, choosing,
exertion, and outer compulsions is opposed to an effortless life in
complete harmony with our environment, one in which our actions

seem to come of themselves and nevertheless always are the "right" actions.

It has taken me several sentences to begin to articulate this duality, but Tanzan and Ekido from the Zen story quoted above convey it succinctly. In fact, they are embodiments of this duality. Characteristically they are both monks, one being *monks as they are*, the other *monks as they would like to be*. This duality, though perhaps only implicit, is present and necessary in all of the versions of the ideal of spontaneous mystical action referred to above. The Bodhisattva's effortless action is contrasted with "human laboring." The "without a why" of Eckhart and Angelus Silesius contrasts implicitly with all the "why?s" which bedevil us and the mystic in actual life. And the effect of Silesius' poem on the rose depends on the implied contrast with a more complex and self-conscious form of life, one with which we are all too familiar.

The ideal of spontaneous mystical action is a vision of another, easier, more harmonious form of life placed by monks and mystics of the way of unknowing at the end of the path along which, with difficulty as well as with joy, they are moving. It is a highly specialized and also highly refined dream of paradise, the antithesis of which is real contemplative life. Simply as an ideal or dream it rests, as we have just seen, on a profound duality, one created by the intellect, and as such it is a departure from the negative way. The departure is magnified and becomes, in fact, a return to positive ways when it is also asserted that the ideal can be realized and that there is a way to realize it. For to assert that the life of spontaneous mystical action is the life that awaits us once we have "completed" the way of unknowing is to make a fundamental and strikingly optimistic assertion about the world. With such a sweeping claim we are far removed from the negative way and clearly back within the intellect's world of "positive" religion, philosophy, and metaphysics, of the dualities and assertions that constitute them.

It may be true, of course, that we human beings *can* empty ourselves of intellect and will; that the principle of spontaneous mystical action then fills this emptiness and becomes the source of effortless, conflict-free activity in perfect harmony with the world, and that consequently the problem of the negative way's self-dissolution has been "solved." But such a hypothesis about the world is not compatible either with the aim of this essay or with the evidence offered by real mystical life. My purpose is to explore where the way of unknowing leads us. As we have now seen, the idea of spontaneous mystical action departs from this way and brings us back to ways of knowing. But apart from my purposes, the basis for expecting that spontaneous mystical action is a genuine human possibility is tenuous at best.

On the whole the traditions themselves do not portray spontaneous mystical action as an achievable goal, and historical reality offers little if any evidence for it. The claim joins the ranks of the countless other propositions about the world which the intellect has advanced. The idea of spontaneous mystical action conflicts, finally, with one of the basic points I suggested first in Part II: We never pass decisively beyond the intellect with its words and concepts. The dream of spontaneous mystical action beckons us as the radically new condition that awaits us if only we succeed in completing the way of unknowing by passing entirely beyond intellect. In reality, however, that process of eliminating and going beyond the intellect will never be even remotely complete.

Even on the way of unknowing we remain enmeshed in words, concepts, doubts, anxiety, and inner conflict. Far from completing it, we are and will always remain novices on the way of unknowing. As much as we may struggle with the intellect and its words, we will never be free from their hold over us, and so the life of the way of unknowing is, at best, a frontier life at the border of words and mystery. As we struggle on the way, the ideal of spontaneous mystical action presents itself to us as its paradisiacal completion, an imagined transformation of our lives into an effortless, harmonious unity. But we will not reach that promised land of completion or become "someone else." We will complete nothing, novices that we are and so destined to remain at the beginning of the way. And the ideal of spontaneous mystical action, we finally see, is itself a contradiction—a mirage. It offers itself as the transformation that occurs when the intellect is entirely dissolved, yet it is itself a creation of the intellect. It poses as a new form of existence and action, but it represents in fact a return to the intellect and its dualities, words, images, and assertions about the world. Like "inactivity," like the "sacred," like "silence," it is, we finally realize, only one more temptation along the way.

As a human possibility, the ideal of spontaneous mystical action is a fiction and a self-contradiction. In both the past and our own time, however, it has exerted a powerful appeal, and in trying to explain this fascination two factors are of great importance. First, traditional Buddhism is a religion or a practice the clear goal of which is liberation. The basic teachings of original Buddhism were that life is suffering, but that suffering can be overcome by traveling the eightfold path. Similarly, traditional Christianity is a religion of salvation, the assertion that the sin and suffering which define our lives have been or can be redeemed by the suffering of Christ, and that "soon" a transformation of the world or at least of the redeemed individual will occur. Buddhism, Christianity, and most religions with written traditions assert an ultimate harmony, the overcoming of all conflict, suffering, and evil, whether in the Buddhist *nirvana*, the Christian heaven, or some other form. To live within these traditions is to live with certain more or less unspoken assumptions—and one of the most powerful of these assumptions is the association of religion with ultimate harmonies. The forms of the way of unknowing that have developed within these traditions have inherited and preserved these powerful expectations. As we have seen, the ideal of spontaneous mystical action, problematic as it may be, is the traditional way of unknowing's *version* of ultimate harmony, the specific way in which it fulfills traditional expectations of a final perfect state.

This historical factor having to do with what we more or less automatically expect of "religion" undoubtedly is one important reason for the great appeal of the ideal of spontaneous mystical action in both the past and the present. A second reason, one related to the first, is our very human tendency to prefer the imaginative, vicarious experience of perfection to immediate awareness of our own all-too-real imperfection. I have suggested that spontaneous mystical action is a humanly impossible goal—that it is, in fact, a self-contradiction, a supposed transcendence of the intellect rooted in the intellect. It is a "perfection" we can experience only in the imagination, and then only confusedly and imperfectly. And so the travelers on the negative way, eager to participate in perfection in the one way possible for them, lose themselves in the contemplation of the Bodhisattvas, just persons, and Zen masters of spontaneity they themselves can never be.

We are close here to what can be so quickening for us in Eckhart's sermons, the great Mahāyāna sutras, and Zen stories. They are relentless and endlessly creative first of all in their pursuit of the way's central negative aspect: ferreting out the intellect's subtle presence in the most unexpected places, then demolishing with a few powerful strokes the very foundations on which we had thought they stood. They offer us previously unimagined perspectives in which the intellect's hold is at least loosened, taking us to the outermost reaches of our capacity, then always returning, sooner or later, to the absolute ineffability, the humanly unimaginable plenitude of just this moment and place. They create an emptiness, a mysteriously fertile desert place which at the same time is this world at this moment; they then populate this reborn world with beings somewhat like ourselves who nevertheless are unreservedly at home in this world beyond words, who exist in perfect harmony with it and act with pure, effortless spontaneity within it. And we ourselves are quickened and renewed, if only inwardly and imperfectly, by this fleeting glimpse of a concretely imagined life entirely beyond words and rationales, a life which for a moment seems almost within our grasp.

I suggested in Part I that contemporary Westerners may naïvely tend to see the hard work of spiritual paths and inner transformation as quickly and easily achievable. We also may be unusually prone to substitute an imagined spiritual life for one that is actual. Writing in the United States, I am especially aware of living in a society in which there is little connection between stated religious beliefs and what is called "real life." As defined by its majority, the United States is a land of Christian consumers, adherents of the Sermon on the Mount who appear willing, even eager, to engage in the nearly full-time pursuit of material goods and security. This remarkable paradox is possible only where there is virtually no connection between fine words, imaginings, and occasional symbolic actions, on the one hand, and "life" on the other. In such a society it comes to be understood that religion, apart from clearly demarcated rituals, is a purely inward affair, a matter of aesthetics and the imagination, having no real connection with our actions and lives in the world. If this is the starting point from which we subsequently encounter and learn to value the sutras, Zen stories, Eckhart's "without a why," and Angelus Silesius' rose, we may then value them primarily for the contribution they make to our inner, purely imaginative experience. And we may be inclined to let the matter rest there, as if the vicarious imagining of impossible perfections were the true center of religious or mystical life.

This tendency to construct and then dwell imaginatively in purely symbolic images of perfection is not, however, peculiarly Western or contemporary. The numberless Mahāyāna Bodhisattvas, all the fully enlightened Zen masters, Eckhart's "the just," and Angelus Silesius' rose are all, as we have seen, products of the major traditions themselves. It is clear, in other words, that the greatest expressions of the negative way that have come down to us from the past share our propensity to substitute imagination for reality, to use words and images to create purely symbolic images of perfections and then to try to dwell vicariously in those images. In the nineteenth century, Søren Kierkegaard ironically made the point about philosophers (especially Hegel) that they constructed magnificent edifices of thought in which they could not actually live as flesh-and-blood human beings. We have now seen considerable evidence of a similar tendency in mystics of the negative way. In the past, tremendous energies have been poured into the creation of images of perfection, vast edifices that can only be entered imaginatively, edifices that are not and could never be genuine expressions of spiritual life as it actually is. And we in our turn tend to gravitate toward these imagined perfections and so to make the mere imaginative glimpsing of conflict-free wholeness, which in itself is one of the tradition's great achievements, the focal point of our contemplative lives.

We might consider that this imagined perfection is to be taken only as an ideal, a source of inspiration. But if we simply legitimate the tradition's imagined embodiments of spontaneous mystical action in this way, we forget two things. First, the ideal itself is a creation of the intellect, and so even as a "mere ideal" it is a departure from the way of unknowing, a return to the world of the intellect and its symbols. Second, it pictures the negative way as having a culmination, and it further portrays that completion as a condition of perfection, the condition of *masters.* In doing this, it diverts us from awareness of our actual condition on the negative way, our perpetual "beginner" status, whereas further movement on the negative way most likely will come, not from imagining states of mastery that depart from it, but from the continued exploration of the reality of our novice state. On a purely practical level, moreover, the cultivation of dreams of mastery leaves us singularly unequipped to deal with reality's negative aspects when they do force themselves upon us, making us realize that we ourselves are nothing like the harmonious, conflict-free masters we have been imagining. Despair and self-accusation are the likely result of being forced to measure our actual lives against this phantom.

Our tendency to prefer the imagined vicarious experience of an unreal perfection to the actual living through of the complexity and ambiguities of real spiritual experience has yet another unfortunate consequence: it often distorts our relation to the tradition itself, to those followers of the negative way who have preceded us. This distortion is most evident if we look specifically at the way we usually approach historical Zen, the tradition that has surpassed all others in the energy, creativity, and subtlety with which it has pursued the negative way. For there is a remarkable blind spot in the way we tend to approach Zen, especially classic Chinese Zen, and to present it to others. These portrayals are invariably based on the collections of anecdotes and dialogues that most people find such an appealing aspect of Zen. What is striking is that the question of the historical authenticity of these accounts seldom if ever surfaces. Are these encounters real or imagined? Did these masters actually exist as portrayed in these accounts, or are they fictional?

Writers on Zen show little interest in this fundamental question, and we typically do not either as we read their accounts. In his numerous and now classic presentations of Zen to the West, D. T. Suzuki characteristically takes all the accounts at face value and ignores the "historical" question. This is also largely true of works that explicitly present themselves as histories of Zen, as in the case with Heinrich Dumoulin's *A History of Zen Buddhism*. Dumoulin's book is scholarly and presents itself as history. It is by no means a partisan apology, and it does, for example, discount reports of miracles. But Dumoulin relies primarily on the traditional collections of stories and dialogues as if they were reliable historical documents, even though in the case of Chinese Zen the documents we have were composed centuries after the incidents they presumably recount.

This failure to confront the question of historical truth tends to skew our relations with Zen, leading us to confuse its own realities and imaginings. For we focus almost entirely on the enlightened masters the texts portray, and we easily identify Zen's early masters, of whom we really know next to nothing, with the largely fictional masters these texts create. We simply do not have sound evidence for drawing even tentative conclusions about those early Masters. The fact that Zen stories generally portray them as perfect masters, realizing to the full the ideal of spontaneous mystical action, merely suggests the imaginative and utopian nature of these texts. Our failure to ask the question of historical truth leads us on, however, to the pleasant notion that dozens or hundreds of fully enlightened Zen masters, fully harmonious within and without, populated the China of the seventh, eighth, and ninth centuries. Though we may consciously "know better," we forget, when we read the Zen accounts, that this is an *imagined* culture, and so at the same time we forget that the true human reality is not these enlightened Masters, but the much more frail human beings who have imagined them. For Zen's historical reality is not these imagined Masters but its living novices, human beings like us. These novices have created for themselves, and for us, a series of wonderful folktales of the way of unknowing.

There is an amazing creativity and subtlety in this ideal culture they have imagined, a fictional society based not on economic necessity or power politics but on the negative way. The intellect's hold on us is infinitely ramified, a fact which offers endless possibilities for exposing it, and in this exploration our anonymous authors are wonderfully subtle and energetic. As we have seen, the notion that there are such things as enlightenment and the way must be continually deflated. Lest we suppose that there is something special to hang on to, we are continually reminded that there is "nothing." Lest we fall into the trap of supposing that silence, then, somehow gives special access to suchness, our fictitious masters are portrayed as equally at home in speech, silence, and physical acts. Lest we suppose that awe, ecstasy, and reverence, as opposed to more everyday emotions, are the proper responses to mystery, we are shown masters who specialize in the comic and in disrespect for the sacred.

I have suggested that these masters usually are portrayed as fully enlightened embodiments of spontaneous action, but sometimes the awareness of human incompleteness breaks in, as in this exchange on "substance" and "function," which I take to correspond with inner enlightenment and spontaneous mystical action respectively:

> Once when all the monks were out picking tea leaves the Master (Kuei-shan) said to Yang-shan, "All day as we were picking tea leaves I have heard your voice, but I have not seen you yourself. Show me your original self." Yang-shan thereupon shook the tea tree.
>     The Master said, "You have attained only the function, not the substance." Yang-shan remarked, "I do not know how you yourself would answer the question." The Master was silent for a time.

Yang-shan commented, "You, Master, have attained only the substance, not the function" (Chang 1969, 204).

Portrayed here is a fragment of an imagined ideal culture, one that revolves entirely around the way of unknowing. In their preoccupation with it Kuei-shan and Yang-shan are certainly serious—it is, after all, the perpetual center of their conversations. But there also is playfulness in their talk, and this playfulness adds a generous measure of ironic humor to their use of such grand terms as *substance* and *function*, which otherwise might be metaphysics and jargon. The scene, moreover, one of picking tea leaves and then of shaking the tree, ensures that we do not take these philosophical terms too seriously. There appears, finally, to be a mutually understood recognition and acceptance of human incompleteness. Yang-shan can act, but is there anything "behind" it? The master, on the other hand, appears to have something "inside," but then why can't he say or do anything? To neither of them, however, does this situation seem to be surprising—they take their human incompleteness in stride. Tomorrow, undoubtedly, they will continue with their outdoor work, their pursuit of the way, and their conversation.

Kuei-shan is said to have died in 853 C.E. This conversation with Yang-shan appears in *The Transmission of the Lamp*, the first "historical record" of Chinese Zen compiled by Tao-yüan in 1004 C.E. (ibid., xiii). It is stretching credulity to suppose that this conversation ever took place. It is also stretching credulity to suppose that the culture this conversation and thousands like it portray ever existed. In ninth century China there was no subculture built entirely around the way of unknowing, one in which ambition, desire, uncertainty, inner conflict, envy, and questions of economics and politics played only marginal roles, in which devoted seekers of truth were guided by others who led lives in which perfect inner clarity expressed itself in spontaneous and harmonious acts. The Zen culture of these texts is an imagined utopian culture, religious "literature." We easily recognize Mahāyāna Buddhism's Bodhisattvas and their marvelous deeds, thoughts, and Pure Lands as products of the mystical imagination. Zen's great masters, as portrayed in the traditional texts, are the Zen equivalent of those Bodhisattvas, though these masters are the protagonists of an earthier, more "realistic" literature. Undoubtedly it is the realism of the Zen accounts that encourages us not only to be drawn toward this imagined perfection but to blur the line between it and historical fact.

Like the vast literature of the Bodhisattvas, that of the Chinese Zen masters was created, more or less collectively, by many anonymous authors. It is safe to assume that in their personalities and lives these authors resemble us much more than they resemble the masters they created. We and they are real human beings after all, and the masters of their accounts are not. In both their personalities and individual biographies they undoubtedly displayed great variations, from inner harmony and good fortune to inner conflict and great misfortune, and in this respect they are just like us and just like their non-monk contemporaries. Among them were stable characters, energetic and happy ones, melancholiacs, and depressives, monks in the best of health and monks perpetually sick and in pain. Surely they were much less centered, less harmonious, and more complicated than the characters they created. And what is most significant for our purposes, they were not by any means the fully enlightened masters of spontaneous mystical action their imaginations invented, but rather novices on the way of unknowing. They were Ekidos, not humanly impossible, chimerical Tanzans.

Once we have changed our perspective from imagined utopias to human reality we see, in fact, that what is special about these monks is not that they had completed or mastered the way, but the mere fact that they had set out upon it—that is the full measure of their claim on our attention and gratitude. And though some of them, by force of circumstance and personality, seemed more harmonious and spontaneous—that is, more like Tanzan—than others, we need not take this to mean that they were farther advanced on the way. After all, isn't the dichotomy harmonious/disharmonious just one more of the intellect's innumerable dualistic creations?

A culture of novices struggling on the way of unknowing collectively imagined a humanly impossible culture revolving around enlightened masters who have actually completed the way. Into the imaginative creation of this appealing though ultimately self-contradictory culture went many different motives: the tendency to construct imaginative perfections and paradises; our desire to escape conflict, suffering, and boredom; love of the way of unknowing; the desire to free oneself and others from the intellect; an at least temporary victory over the intellect expressing itself playfully and imaginatively;

pleasure in literary composition; our propensity to imitate and to complete. Some of these motives subsequently lead us, however, to ignore these novices entirely in favor of the masters they have imagined, for we may be especially prone to dwell vicariously in imagined possibilities or even impossibilities. But these novices are the human reality of Zen, the actual, concrete tradition we can recall and inwardly address. We should not turn away from them, just as we should not turn away from our own difficult and complex lives.

## PART V: THE MYSTERY OF ACTION

HAVING TURNED AWAY—NEAR THE END OF PART IV—from that utopian and mythical culture of enlightened masters whose every act shines forth as realizing perfectly the ideal of spontaneous mystical action, I looked instead at the culture of the novices who created them. Continuing to reflect on these creators, we may be led to glimpse or experience one of the unexpected and most precious gifts of this and other forms of mystical life: our kinship and bond with those novices in what Christianity traditionally calls the "communion of saints." For they live the complex and difficult lives that are inevitable at the border of "the mystical," just as we do. Within a mystery that transcends the divisions of time and space, they and we are kin who walk together the same path. As we continue on the way of unknowing, we will often be grateful for, and nourished by, this profound bond.

If we turn our attention, however, to our reflections on the way of unknowing itself, and to the problem of the way's seeming self-dissolution, we find ourselves at an impasse. I pointed out in Part IV that the tradition typically does not even attempt to portray the ideal of spontaneous mystical action as an attainment to seek in actual life. Additionally, and still more seriously, the ideal of spontaneous mystical action involves the creation of new dualities and comprehendings. This means that it cannot represent the realization of the way of unknowing, for it is a departure, a return to *positive* ways. Our goal has been to explore the way of unknowing as a form of mystical life, but now we are at a standstill. As something we can describe and understand, the way of unknowing has dissolved itself, leaving us with "nothing." We have apparently raised a question that has no possible, plausible, or even conceivable answer.

Before yielding to this apparent impasse and turning away from the way of unknowing, let us note, however, that the preceding sentence merely repeats a sentence from Part I. Let us note that in the course of this reflection we have experienced and overcome such an impasse once before. What brought the intellect to a halt then was this question: "Why does the world exist?" But then we also observed that the mystic, unlike the philosopher and unlike the rest of us, chooses not to turn aside from the mystical, but rather to abide with it and dwell within it. We can see now that our continuing exploration of the way of unknowing has brought us to a similar impasse, only this time "the mystical" is something that strikes us as much closer to us, as much more intimate, than the existence of the world. It is our very *life* as a life on the way of unknowing. The mystical is now all our actions, is that miraculous event or act each one of us *is*.

In Parts I and II, I wrote that the mystic on the way of unknowing is always a novice, a pioneer, a perpetual beginner. Recollecting this enduring quality of all experience on the way, we can now apply it to the mystic's relation to his or her own life and acts. Here, too—in my perception of and response to that mystery that is my own life and acts—all seeings are, as it were, my very first glimpse, all "progress" always just the very first step, all dilemmas and questions the very first. I pointed out in Part II that the mystic on the way of unknowing must apply the negative way to the way itself. Having done so, the mystic will no longer be able to name, describe, explain, or justify that way and that life. Hinduism's portrayal of the *jīvan-mukta* as having passed beyond action's sphere and various versions of the ideal of spontaneous mystical action are attempts to go beyond this, to "resolve" the impasse and dilemma created by the way's self-dissolving quality. But now these "solutions," too, have dissolved. Once again it is clear we are pioneers and novices; once again we are back where we began.

Further, as we continue to reflect on life and action, we may experience the ever-widening dissolution of the names, descriptions, explanations, and justifications we apply to *all* our acts. I wrote earlier that when confronted by the question of why the world exists, we soon become uneasy and restless. Eager to get back to our "real lives," we readily accept any proposed answer, no matter how superficial or patently inadequate that explanation may be. So it is with our own lives and acts. Avoiding questions and reflection, we seek to get on with our lives, carrying with us a handful of ready-made and ill-examined descriptions, explanations, valuations, and justifications. These catchwords, the common currency of self-explanation, enable us to pretend to others and to ourselves that we understand our acts and our lives, just as we pretend among and to ourselves that we have a good idea of "why" the world exists. But if, instead of hurrying back to our "real lives," we continue to reflect on life and action, we find that our supposed self-knowledge, like our supposed understanding of the world's origin, melts away.

If I seek, for example, to name, describe, explain, or justify what I have done today, I will quickly arrive at categories and pictures of action radically different from the internally diverse accounts that would be offered by individuals from a dozen distinct cultures. Confronted by this fact, can I maintain that *my* account is the right one? For that matter, can I go on assuming that there is such a thing as a "true account"? Or if I ask how it is that I can do the most familiar and everyday things, like remembering my own name, or why it is that I got up this morning just when I did, I find that I soon arrive at "explanations" that I cannot explain, or at several competing, equally plausible explanations, or at explanations based on nothing but hearsay and speculation. I begin to realize that explanation is an unending dreamlike movement toward a goal—the "explanation"—that recedes infinitely, moving away again with each "advance" I make, and that each temporarily satisfying explanation merely provides the material for a new question. And as my habitual explanations melt away, I begin to see that my acts and my life are not safely enclosed within a sheltering context of explanation and justification. Instead it begins to seem that each of my acts, that my *life* is an event that is indescribable, inexplicable and unjustifiable, an event that is just *given*. I wrote in Part I that the intellect, having asked, "Why does the world exist?" eventually runs up against the irreducible and impenetrable fact of being. Now, having arrived at the end of our fragile and invariably questionable self-explanations, the intellect finally halts before the inexplicable and irreducible fact of "my life," and before the impenetrable givenness of each *act*.

The Uncertainty Principle asserts that the movement of atoms is influenced and altered by our mere observation of them. We can now see that the mystical, observed and experienced in contemplation, inevitably dilates, stopping only when it has encompassed awareness's entire contents. Earlier I noted that the intellect's failure with regard to the "why" of the world soon spreads to the "what." Now we have seen that process repeating itself in another realm. We have seen mystery, within which the way of unknowing already has dissolved—spread out to encompass all our acts, our entire life and self: On the way of un-knowing, after all, we are to know *nothing* either of "things above" or of "things below." What will be the mystic's reaction to the impasse I have described and to this dilation? Earlier I described how the mys-tic, unlike the philosopher and unlike the rest of us, abides with the mystical, even though the intellect is entirely helpless in relation to it. Now that process of abiding and immersion is repeated, with just this difference: This time, "the mystical" is the mystic's own life, the mystic's own *acts*. Earlier, I became a novice beginning to dwell in the world as in a mystery. Now I grow out of my own seemingly compre-hended life, out of my own seemingly familiar and intelligible acts. Novice-like once again, I begin dwelling within my own acts, within my life as it is at this very moment, as a mystery. This means that I turn aside from my fascination with descriptions, explanations, and evaluating assessments of my acts and life, and attend instead to the pure act each act—and my entire life—is. It means I begin to dwell within the mystery that action finally transcends all namings, descrip-tions, explanations, and valuations, the great mystery that action is prior to the *logic* of action. It means that the pure mystery I call "my life" and those pure mysteries I call my "acts" are what is real, and the words I think or utter about them a kind of dream, one way—"mine"—of dreaming that life and those acts.

What would such a life be like? Is it possible to live, not as a seem-ingly self-transparent, self-elucidating "I," but as a mystery whose scent, more than anything else, is the scent of "the mystical"? Can there be action free of all context, a pure act unframed and unsupported by any "logic of action"? Such action is not only possible but actual. In-deed, the supreme example of such a pure act is the event that formed the starting point of this reflection: the creation, the coming-to-be of the world. That is the supreme event, making possible all other events. And it is the great example of action prior to any logic of action, for in that "nothing" out of which something emerges, there clearly can be no "cause," "motive," or "material," that might then provide the basis for a description, explanation, or assessment. In that nothing there can be just "nothing"—and that is precisely why the "illogical" emer-gence of "something" is the mystical.

Because the coming-to-be of the world is the supreme and original exemplar of event as mystery, the mystic on the way of unknowing can embrace it as the archetype upon which all the mystic's acts are modeled, and within which they participate. On the way of unknowing, my life, just like that primordial, mind-breaking coming-to-be, is a mystery. As I act—as I make a difficult decision or simply reach out through a summer day's tranquillity to pick up a stone from the shore—my act echoes and somehow replicates that supreme act. Earlier we saw how the mystic, having decided to abide with the mystery of existence, begins to discern and enter into the previously unsuspected depth of the world. Now I begin as well to awaken to the mystery and depth of my own acts, of that most intimate and unknown thing I call "my life."

AS WE BEGIN, LIKE A HATCHING CHICK, to break out of our customary descriptions, explanations, and evaluations—out of all our "comprehension"—of our acts and lives, and as we then begin to discern and abide within action's mystery, we might be said to have "progressed" beyond the assumptions and habits that earlier led us to construct a remote, dualistically conceived ideal of mystical action. That advance is twofold. First, our awareness no longer is contained and shaped by the intellect's distinction between the perfect and imperfect act, and between the novice (that is, us) and those masters who, having reached the highest summit of the path, flawlessly realize the ideal of spontaneous mystical action. For now acts are not "perfect" or "imperfect," not "flawless" or "clumsy," not "this" or "that." Now all verbal distinctions are swallowed up in the pure mystery of the act, of the finally unnameable event both you and I right now are. Second, we have now begun to realize that the "mystical" quality of action is not a supreme skill or mastery to be achieved. For "the mystical" already is present in all action, and so our seeking to acquire it is an attempt to duplicate—superfluously—what is already there. Instead of seeking to achieve the mystical act, we need only become alert to the mystery that already pervades all our acts, just as we awakened earlier to the mystical quality of the fact *that* the world is. To be journeying on the way of unknowing, to lose oneself in recollection, to move a ladder or pick up a brush—all are, first of all, great mysteries. "How wondrous this," exclaims P'ang Chü-shih, "how mysterious! I carry fuel, I draw water" (Hyers 1973, 87).

In these two ways we have "advanced," but here as before we soon discover or are reminded that life on the way of unknowing is not a steady progress or an ascent toward an attainable or even verbally specifiable goal. It is repetition, a continual beginning over; it is again and again to awaken as if for the first time to the subtle and infinite mystery that pervades each space, each moment I occupy. Here, as before, we do not move "forward" toward answers and explanations. We don't "explain" the world's existence, or our own acts and lives, and then "move on." We don't seek answers to the questions of why the world exists or how action is possible. Instead, we slowly begin to realize that our questions are not the first steps of a limited question and answer process; they are infinite koans which, sooner or later, bring verbal awareness to a halt, so that mystical awareness can burst out of all answers and all questions and dwell in the inconceivable.

Of course these haltings and burstings, like all else in life, are provisional—most likely they will be followed by an equally provisional return to a less alert condition. This fact and the related fact that life on the way of unknowing is a continual beginning over and rediscovery suggest to us both the importance and the nature of the mystic's ongoing "work" in relation to the mystery of action. It is important because the ideal or dream of spontaneous mystical action performed by someone else, or by me in a remote future, is replaced by the *work* of awakening to the mystery that pervades all action. The nature of that work will be analogous to that undertaken by the mystic in relation to the "why" of the world. Here, too, we will attend closely to the spreading failure of the intellect, this time as it broadens out from the actions and life of the way of unknowing to include all acts and all life. We will continually discover, and then dissolve, previously undetected stores of self-comprehension. We will find that new and subtler forms of self-knowing are continually forming within awareness, and we will work not to let awareness be encompassed and molded by them. In all this we are working to learn, slowly and haltingly, to be an event outside and greater than all understanding, a mystery we cannot begin to comprehend.

The fact that the mystic's relation to action and the very life of unknowing, like is or her relation to the mystery of existence, is one of abiding, repetition, and immersion—and not one of steady progress toward solutions and goals—deepens our awareness that the way of unknowing remains always a life at the border between the seemingly known and the unknown, and between words and the wordless. In the mystic's relation to action, as in the mystic's relation to all things, there will be frequent crossings and recrossings of that border. Having wandered for a time on the other side, and having abided there in the mystery of action and of the life of unknowing, the mystic may return and attempt to communicate something of that mystery in words. Further, circumstances, choice, or necessity will frequently bring him or her back to "this side," where for a time he or she will make choices and carry out actions, and these will be accompanied by the words, descriptions, explanations, evaluations, and justifications the rest of us use when we choose and act. For choosing and acting are inherent in human life and, as we have seen, on the way of unknowing there exists no mechanism of spontaneous mystical action to which the mystic can turn over the responsibility for choosing and acting. This means that as the mystic returns across the border from the wordless to words, he or she will choose and act as we all do.

Indeed, the very fact that the mystic now is compelled to attend to the deliberating, reasoning, and assessing—the "logic"—which accompany human choice and action means that the mystic now discovers a dimension of the mystical, and of life in the mystical, which reflection on the "why" of the world fails to disclose. The question, "Why does the world exist?" leads in reflection and contemplation to a discovery of the mystical. Reflection on the question of how action is possible deepens and widens that awareness. But the inevitability of choice and action also leads the mystic to seek to realize the mystical in choice and action, as well as in reflection and contemplation. We have seen that the mystic can do this by abiding in the mystery of all action, and by seeing in all action a reflection or reenactment of the supreme event-mystery, the coming-to-be of the world. The inexplicable emergence of something from nothing is the quintessential example of action prior to the logic of action—indeed, of action not framed or supported in any way by any "logic." But for human beings, defining, weighing, explaining, assessing, deliberating—that is, logic—are essential elements in the choosing and acting process.

Here the mystic is challenged to realize the mystical in choice and action on a particularly difficult and subtle second level of action. On the one hand, the mystic will reflect, weigh, evaluate, choose, and then act—more or less adeptly, more or less successfully—as we all do. But at the same time, all this will take place for the mystic within that greater realm that is the mystery of existence and action. There *will* be reasoned choices and actions that can be unfolded in words; there will be, that is, a "logic of action." But that logic, in turn, will be a logic that hovers in nothing. The logic itself—the verbalized "why" that accounts for my choice and act—will be a logic which, finally, is inexplicably just "there," precisely as the world, inexplicably, is "there." Finally, in fact, that logic simply adds to mystery. Just like carrying fuel or drawing water, it is simply one more manifestation and realization of the mystical, whose supreme archetypal manifestation is the coming-to-be of the world. When choosing and acting, the mystic will consequently have "reasons" for acting, as we all do. But at the same time, the mystic will be abiding with and awakening to the fact that—as for those reasons—there is no reason, no Eckhartian "why."

As we have seen, the mystic's frequent crossings and recrossings at the border testify to his or her complex and constantly shifting relationship with words. For, on one hand, the mystic enters mystery just by passing beyond words; and, on the other, the mystic often returns to this side in order to convey something of the wordless by means of words. If we ourselves journey on the way of unknowing, this ambiguous tension will carry over into our attitude toward those other travelers who use words in this way to suggest and describe routes, to call attention to important sites, and to "map" the wordless. There will be times when we need above all to break out of their words—they are, after all, "just words"; and we often need to break out of *all* those words which, instead of pointing toward the wordless, tend to divert us from it, or even to bury it under words and knowing. But there will be other times when the words of those other possibly more experienced travelers are most wonderfully able to deepen our awareness of mystery, and to impel us toward or into the wordless.

So it has been here—in relation to that mystery, action. In Part IV, it seemed necessary to break out of the tradition's ideal of spontaneous mystical action. That unrealizable dream simply reinforces our inveterate tendency to imagine that we can map the wordless and to see dualities where there is neither one nor two. It strengthens our inclination to move toward answers and solutions, rather than to let the very questions themselves dissolve in mystery. But then, having freed ourselves, if only temporarily, from our propensity to use spontaneous mystical action (or any other conception) as a way to comprehend the life of unknowing, we can listen to and be stirred by the tradition's words afresh. I have quoted the eighth-century Chinese Zen monk, P'ang Chü-shih, and referred again to Eckhart. If we now reconsider Meister Eckhart's formulation —"without a why," or perhaps simply "no why"—we see that it points us in a most succinct and quickening way toward the pure act: action not framed, supported, or delimited by any logic of action, action free of all context. And if we then look more closely at Eckhart's words, we discover that he often calls attention to the likeness, or even identity, I have also touched upon here: that between the supreme event—the coming-into-being of the world, the "creation"—and the event you are and I am right now. Indeed, Eckhart often describes this identity as complete. When reality is known most truly—that is, when it is "known" outside of time, words, and knowing—it is seen that reality is just "one life and one being and one act" (Eckhart 1979, 185). That act is the creation, the coming-to-be of all things and events which is taking place "right now" in a "now" outside time. In this perfect oneness, the event I am is not anything other than that "one act," that timeless coming-to-be. "In my eternal birth," Eckhart writes, "were all things born, and I was the cause of myself and of all things" (ibid., 308). This oneness—the fact that the event I am and the one supreme event are but one event— makes it possible for me, like God, to act "without a why."

These reflections on action and on the relation between the mystery of action and the mystery of existence, point us toward one of the way of unknowing's most important qualities. The world it enables us to enter is mind-breakingly vast and manifold, but at the same time it is, as the end of the last paragraph intimates, a place of the most subtle simplicity. For on one hand, of the many important questions and topics the way of unknowing suggests, we have considered here just two: the questions of why the world exists and how action is possible within this form of mystical life. I have not even alluded to numerous other questions and themes relating, for instance, to the nature of the self, the nature or "non-nature" of the wordless itself, the mystic's evolving relationship with the world our five senses discover or invent, the question of how it is even *possible* for any actions or words to somehow participate in or disclose the signless. As for the two questions I have considered, what is true elsewhere on the way of unknowing is true here: I have scarcely begun—or, strictly speaking, I have not even begun—to fathom or explore them, for they are unlimited, and the end of reflection upon them is still an infinity away, just as it was before this particular reflection began. As we reflect further on the very questions themselves, and on the process they set in motion, we begin to sense that they—and perhaps *all* questions—are not so much questions as koans. Questions—so at least we dream —lead to answers. They are settled and laid to rest by those answers. But the questions we have been considering set in motion an unlimited reflection—for words, sentences, and possible "answers," like space, are infinite. There are just two possible ways, therefore, in which reflection on these questions can come to an end. One possibility, described in Part I in relation to the question of why the world exists, is simply to abandon the question. Doing so enables us to return to our real lives or, alternatively, to take up other, more meaningful questions, those amenable to the intellect.

The other possibility is to continue to pursue the question wherever it leads us, to "work" at it with all our energy. In this way, we let the question become a koan. Such questioning will not end in mere abandonment, and it will not end with an answer—there are no answers to infinite questions. It will end in only one way: The frustration, the bewilderment, the laughter, the awareness of words' strangeness and frailty, the sense of constriction, the sense of mystery—all will accumulate in the questioner until one day that questioner gradually or all at once finds him- or herself breaking out of that question and out of all words, just as one day—inevitably and *unknowingly*—the chick breaks out of its shell. The chick will have come into what we humans call "the world." The questioner will have been released by that koan into the wordless.

Since it contains numerous infinite, and infinitely varied, reflections and experiences, the way of unknowing resembles in its constantly changing multiplicity the seemingly familiar world, this vast kaleidoscopic universe with its "ten-thousand things." Yet it is equally true that the way of unknowing displays that perfect simplicity the tradition frequently attributes to God. On this way we sometimes will delight in or be bewildered by its boundless manifoldness. At other times, it will be as if all things and events are united. All become, mystically, one. Discovering this, we become more and more aware of the fact that life on the way of unknowing is not a continual and rapid journey from one new sight and experience to another. It is life in just a few "places"; it is immersion in a mere handful of great and abiding mysteries.

Here I have reflected on two questions: "Why does the world exist?" and "How might one actually live a form of mystical life that seems to dissolve itself?" One question reaches out toward that most remote and obscure happening: the ultimate origin. The other directs our attention toward those most intimate realities: my own life, my own acts. Exploration of these seemingly divergent questions leads us into the most diverse areas. Following the first, we soon find ourselves pondering the hypotheses of modern physics, medieval reasonings about existence and God, ancient creation myths. The second question naturally leads us to explore Taoist, Christian, Hindu, Buddhist, and other forms of the way of unknowing. It leads us to reflect on all action, and on the rationales used to explain and justify various forms of mystical and non-mystical life. Yet these two divergent, inwardly multifarious reflections, which wind slowly over great distances and through the most diverse landscapes, have at last flowed, river-like, into a single all-subsuming reflection on one boundless act. It is the undivided and uncontained act that—right now—fills you, me, and all things: the timeless, seamless, inexplicable act of *being*. It is the great mystery of the verb, the mystery of the pure act, of the unlimited pure act. It is the supreme act all our little and imperfect acts—somehow—perfectly enact and duplicate. Reflection on the why of the world becomes at last an abiding with it. Reflection on the how of my own acts becomes at last a dwelling with and within it. Our lives in words—our lives on "this side"—are lives in a constantly shifting multiplicity. But the mystic on the way of unknowing might move for an entire lifetime within this great mystery as a fish moves all its days in one sea.

# PART II
# WAYS INTO MYSTERY

# THE GOD IN THE MOMENT

ENCOUNTERING THE PHRASE "the God in the moment" our minds may quickly scan to more familiar sounds such as "to live for the moment" and "seize the day," but, in fact, these latter expressions have an entirely different source and actually mislead us about their relationship with time. For when we live "for the moment," our awareness, desire, and joy are not in reality focused on the moment itself, but rather on something else—an experience, a person, an action, a thing—that is filling the moment. Clearly there is a way, a relatively superficial way, in which living for the moment differs from living in the past or for the future. To live in the past is to fill the present moment with memories, and to live in the future is to fill the present moment with thoughts and dreams of that future, and of the actions we imagine will bring it about. But whether living in the past, for the moment, or in and for the future, we are only varying an underlying action that is always the same: we are using one thing or another to fill the present moment itself, which we experience as a void to be filled. If we should sense, however, that there is a god in the moment itself, the situation would be wholly changed. Then we would no longer experience the moment itself as an emptiness that must be filled—or, even worse, as time to "kill"—but rather as a hidden fullness to be uncovered, a great unexplored gold field in which we might happily become lost.

How do we usually relate to the moment itself, separated out from the assortment of actions and experiences with which we ordinarily try to fill it? No one has described better than Pascal that hidden ocean of disquietude that begins to stir if we turn aside from our "diversions" and just sit quietly with the present moment, with who we are *right now*, and with what our condition is *right now*. No one has described better than he how we therefore flee this disquiet, escaping into the past or, more likely, into the future, a doubly *unreal* future. "We never keep to the present," he writes,

> "We recall the past; we anticipate the future as if we found it too slow in coming . . . We are so unwise that we wander about in times that do not belong to us, and do not think of the only one that does . . . The fact is that the present usually hurts . . . The present is never our end. The past and the present are our means, the future alone our end. Thus we never actually live, but hope to live, and since we are always planning how to be happy, it is inevitable that we should never be so" (Pascal 1966, 43).

To this Pascalian diagnosis I am only adding the following: to live "for the moment" is simply one more way in which we try to fill— and so cover and conceal—that ominous void, that embryonic disturbance that the moment itself is.

To propose amidst such thoughts that we can find "God"—that unencompassable source from which all things flow, we ourselves, our energies, and our lives included—in the moment itself creates a paradox. It suggests that when we turn away from the present moment itself, as we almost always do, we are turning away from our highest good, indeed from "the highest" itself, that is, God. In part this may be because we do not know that there is a god in the moment, and an additional factor may well be the fact that we have within us—Aquinas called it *acedia*—an aversion toward God and our own supreme good. It is also true, of course, that in shunning the present moment itself we are also in flight from ourselves, not only in the sense that "God is closer to us than we are to ourselves," but also because we fear, even for a moment, to acknowledge openly to ourselves what our condition is—all our being, our "substance," after all, resides more in the impressions we make on others, in our own chatter about ourselves, and in our Pascalian anticipations of a never-to-be future than in anything real within ourselves that we can point to right here and right now.

This being the case, how might we then begin to explore whether or not, and in what sense, and by what means, we might be able to find "God" in the moment? Clearly, we will have to reverse completely our habitual response to the moment itself; instead of fleeing it, we must face it and attempt to approach it. But here, too, we will do well to recognize with Pascal that "We are floating in a medium of vast extent, always drifting uncertainly, blown to and fro" (ibid., 92). This means that we will not be able to find someone who can give us a map of the way; there is, indeed, no "way," and all our supposed maps do not exist in God or in the order of things, but in our own heads. It also means that we cannot control this venture, for we do not so much as understand it—it is we, after all, who cannot even explain how it happens that the world, or "God," or anything at all exists, just as we cannot explain how we can remember, from one moment to the next, our own names. It means that when any of us seeks to approach the moment, it is finally as if humankind were in this place for the first time. In this uncharted expanse we call "the world" we can therefore only speak provisionally and clumsily to one another of possible trails, resting places, obstacles, traps, feeding places, and milestones we have found. I will attempt here to describe two parts of such a pathway leading to the moment itself and, finally, the god who can be found therein.

## THE FISH IN THE FLOWING STREAM

THE FIRST THING WE CAN DO IN OUR attempt to find our way to the god in the moment relates to the moment itself. We must get through to that still place in which we can dwell quietly, and alone, with the moment—let us call this "grasping the fish in the flowing stream." To begin this work, we attempt to sweep aside and pass beyond all those undertakings and preoccupations under which we have heretofore buried the moment itself. We will not allow ourselves—and the moment—to be "occupied" by regrets, pleasant memories, self-accusations, or futile reconstructions of what we should have said or done. We will no longer avoid the immediate reality of the present moment itself by reducing it to being merely the foundation of an imagined future. Thus our awareness will not be diffused through the vast reaches of past time and future time, but will instead be collected together, concentrated in that vanishing point that is "right now." And we will not blot out this elusive "right now" with doings that are just "for the moment"—instead we will try to bring awareness to rest in the transparent presence of the moment itself.

The world and our own inner swarm of impulses to fill the moment are loud and unrelenting. Like an undiscovered diamond, the moment itself is mute and hidden in darkness, something we must excavate from the seemingly tomblike depths of the world. Consequently it is a difficult work and a genuine achievement just to reach that place of stillness. Many traditional forms of meditation in both East and West seek among other things this ingathered and composed dwelling in the moment itself. The "just sitting" of Sōtō Zen in particular, free as it is from any "goal" or "purpose," is an attempt simply to *be* —or to neither "be" nor "not be"—in the right here right now.

As we succeed in penetrating through the barriers that separate us from the moment itself—an achievement that, like all our successes, failures, and very selves, is always only temporary—we will find ourselves changing in unexpected ways. It happens, for instance, that as we dwell in the presence of the moment itself, our very sense and understanding of that mystery we call time can be transformed. For once we have brushed off the last particles of dust that cling to it, once we are in the presence of the pure moment itself, nothing remains that might distinguish this particular moment from any other. The present moment I can dwell in right now, and someone else's "present moment" five thousand years ago, are moments veiled and filled by different events and experiences, but in themselves those moments cannot be distinguished—each is just a pure presence, a mysterious "now."

Since the moments are identical in themselves, since we can differentiate them only by reference to something else, that is, the coverings or "fill" that obscures them, there is no reason not to see the moments themselves as the same moment. Thus we—along with Annen, an eminent ninth century representative of Japanese Tendai Buddhism who taught "all times identical with one time"—are led to reinterpret time as the constant, endless reiteration of the very same "moment," a pure constantly returning "right now" which, however, is choked and covered over by ever new particulars. But there is no reason to stop at this image of an endless staccato repetition of the selfsame moment. We can simply go on and say that there is one single moment, a moment that abides and is eternal, a moment outside time through which, however, the motley, swiftly changing flow of individuals and events streams. This is that still point that, making time possible, is the "host" of time and of all things, but that also offers us a vantage point and a place to dwell "beyond time." It must be that eternally present now to which Meister Eckhart and others refer.

The only reasonable expectation—to reflect very widely for a moment—is that there should not be anything at all, yet the world unaccountably exists, and we as well. This all-encompassing mystery is the paradigm for all the paradoxes and unanticipated turns that await us on our wandering. Thus we have just reached into the stream of time and found something changeless and abiding, and we have found it precisely by probing into that which we thought more fleeting and insubstantial than anything else: the moment itself.

What is this enduring something through which time and all things pass? We can hardly continue to call the place we have now reached "the moment," remote as it now is from the usual connotations of that sound. Nor can we comfortably think of it as a "thing," "it" being so unlike what we usually think of as "things." Indeed, if we name it anything at all, and if our minds then quickly come to rest in that name, we simply betray the fact that we have not yet fully adapted ourselves to this new place, for we still assume, presumptuously and naïvely, that we can easily catalog and name the world and that our language therefore is a kind of roll call of the real. When, however, we come into the presence of the moment itself, of that enduring something through which all else quickly passes, we are confronted by something that, like the existence of the world itself, is a mystery against which our words and minds shatter. What then can we say? We can only say, awkwardly, that when we have broken through all the particular coverings and so dwell, if only briefly, with the moment itself, we sense— but do not comprehend—a presence that cradles and somehow contains all these particulars. It is a silent, resting, transparent, imperishable center that can be reached from all places and all times. It is a presence of which it makes little sense to ask whether it is living or dead, whether it is a "person" or a "thing." Because it is enduring and unfailingly the same, it extends unimpeded through infinite time, and I can as it were ride anywhere along its endless rails, visiting all "moments." It is that single moment of time—though we can no longer call it a "moment" or "time"—that is the innermost being of all times at all places. From English translations of Sanskrit, Chinese, Japanese, and other languages we have added to our vocabulary words like *thusness, suchness,* and *just so-ness.* These sounds, perhaps better than any other, evoke that mystery that becomes manifest when we reach the center of the moment itself.

I am putting together words, phrases, images, elusive scraps of inner experience, curiously linked sounds—or on this paper, no one really knows how, such sounds, pictures, and memories are being brought together—in an attempt to describe two phases of a movement that can lead us toward the god in the moment, a "being" alien to our understanding, but nevertheless closely akin to our own usually covered-over inmost reality. I have now described the first: to grasp the fish in the flowing stream. To achieve this we must sweep aside all our particular memories, actions, experiences, dreams, and plans, thus clearing a path for ourselves to the moment itself, that eternal "now" in whose presence we quietly inhale and exhale the "just so."

## THE NEEDLE'S EYE

HAVING COMPLETED THIS FIRST WORK, we find ourselves, however, not at the end of a journey, but rather at a frontier where the peripheries of two worlds mingle. Behind us lies the world of change, for we have turned away from the constantly shifting contents of the moment and dwell now instead in the changeless, abiding presence of the moment itself, the unchanging host of all change. And behind us lies as well the world of particularity and distinctions, for awareness is now withdrawn from the coverings and fill that differentiate one moment from another and has converged instead on that pure just so-ness far beyond all division and distinction.

But all our supposed knowledge, all our means of comprehension, of getting our bearings, and of expressing ourselves are inextricably enmeshed in that old world of particularity, distinctions, and change. We have always attended to how places and what is in them differ from one another, but not to the way in that all places are just "place." We know our way—in infinitesimal detail—around time, but are confounded by the pure moment itself. Without a thought we distinguish, for example, before from after, the present from both the past and the future, next Friday from next Tuesday and from last Friday, a second from a year, a lifetime, and a millenium. The following, however, must be obvious: once we come into the presence of the pure moment itself, the eternal now, all markers such as *Friday, three years, 1990, his-tory*, and *the creation of the universe*, and all the sounds we use to tame and plot out time begin to dissolve—how, after all, can this intricate house of cards we have built withstand contact with that "eternal now"?

It is obvious that the eternal must finally overwhelm all our childlike efforts to turn it into "time," yet "time" clings to us and to the people and things around us. This is because the place in which we enter the presence of the moment itself is also a frontier area between two worlds, and nothing is easier for us than to drift back into the world from which we came, the world of distinctions, change, and the unflagging impulse to fill the moment. If we wish, however, to enter that other world wherein dwells the god in the moment, we must press on past the frontier and undertake the second part of the work—I will call it "passing through the eye of the needle."

To accomplish this we must somehow enter into and pass through that tiny point which the moment itself is. Having pressed through the eye of the needle, and having then flowed out into the unimaginable world on its other side, we find ourselves in that absolute mystery which is "God's" world. Already time in its myriad aspects, having come into contact with the eternal now, the pure just so-ness of the moment itself, has melted away. Now we must extricate ourselves from all the categories, structures, and assumed familiarity, that is, all the *comprehension* with which we have diminished and defaced the world. That absolute and unthinkable "infinity" we now seek to enter is not just a temporal infinite, such as we have already explored, or a spatial infinite, but an absolute otherness and edgelessness, the wholly unbounded, a reality that our yardsticks and watches certainly cannot measure, but which all our powers of description, conception, and imagination also cannot grasp or even touch. To enter this other world—that is this very place, no longer distorted by our understanding of it—we must, however, enter into the moment itself and then come out on its "other" side. But we can pass through this needle's eye only if we ourselves have been reduced to a mere point. We can become such a point by freeing ourselves of our entire repertoire. What do I mean here by "repertoire"?

In one of his most famous sermons Meister Eckhart describes the condition of inner poverty we must achieve before we can experience the presence, or the "birth" in our soul, of that god beyond all gods, names, knowledge, and conception. We must, he says, not have anything, know anything, or want anything (Eckhart 1979, 303). Let us note, however, that if we have seized the fish in the flowing stream, if, in other words, we have found our way into the presence of the enduring and changeless moment itself, we have already achieved the first and last of these three freedoms. We will no longer have anything, for while approaching the miraculously abiding center of time we will have uncoupled ourselves from our past and from whatever inward possessions, reality, and status, especially spiritual status, we have accumulated in the past. And we will no longer want anything, that is, we will also have broken free from the future, so that our awareness and life will no longer be shaped and animated by that imagined future, whether conceived as the next moment or the next life. Having separated ourselves from all that we *have* become and acquired in the past, and from all we *want* to become and acquire in the future, we simply *are,* right now, having suddenly become a much more fluid "something," aware only of the moment itself and of the just so-ness that is its taste and smell. And as we abide in that elusive, hard to name "suchness" that permeates the moment itself, we begin to be aware of a new way of being with things.

The awareness emerges within us as we realize that this frontier area does not belong to any familiar, transparent, named, mapped, describable world, a world our minds can grasp and encompass. Instead, we sense something edgeless, undefined, unnamed—now *we* are the ones who are encompassed and it is *we* who squirm in the grasp of the unknown. Mircea Eliade and others have described those centers of the world—the world tree, sacred mountains, temples—through which pass vertical pathways giving access to heaven, hell, the sacred, other worlds. We have now isolated an analogous place within *time*, a temporal sacred point that, if we enter and pass through it, gives us access to another world. But to enter into that point and so to pass through the eye of the needle, we must divest ourselves not only of our past and future, but of that now suddenly much less self-evident "knowledge" with which we have feigned to know our way around time and the world. We must, in other words, get rid of our "repertoire."

Our repertoire includes everything we say, think, or do that embodies our assumption—an assumption that comes to us naturally, but which nevertheless is astonishing and even comic to honest reflection—that we know where we are, that we have our bearings, that we have maps and calendars that enable us to know, if perhaps only roughly, the true contours of time and place and also to comprehend what transpires, and what we ourselves do, *in* time and place. This unreflective sense of being oriented, of being in the known, mapped, and familiar, is a distinguishing feature of awareness that has not yet passed through the needle's eye. To it corresponds a picture of the world, and even of "God," as something limited, something we can name, categorize, and describe, an ultimately passive and transparent reality that our words and our understanding can penetrate, illuminate, encompass, grasp, and lay bare. But there can be no place for such awareness and for such a rendition of the world on the "other side"— how can we pin down a *when* in the eternal, or a *where* in the infinite? How can we even roughly sketch a *what* in the unnamed and indescribable?

Our repertoire—all the ways in which we display and assert our imagined understanding of things—has two dominant means of expression. One of them is language, the medium for what we both think and say. Its names, definitions, categories, descriptions, explanations, narratives, images, and analogies create a vast network, an apparent catalog and great mirror of reality; and when we then use it we imagine, automatically and unreflectively, that we are thinking about, or talking about, "the world." Our spontaneous faith in language as an enactment of our understanding makes possible that interminable, dizzying, even slightly mad homily that is all that human beings have said, are saying, and will say about where, when, and who we are, about outer limits, about the beginning and the end of "the world," about just what we should be doing during these few moments that are ours, about what "matters" and what doesn't, about how we should act toward others and what criteria we should use to evaluate ourselves, about the nature of "God" and spirituality, even about what we should do if it turns out that none of these questions have answers and if the world, therefore, makes no "sense." Before we can pass through the eye of the needle we must, however, leave behind this entire part of our repertoire, abandoning our original faith that the truth of things can be poured into and carried within our words, our formulations, our images.

Second, our repertoire also includes a vast array of actions that seem to us to enact our understanding of the world and of what life is "about." In the contemporary world this feigned understanding of what is to be done can manifest itself in time-devouring efforts put into careers, advancement, and becoming "secure," as if these were the

obvious goals to seek. In the spiritual realm such supposed comprehension of what is to be done and how it is to be done can embody
itself in ritual, in meditation, in specific postures, in the *suspension*
of action, in silence, even in Zen's "just carrying wood and drawing
water," if these everyday actions are accompanied by the thought: "This
is it. This is the way to *be!*" All such actions and suspensions of action
enact the old presumption that we are at least somewhat oriented and
know our way about. Carrying this presumption within us, we do not
experience time as a thought-stopping mystery, but rather as an emptiness we fill with our actions, an empty stage on which our feigned
comprehension of life is enacted. But all these actions, too, belong to
our repertoire. To pass through the needle's eye, we must leave these
feigned embodiments of our knowledge behind.

Our individual repertoires, with all their thoughts, utterances,
actions, and poses, are manifold and infinitely complex, like the brain
itself or the tip of a blade of grass. When combined with our imagined attainments and possessions, our desires and plans make an
imposing list. The moment itself, however, is infinitely small, a tiny
point, nothing more, as it were, than a speck of pure potentiality wedged
between the two massive, all-consuming unrealities of the past and
the future. We can pass through this infinitesimal point—and so pass
through time—only after we, having left behind past acquirements,
future hopes, and our entire repertoire, are distilled entirely into that
single point that is our innermost center. This point, a sliver of pure
thusness lodged deep within us, is never entangled in or affected by
our achievements, plans, repertoire, or supposed knowledge. It remains
something hidden, unnameable, and indescribable, a point of pure
mystery, Eckhart's divine spark. Having become it and it alone, we can
pass through the needle's eye.

## TIME'S ETERNITY, ETERNITY'S TIME

WHAT PLACE DO WE THEN ENTER WHEN, having entered into and passed
through the pure moment itself, we emerge out into that other "world"?
And what becomes of us in this unencompassable, unthinkable place?
Of course, we cannot respond to these questions as we were once accustomed to respond to questions, for we have left all our presumed
knowledge, and all the utterances and actions that purport to embody
that knowledge, behind. From now on speech is not the manifesta-

tion in sound of our knowledge, but can only be an attempt to voice our unknowing, our disorientation in a place beyond time, words, and thought. We might say, for instance, that we are in the eternal, the infinite, the unmapped, or the unlimited. We might recognize, further, that these are not names in the usual sense and that in using them we only wish to be making it clear that we are *not* in time, the finite, the mapped, the limited, or anything else we can name. In this way, then, we will simply be pointing to the fact that this is a place from which all words are banished and that we gain admittance to this "place" precisely by turning in all names and words.

But here, too, there are dangers, for we are still inclined to image eternity as something opposed to and therefore limited by time, and we will also tend to continue seeing "the infinite" as something known and distinct from "the finite." This "eternity," however, cannot be limited by time, but instead will include it. This infinite includes both the infinite and the finite. This "unknowing" contains all confusion and all lucidity. Indeed, the world we find ourselves in on the inconceivable other side of the moment is not opposed to, but, in fact, mysteriously includes and embraces, the world it seemed we had left behind. It is simply the mystery in which we have always been, mystery no longer buried under our make-believe comprehension of it. It is the diamond-like transparency of eternity no longer encrusted by time.

And what then is our own condition in this place that all our words only obscure? I said above that we must become a point of pure mystery before we can pass through the moment itself into that unthinkable element beyond place, time, and name. After making the passage we will continue to be just that "point"; we will not, in other words, return to our old repertoire or acquire a new one. Yet we will be increasingly aware that this point, too, is nameless, unknown, without measure, and so itself a great mystery. Lacking contours and edges as it does, how, in fact, can we distinguish it from the infinite? We can try, once again using negation, to indicate our transformed condition as follows: just as I am no longer in a "world," a structured cosmos, so I no longer have anything like what I once thought of as "a life" or as "my life," that is, a personal history I create and accumulate, or pretend to create and accumulate, through time. Here all maps, and also all biographies, fray, disintegrate, and are soon swept away. In this place outside all time and all knowledge, we will no longer feign to have a past, that is, a personal history we can narrate, a time during which we amassed and became what we now "have" and "are"—now, after all, we are in the Eckhartian condition of having and being nothing. And we will have no objectives or goals, no dreamed of life to come, no future across which we are stretched, acquiring thereby a would-be reality. And in the present we will no longer identify ourselves with any words or actions that embody our supposed comprehension of what we now have and are, and what we are on our way to gaining, achieving, and becoming.

This withering away of everything I once thought of as "my life" may be what early Buddhists wished to point to when they spoke of *nirvana*, that is, "extinction," for during this process all that I have acquired, done, and become—and all I hope to acquire, do, and become—go out like an extinguished flame. And further: recalling early Buddhism's outright denial of the ego, or self, we may also be led to dwell specifically on all that is problematic in the possessive pronoun inhabiting the phrase "my life." "I," that is, "my consciousness," was once the apparent center of the world, the fixed point from which all was named, known, and weighed, the castle in which all decisions were made. Now, since there is no longer a cosmos for it to comprehend or a life for it to plan and manage, there is no longer a significant role for this old "I" to play. Sensations, feelings, thoughts, memories—this "activity" still goes on, but it is no longer mine. And this activity, the mysterious conscious life of this body, is now just one more thing I do not understand and cannot even properly name—it is simply one of innumerable links in a chain whose beginning and end I cannot comprehend and whose nature I cannot describe. And as for this "I" itself, this "I" that once fretted about its present condition, that dreamed of its future, and that feigned in both reflection and conversation to be in charge of a "life," that "I" is now being burned away in a refining process the Buddhists called extinction and John of the Cross annihilation, that is, the "perfect" annihilation of the understanding and the will.

To the "I" in its heyday, surveying the world and shepherding its alleged life across the volatile and dreamlike fields of time, nothing seems more unthinkable than that it should be dislodged from it seemingly rightful and self-evident place in the very center of that life. After we pass through the eye of the needle and emerge on the other side of time, however, this once dominant figure gradually fades from the scene. Even more remarkably: as "my life," together with the "I" that perceives, owns, and manages it, fade away, the name-resistant presence that remains will for the most part not regret or even notice the disappearance. That presence's attention has been caught by something else. Awareness no longer holds "my life" in its loving and anxious hands; instead, its attention is turned *outward* toward something that flows steadily against it and even into it from without. That "something," which is even more resistant to names, is the god in the moment. What can we say, or not say, of this divinity?

We can say, clumsily, that this god, unlike many others, is a god found on the other side of time and in a place that is beyond the future—"it" is the unthinkable eternal to which the only access, always, is just right now. Just as we might expect, we bring to our spiritual lives those habits and assumptions that mold the rest of our lives. This means that much of our religious life, too, is laid bare by the Pascalian analysis quoted at the beginning of this essay. Our gods are gods of the future, gods who will enable us *someday* to be happier and better than we now are. We do not live, spiritually, right now, but dwell in a perfect—and hypothetical—spirituality that will be ours, we tell ourselves, at some future time. Someday—later in this life, or in the next one, or after hundreds of thousands of lives—we will be saved, enlightened, free, integrated, whole, joyful, and with God. But in all this we are still just working to create for ourselves, albeit on the spiritual plane, an individual life pivoting around an "I," that is, a planned, describable spiritual history through time. This means, however, that we are not yet beyond time, and since we—to paraphrase Pascal—are always planning how we will come into God's presence, it is inevitable that we never will.

We can also say that the "god" whose domain we enter when we slip through the moment itself transcends, absolutely, our entire repertoire. Indeed, since a condition for coming into the presence of this god is precisely that we should have left our entire repertoire behind, we can say that "God" is simply that "something" in which we dwell when all our knowing, and all the fictitious embodiments and enactments of our knowing, have been burned up. Hence there is no way in which we can think, utter, or describe God, no way—whether by means of speech, silence, action, or non-action—by means of which we can enact a supposed comprehension of God. Even to *name* God as we usually name persons and things is to entangle God with the unreal and to return to our old repertoire ways, for it is with naming, first of all, that our imagined familiarity with the world, and with God, begins. When we grasp the fish in the flowing stream and so dwell in the pure moment itself, sounds like *thusness* and *just so-ness* can at least suggest the abiding fullness and mystery we breathe there. But when we pass through the eye of the needle, we leave all our words— indeed, our entire repertoire—behind, and so if we wish to look for a word to allude to the presence we meet there, we must seek out a word that is in a state of absolute tension with all other words. It must be a sound whose very utterance evokes the dissolution of all repertoires, the abolition of all names. It must be a word that breaks in upon our usual named, known, mapped world and reveals it as being uncharted, unknown, and nameless. It must burn up and leave behind all the great dualities of time and the eternal, finite and infinite, real and unreal, this world and the other, so leaving us bedazzled, right now, by an unthinkable oneness.

In English the one possible sound for this work is *God*. It is true that the word *God*, just like our spirituality itself, has often become entangled in our repertoire, in our make-believe knowledge, in time, and in our fantasies of the future. The name 'God' then becomes a name just like any other name. It is then imagined that we can comprehend God, that we can know what, or "who," God is, what God "does," and how we should respond to God—this is the God Eckhart says we must get rid of. But others have struggled precisely to liberate the sound *God* from all entanglement in our repertoire—in Christianity the traditional name for this effort is the negative way, and to it corresponds, in Buddhism, the Mādhyamika, that is, the "middlemost" way. The followers of the negative way have sought to leave *life, religion, being, nonbeing, time, eternity*, their entire repertoire, and all gods trapped in that repertoire behind. Breaking out of the tiny world of our knowing, they then find themselves in the unbounded and unfathomable world of God, a world that at one and the same time is totally real and wholly unthinkable. Such appears to have been the experience of Dionysius, who writes of God:

> We can understand nothing about him, nor is he knowledge or truth or kingdom or wisdom or singularity or unity or Godhead or goodness. Nor in the sense that we understand 'spirit' is he spirit; there is no sonship or fatherhood, nor anything else that is known by us or by anyone else. He is none of the things that have no being, none of the things that have being" (*CU*, 217).

Those who "close their eyes that they may see," he writes, are filled with "the most beautiful splendor" (ibid., 206).

It is a paradox that we must close our eyes in order to see and that we must leave behind all our knowledge before we can begin to sense, haltingly, where and who we are. It is a paradox that I begin to live only when the sound *my life* has become a curiosity long since fallen into disuse. It may be that in our immaturity all our imagined knowledge was a necessary protection for us, a cocoon, a shell shielding us from the experience of edgelessness and of God. But at a certain point this little egg-world—the cosmos; the universe; dharma; the way things are; that vast articulated web of things, other people, ourselves, the world, and God as we "know" them—becomes a prison. If we then break free, or even clumsily fall out of this confining shell, this soft, entangling cocoon that pretends to be the world, we find ourselves in the unconfined, the limitless, the unsayable and unthinkable world of "God." Here we are dazzled by that splendor to which Dionysius refers. Here we are finally led, in the words of the Upanishads, from the unreal to the real. We are given a knowing that is not knowledge. A food that precedes the very idea of food nourishes us, and an energy prior to all "energy" flows through us. Our unknowing mysteriously commingles with and so knows the unknowable God. And we ourselves begin to undergo a transformation we will never understand and for which we will never be prepared.

Again, we have at our disposal various sounds, slogans, and categories. They are containers into which we may be tempted to pour, and so misunderstand and lose, this experience of God. Salvation, enlightenment, liberation, wholeness, perfect harmony, spontaneous action—these are some of the sounds we use to domesticate "God" and to twist our relationship with God into something we can name and describe. Using them, we cut ourselves off once again from God and the experience of God, just as we lose touch with this place by thinking of it as *the world, the universe,* or *being.* In the course of this essay I have referred to the fact that we typically use these spiritual sounds to dream—in a way laid bare by Pascal—of namable, knowable, *future* perfections. I have also attempted to explore or at least point to the following: our incessant need to fill the moment; the process of coming to dwell in the presence of the pure moment itself, or grasping the fish in the flowing stream; the process of entering into the moment in order to emerge on its other side, that is, passing through the eye of the needle; the leaving behind of our repertoire; the disintegration and disappearance of "my life"; the gradual turning of my attention away from the known and from my life in time toward an edgeless God whose waves wash uninterruptedly against me. In the wordless world beyond the eye of the needle we no longer know what "speech" is, or "silence"—how then can we propose that one is to be preferred to the other? It is possible, then, after bringing together and reflecting on these things one more time, to inscribe the following conclusions in the flowing stream.

## THE NEEDED ERROR

OUR USUAL DREAMS AND CONCEPTIONS of spiritual perfection are just the antitheses, the ghostly negatives, of our usual condition. For, ordinarily, if we put aside our busyness in order to take a look at ourselves, we see that we are dissatisfied, restive, fragmented, torn, self-accusing—a scarcely real, quickly vanishing atom. Still living in the world of words and distinctions, we conjure up the reverse image of ourselves, a condition in which we are joyful, at peace, whole, harmonious, immortal. In all this we are still enwrapped in the cocoon of our repertoire. We still imagine, in other words, that we can name and describe the world, ourselves, and our spiritual lives, only we now add to our repertoire world by adding to it images of a perfect condition contrasting sharply with our present state. And we are still acting in conformity with the Pascalian diagnosis, for we imagine this perfected condition as one that will *someday* be ours. In all this, however, we are just like a chick that, still enclosed in the egg, thinks it knows what the world is like, for we have at that point no more knowledge of other "worlds" than does the chick in the egg or the butterfly still working free of its cocoon. The transformation we experience when, leaving behind all our repertoire and passing through the pure moment itself, we flow out into the realm of God cannot be thought or imagined ahead of time, for it can never be thought or imagined, not even when we are within it. We cannot apply to it words like *salvation, liberation,* or *enlightenment,* for these sounds have their home in the old repertoire world—they are just the shining obverse of the familiar coin of that realm. But now that entire world—with all its the dualities of liberation and bondage, harmony and contradiction, salvation and perdition—is gone. What remains is the unimaginable world of God.

Further—and still speaking in this place in which speech is neither tenable nor untenable—if we can say one thing about life in that
old, named, comprehended world, it is that there always was in its very
marrow, and in ours, a lack, an absence, a perplexing and seemingly
ineradicable flaw. That world was instrinsically flawed because it hovered
before us as a passive object waiting to be named, known, and acted
upon by us. The world was a thing, a dead thing that we brought to
life by our naming of it, and *within* which we then had to create and
to unfurl across time our own "lives." Hence our fear of emptiness,
our unwillingness to look honestly at the world and at ourselves, our
incapacity to dwell in the moment itself and be nourished by it, our
constant need to fill the moment with the actions and experiences that
constitute "my life."

Here we have reached a place within us that lies below, and also
explains, that urgency to fill the moment that was the starting point
of this essay. I referred then to an underlying disquietude that is the
origin of this urgency; now we have a context in which to place it. Down
the very center of all our nerves there flows as it were a filament of
pure absence; an animal dissatisfaction, unrest, and fear; a premoni-
tion of doom; a dismal admission, in the midst of life, of inevitable
defeat. Pascal has explored this, too. For him this emptiness manifests
itself as awareness of "the eternal silence of these infinite spaces," a silence
that fills him with dread (Pascal 1966, p. 95). In a similar vein he refers to the "infinite abyss" within us, and also to our "wretchedness."
It is this obscure yet troubling abyss that makes it so difficult for us to
sit quietly, just letting time flow through us. For Pascal, in fact, "The
sole cause of man's unhappiness is that he doesn't know how to stay
in his room" (ibid., 67). And he goes on to describe more effects of
this inner abyss:

> "The only good thing for men therefore is to be diverted from
> thinking of what they are, either by some occupation that takes
> their mind off it, or by some novel and agreeable passion which
> keeps them busy . . . Thus men who are naturally conscious of
> what they are shun nothing so much as rest; they would do any-
> thing to be disturbed" (ibid., 67-68).

This disquieting if not frightening emptiness within can explain,
therefore, many things. It explains why solitude, as much as we may
sometimes long for it, easily takes on a menacing, disintegrating as-

pect as we actually begin to approach it. It explains our relentless need to fill the moment with memories, experiences, actions, dreams, plans. It explains why we would rather experience pain, which fills the void, rather than confront that inner abyss itself, an abyss which, through the fear it engenders, we can now see as the true creator of "my life." But we can now go farther and say that this absence within us is only an interior echo of what is profoundly flawed in our sense of the world around us, the fact, namely, that we experience it precisely as "the world," that is, as something we are in a position to name. We can express this by saying that we have eaten of the Tree of Knowledge, in which moment the world as it is, that is, "paradise," was destroyed. For in our most fundamental relationship of all—our relationship with this place—we have naïvely taken what is around us as something passive that we can name, something transparent and familiar that we can comprehend, something that does not act upon us, but offers little resistance to our knowing, and controlling, action upon it.

If, therefore, we ever put our busyness aside in order just to be, right now, and to attend to where we are, right now, we should not be surprised if the world seems to hover around us, oppressively, as a flawed world, a world that is passive, inert, profane, lifeless. And it should not surprise us if the world is chillingly silent, or if we are filled with dread by what strikes us as "the eternal silence of these infinite spaces." For we have silenced the world by feigning to name and comprehend it. With our chatter we have drowned out its mysterious and quickening voice. Thus we have obliterated and so lost paradise—that is, our home, our "friend"—by superimposing upon it the world. Further, we have killed God, and then we have entombed God within our knowledge of God. In so doing we have lost all contact with the god-world, that edgelessness in which even the "sacred"—and its opposite, the "profane"—are swallowed up, and so we are reduced to searching for the divine in limited, identifiable gods, persons, and things. Or else our sense of "the sacred," severed from its root in the boundless, withers away altogether, and we are then simply left with that awareness of an intrinsic flaw, an absence in the very marrow of the world and in our marrow, a sense of absence which then leads us to experience the moment itself, too, as an emptiness we must hurry to fill.

But as Pascal writes: "this abyss can be filled only with an infinite and immutable object" (ibid., p. 75). That unthinkable "infinite object"—God—can fill the abyss only when "it" comes to life once again, breaking free from the names and knowledge under which it lies buried, only, that is, when I have passed through the eye of the needle, leaving all my knowledge and all my repertoire behind. What takes place within me then is itself something unknowable and unnamable— it is not *salvation, enlightenment, liberation,* or *the great bliss.* If I look for words to point to it, I will be led toward words that are shorter, simpler, more modest. I will simply say that I certainly cannot explain it, but now everything is very different when I sit quietly with the moment, the world, and "God." Now when I just attend to this place, I am aware of presence, not absence. When the world was inert and God obliterated by my knowledge of God, consciousness always searched restlessly for some object to occupy it. Now it is *already* occupied, for just as I sit quietly, doing nothing, "occupied" by nothing, God pulses against me and through me. I no longer need to seek out something to attend to. That something—God—is already acting upon me as a given, a gift. I cannot explain, but can only clumsily report this transformation of the world from something known, passive, limited, and riddled with emptiness and defeat, into an unexpected, unthinkable, inexhaustible something washing against me. I can say that the mystery in which I now find myself—God—breaks against me with a life that awakens new life within me, whereas my life was once being slowly drained away on great fields of vacancy. I can say that I am no longer waiting for something—"my future"—to happen, or to result from my present efforts, for at this very moment I am enfolded in an unthinkable event—God—that is already taking place and that indeed has already been taking place eternally. I have not been saved, liberated, or enlightened. But instead of being terrified by Pascal's eternal silence, I attend spontaneously to a sound— the Upanishads call it "*the* sound"—that is an eternal, unvarying, soundless hum or "om" superceding all sounds heard by the ear. Doing and thinking about nothing, I am filled. I remain motionless, letting the ocean break against me and over me. I can say that I am aware of a nameless presence—God—somewhere close by in the Garden's evening stillness. Or simply that God is an abyss, edgeless on all sides, bottomless, horizonless, into which I can perhaps safely fall.

## THE CHOICE OF ATTENTION

I HAVE ALREADY STATED THAT THESE WORDS are written in the flowing stream and vanish as quickly as they appear. They can scarcely reach what is abiding in time's flow—that eternal, changeless moment on which time itself merely feeds—and so they most certainly cannot reach God, in whom both time and eternity are dissolved. Nor can we ourselves attain to God if we cling to these words or any other. Yet it may be that we somehow need error—the "comprehended" world—in order to reach God, who is inconceivable truth. Certain Tantric adepts claim that our desires, which keep most people trapped in illusion and bondage, can be used by the wise as vehicles of liberation. Certainly it is just as plausible to suggest that words, which usually entangle us in word-worlds and in our repertoires, can be used to point us not only to liberation, but also toward God. For it is as if we must start with something, and what we start with in this case is time, the familiar word-world, and the lives we parade across time and the world. When then this little bubble-world vanishes, it leaves behind an opening, a space temporarily freed from all comprehension, into which God therefore can immediately flow. Let us acknowledge that our experiences of the Garden and of God are almost always of this transitory and imperfect kind. We are continually twisting and flailing around in time, our words, our knowledge, our lives, and ourselves. But sometimes all this twisting and flailing around results—we do not understand how—in the creation of a small and temporary air space, a clearing, a pocket of pure mystery that God instantaneously fills.

In a spirit of Pascalian honesty and self-examination we would do well to acknowledge still more: we—and here we can include Dionysius, Eckhart, and Pascal—are seldom in the Garden or with God, even for those fleeting visits or revelations of the kind I just described. We seldom see, if even for a moment, that "most beautiful splendor" to which Dionysius refers. In part this is because life in God's presence cannot be *one* namable or imaginable thing more than any other and so, finally, it cannot be "the Garden" any more than it is the fallen world or perdition, nor can it be a "beautiful splendor" any more than it is a place of emptiness, weeping, and despair. But in truth we are seldom even close to these dualities in their pure form, not to mention beyond them. Indeed, we are seldom even as far as the eye of the needle, the pure moment itself that opens up on its elusive other side into God's world. The truth is that we are all too often back at the beginning, back where this essay and the Pascalian analysis begin, back, that is, with the moment itself and our unease about it, back with ourselves and our more or less confounded minds and divided hearts, back with the relentless impulse to just cover this discomfort, or pain, with sights and sounds, memories, experiences, actions, projects, dreams, other pain.

So it is that in our spiritual lives—the goal of which is an infinite journey toward God—it is the very first steps that we must repeat again and again. And so it is that we are continually brought back to the same dilemmas, conflicts, and choices. Shall I fill up the moment and simply blot it out with memories, or with the future, or just by doing anything at all, or shall I try to look directly at where I am *right now* and what my condition is *right now?* Shall I try to grasp the fish in the flowing stream? Shall I try, that is, to banish all else and so finally stand alone in the presence of the pure moment itself, that moment in whose unknown depths one can perhaps find God? If this is the path I follow, I will soon be faced by another choice. Shall I use up my time contemplating, dreaming about, and perhaps reading about how it will be when I finally touch God? Shall my awareness become nothing but reveries, images, and words about a future of beautiful splendor, a *conceived* future that does not and never shall exist? Or shall I set in motion that work that I can carry out only by being unreservedly in the place where I am right now, a place in which I am confronted not just by time and my eagerness to fill it, but also by my desire to clear a path through to the moment itself, a place in which I sense that, coming out on the moment's unthinkable other side, I can touch that god who now lies buried under time and all my knowing and doing within time?

This is the choice we face, or evade, each moment. It is the choice between filling up the moment or attending to it. It is the choice whether we will have a life or something else, whether we will dwell stretched out across time, or somewhere else. It is the choice whether to live in what can be said and thought, or to seek the real. As this choice is made, it then becomes the destiny, the event, the chance-happening—or should we just call it the unpremeditated and somehow perfect uncoiling of whatever it is that we are?

# Nobody Knows My Name

## I. "Rava created a man . . . "

THAT REMARKABLE life-fixing blunder to which I will occasionally return later on—the fact that, a few unpredictable moments of unclouded vision aside, we pass our days in those little shells we call our lives instead of in the immeasurable and indescribable reality of God—betrays itself as well in the paradoxes we choose to ponder. We always welcome, for instance, those pleasantly improbable juxtapositions implicit in the proposition that all human actions are outflows from one great stream of energy/desire. Plato was the first to suggest that what ends as a great philosophical exploration began when a vision of earthly beauty rendered someone mad and helpless. Amplifying this Platonic myth of Eros, we can add the commonplaces that today's turbulent longing or boundary-dissolving voluptuousness might reappear tomorrow as an odd sentimentality, or in a dramatic act of self-sacrifice, or as a novel, a banking career, or mystical experience, even, perhaps, as mature love. Still further: in one great infinitely variegated dance hall we can watch women and men, stags and does, fish, Paris and Helen, Penelope and Odysseus, pine trees, turtles, Falstaff and his bawds, philosophers and their Truth, mystics and their Beloved. This familiar hypothesis is sweeping and fascinating. Because of its vagueness, it is untestable and so cannot be disproved. Conceivably it is true. But like so many other pronouncements, paradoxical or not, it is marred by a critical flaw, one that connects it, moreover, to the blunder to which I have already referred. The flaw is the fact that this grand theory about the sources of human behavior feeds our naïve, instinctive belief that we are able to size up ourselves and this place, that we have a somewhat reasonable grasp of where and who we are. It offers us a measured, describable, comprehended world, and so it helps blot out God's unthinkable mystery, the unseen innermost reality of all things. Less familiar, but much more open to that mystery, is another paradox. Compared to paradoxes that help reduce this place and ourselves to known quantities, it is more profound, more dangerous, more liberating, "truer." Like most things that matter, it involves realities we usually choose to ignore. Instead of making this place more familiar and comprehensible, it makes it less so; it makes the world bigger rather than smaller. What is this other paradox? It is that our most searching intuitions of divine being and knowing are strangely intertwined with the obscure fears, the gloom, the debris, the scorned irrelevancies, the shades and hungry ghosts, all the appalling spectral images of vacuousness, abandonment, and craziness that haunt the dark boundaries of consciousness. It is that our profoundest theology sees God as enjoying a condition that, taken as a possible life for *us,* is something we shrink from in horror as the impossible fate we are seeking above all to avoid.

I can explain what I mean by this gloom, these fears and ghosts, and this craziness—and so be in a position to explore the paradox— only in relation to their essential context: that central "blundering" life that these boundary phenomena simply fringe. "All consciousness," wrote Schelling, "is concentration, ingathering, a drawing together of oneself" (Schelling 1861, 74). Beginning with these words translated from Schelling's German, let us continue to ferret out that primary life with the following English words. We instinctively seek to draw all that is fluid, dispersed, and formless about ourselves into a center, to "concentrate" our tenuous, spectral reality into one place. Why? Our goal is to work this "concentrate"—ourselves—into the form of a human being and then to create for this human being a "life." There are — the legend of Rabbi Rava is one—dark tales of golems and homunculi, attempts with the aid of magic to usurp God's role and create a man or woman. Though they are suffused with an aura of aberration, pathetic clumsiness, and doom, these stories exercise a singular appeal, and I see the secret of that appeal in the following fact: the golem legend portrays a process of attempted creation we are all programmed, or perhaps doomed, to undertake. We are all laboring to turn that dispersed and amorphous question we are into human being, to create something living, formed, and real that will correspond with our name, something that can be the proud referent of that spellbinding sound 'I'.

Let us briefly consider the where and the what of these melancholy campaigns. The where is a center, a shared clearing; I will call it the "clear, common light." The place in which we carry out the process of "concentration" is clear because it is a place in which things manifest themselves to us as named, defined, and known. It is common because this knowledge is communicable and so "public," because what happens here can be observed, attested to, told, and retold by all participants. What makes both this clarity and this public quality possible is language, that is, for us, English. English—and the vast but finite world of particular things and events, of "this and that," it evokes—is the medium that joins us together as a public dwelling in the clear, common light. It is also important to note that this public world is also the "where" of almost all the phenomena we usually call "private." For the fact is that we seek reality and definition—that is, we work at creating our golem—within two distinguishable realms of the clear, common light. One is the great public of the community at large: nation, city-state, "community"; the other is the small public or audience of family and intimates, what we usually call the private. This distinction between the great public and the intimate "public" is important, but it is not as profound as the antithesis between this binary public world and the truly private. For both publics are publics of the clear, common light. In both cases we dwell together with others in a world that is "self-evidently" named, intelligible, and utterable, and with both publics English is the key to and medium of that common world. The truly private, however, is another realm; it hovers in obscurity outside the clear, common light, outside the known, outside English. The truly private is furtive, formless, unspoken, uncounted. It is a gopher concealed in the darkness of its tunnel, the scarcely perceptible respiration of a solitary moose—a moose no human being will ever see—

dozing in the cool noontime quiet of the woods. The truly private is a vast world, but since it exists outside the clear, common light, its events don't really "happen." The individual biographies of all bees, a thorough retelling of all the dreams men and women have ever dreamed—these many hundred possible volumes do not belong even in theory to "world history." We will see that the truly private is a black hole that miraculously opens out upon other worlds, even God. Ordinarily, however, we concede to it at the most a shadowy or purely technical reality. A joy we cannot share with someone doesn't meet the requirements to be joy. An untold joke is no joke. An insight that isn't somehow recorded and that leaves no mark in the shared world immediately disappears once again into "nothingness." But a computerized bank statement, an insincere compliment, an utterly baseless accusation—they are "real."

The "what" is our golem project: a curious attempt by soul—for we are all unmeasured, name-transcending "soul"—to turn itself into a particular human being dwelling in the clear, common light. I have said that the clear, common light is a place of definition, communication, and shared knowing, a place in which all things are understood as this or that within the common medium of English. The golem project is our attempt to consummate the work of Schellingian concentration by forming a particularized living this—"ourselves"—that exists in and has a history, a life, its own particular recitable chronicle in that clear light that shines upon the common and the real. Consciousness begins therefore with a positing of its own sad formlessness, of its dispersed, drifting, spectral tenuousness, of itself as a kind of emptiness or hollow potentiality that is nothing now and whose one chance for reality is to become something *someday* in the clear, common light. Consciousness seeks then to "concentrate," to draw itself together, to produce out of this slow haze something definite, a distinct this or that, a formed, named, and known human being. In this work of concentration both being and knowing are of essential importance. We seek to become and then *be* this or that, something definite, but we also want both ourselves and others to *know* what we are and what our story is—in this way we will attain and know our "identity." The clear, common light is the field in which this transformation will take place, and English will be the vehicle of its final consummation, for there exist, in English, sounds that will be able to describe us and tell our story. Thus we are all would-be magicians, perhaps more energetic than wise, laboriously drawing or concentrating our dispersed, drifting purely nominal reality into a central point. We defend this mass, this "embryo," against the setbacks of fate, the assaults of others, the perverse resistance of things, our own doubts and fleeting capitulations. We pack this mass together; we try to press out of it all that is formless, purely private, incommunicable, unknowable, all that is related to "nothingness"; we knead it; we try to shape it into a human figure, a golem, that fully formed individual human being— so perfectly visible to all in the clear, common light—who is to be the true and definitive referent of my name, the subject of my future eulogy. For through my golem I seek not only to be, but always—at the very least—to have been. Once I have succeeded, at some point in the future, in becoming "something," I do not want ever again to slip back into pure formlessness. Somewhere and somehow my golem's existence must be eternally recorded in the clear, common light. It must be forever true that "I" have been.

Clearly there is something quixotic, even messianic, about the golem project—that human being we are working so hard to create is as it were the purely personal messiah of our own particular history. The golem is the savior who someday will redeem me from the formless nothingness, the future-craving pure potentiality, in which I think I begin; my golem constitutes that future reality which is the one possible justification of my present travail. Perhaps there are corners in the soul that are never blind to this fantastic aspect. Perhaps the soul always knows, though with a repressed knowing, that its golem project is doomed, that this personalized messiah will never walk as dreamed and desired, that the celebration of my own individual millennium will never take place. It may always secretly realize that all its victories are paper victories, triumphs in the little world of comprehension and English, but dismal tales of quaint squanderings when overheard in the vastness of unmeasured reality. Yet instinct almost always overpowers bouts of reflection. Our gaze returns, then, to the center, the clear, common light; becoming again the never-ending work of concentration, consciousness—"we"—labors again to clothe its bare name in a few scraps of reality. In "normal" life, consequently, it is only on particular "abnormal" occasions that we are forced out of, or escape, our magician's posture. On these occasions we look around us; we consider other forms and non-forms of life. At the same time that peripheral wasteland that forms the gloomy outer boundaries of consciousness draws closer. The phenomenon most likely to introduce us to these fringes is solitude.

There is a form of solitude—I will call it "tactical solitude"—in which one withdraws for a time from the agitation and distractions of the shared world, but simply in order to engage more efficiently in a particular effort of concentration. In tactical solitude I work in "private" at making things, doing things, or acquiring skills that will contribute to the building up of my golem and that therefore will enable me someday to *be* something in English and the clear, common light. In what might be called "therapeutic solitude," on the other hand, one withdraws on a more or less planned and regular basis in order to "escape" for a while from the collective world, to heal wounds and regain strength, and so to be able to return afresh to concentrating activities in the clear, common light. Both tactical and therapeutic solitude are managed forms of solitude, that is, they are solitudes integrated within and even subordinate to the soul's golem project. They are therefore more public than private, and in them we as it were take the public world along with us into our solitude. But there is another form of solitude—"floating solitude"—in which the tether binding us to our golem project is at least temporarily broken. Floating solitude may be voluntary or the unplanned result of circumstances. I may simply yield to a sudden impulse to do nothing—to drift—or I may find myself in a situation in which I am temporarily cut off from all possibility of working on my golem. Whatever the cause, the soul now has its back turned to those sheltered coves and inlets in which our golem projects, our "lives," normally pass; it is now drifting toward an open sea.

Characteristic of floating solitude is a marked lessening of the hold exerted on us by the clear, common light, by all our shared knowing, by English; there quickens in us an embryonic awareness of other worlds. But what is equally characteristic of this third form of solitude is the suddenness with which discomfort and even the beginnings of panic can set in. Why? Let us reflect again on the Schellingian dictum and on the golem project.

Consciousness, "normal life," is concentration. But in floating solitude the arduous and even Sisyphean work of concentration is suspended and a reverse process of dispersal, of volatilization, sets in. In solitude all the precise contours and secure knowings of the clear, common light begin losing their cogency; what surrounds the soul is disturbingly imprecise, shadowy, fluid, without form, and without the particular certainties of the particular shared world one is now leaving behind. In this way the inviting open sea of floating solitude has now begun to manifest itself as that gloomy fringe that always lines consciousness. But the sensations that penetrate most deeply, sowing seeds of incipient panic deep within, have to do with one's golem, that dreamed of magical result of the life of concentration. For now the soul is in floating solitude and the work of concentration is suspended; the clear, common light is a an obscure glimmer in the distance and English has ebbed. That complex reality that has given birth to the soul's golem project, and that has nourished it, explained it, and justified it, is no longer in operation. And so its life now begins to drain out of that half-finished golem.

The golem, the creation of which has been our reason for being, is now losing its shape, staggering, melting away into the surrounding darkness, or collapsing in a shapeless heap on the ground, a sad and arbitrary heap suddenly inexplicable like the world itself. What is now disintegrating is my attempt to turn myself into a particular, identifiable, knowable, self-knowing human being. What is now coming apart is my individual reality as this or that, my identity, my own attainment of being and knowing, my particular biography, my eternal definition—all the form, substance, story, explanation, and justification in which I have sought to clothe the mystery of my name. And all that remains is something alien to the clear, common light and English and all known forms of being and knowing; all that remains is something indefinite, a formless something that bears a disturbing resemblance to "nothing." It is easy to understand why the soul, faced with perceptions of its own "nothingness," soon turns its back on solitude and returns to company, even bad company, and the shared world. Now it can resume the familiar work of trying to turn itself into "something"; now the sick golem is reactivated by a fresh infusion of its strange life.

In solitude we usually gain no more than a fleeting glimpse of the fringes. Having drifted out into the purely private, we soon get our fill, and usually it is easy to find our way back to the clear, common light and its life of concentration. Consequently, in normal—that is, in nonreligious—life, it is not in solitude but in despair that our most serious encounters with the fringes occur. In despair, as in floating solitude, consciousness has wandered away or been carried away from the clear, common light, and the life of concentration and golem-making is suspended. But despair is never voluntary, and we cannot remedy it easily just by returning to company. Hence we might call despair an involuntary, prolonged, severe solitude in which the soul is banished from the clear, common light and locked within the purely private. "Depression" is an invisible, impenetrable barrier through which we look hopelessly toward an imaginary human world of achievement and lucidity from the gloomy fringes into which we have been cast; in despair we are locked in the truly private as in a hell that is both torture chamber and asylum. It should therefore not surprise us that despair is marked by forms of golem sickness much more acute than those encountered in floating solitude. In despair it becomes a question whether our collapsed golem will ever get up again and resume its clumsy attempts to walk. Indeed, we might define despair as the complete collapse of the golem project. In despair consciousness throws off the exhausting and unavailing work of concentration and looks into the eyes of defeat; in this condition we recognize that our golem will never perform that perfect, messianic walk in front of the others and ourselves, and so we recognize that the dream of establishing ourselves as a vindicated this or that in the clear, common light will never be realized—indeed, it now seems to us that the entire project has been a fiasco from the beginning.

Hence the typical general symptom of despair: the disintegration of the "I" amidst the recognition that it has lost all the being and knowing it has been feigning, both to others and to itself, to possess or to be in the process of acquiring. For now all the others clearly own concrete, individual reality, but I do not. The others already are "somebody" or at least are in the process of making "something" of themselves, but I am not anything—all I have is my name, that tiny, weightless seed I have failed to convert into something. I am nothing, or it might be said that I exist, but simply on a grammatical technicality. For this nominal existence of mine lacks all definition, all palpable form; it is an empty, purely formal reality. My knowing, like my being, is bereft of substance and contour. My opinions and beliefs collapse instantly in the face of the teeming, unhesitating assertions of all the others— they all have won clear understandings of this and this while I know nothing. Transformed by that self-dissolution that is despair, consciousness is no longer concentrating consciousness, but a formless emptiness, a floating, totally fluid subjectivity. It is a nothing that knows only its own—"my"—nothingness.

Though the process is longer and more arduous, we usually find our way out of despair, just as we do out of solitude, and return with a measure of restored optimism to our magician's work of golem-creation in the clear, common light. But what matters here is something else: having examined normal—that is, concentrating—consciousness, and having considered some ways in which solitude and despair carry us out into other realms, we now have a context for and can attempt to define those gloomy boundary areas of consciousness I referred to at the beginning of this essay. What are those fringes? What are the specters that haunt them, the debris that litters them, and the general mood of despair, craziness, and abandonment that suffuses them? Those fringes are a visualization of my own perceived original reality, my beginning. They are the dark, formless waters, the chaos—something prior to all English and all knowing—I am struggling to mold into spatial and temporal form, that is, into a "human being" with a "life." They are that nothingness I will always be unless I can concentrate this nothingness and turn it into something particular and tangible, something that can be talked and thought about in English. They are the cipher, the empty name, the original nature that remains my essence until I have become a particularized being and knowing, until I have recreated myself as an individual that, like all individuals, is a publicly recognized subject of observation, of description, of self-comprehension, of story, of recollection, of eulogy, of eternal definition. The fringes are therefore the dreary, unpromising raw material of my golem. It is from this that I am trying to distill a completed human being dancing its millennium—"my" millennium—in the clear, common light. Someday not one single shred of that original nothingness will cling to my golem—whatever I cannot concentrate into "something" I will cut away. Just like a magician I will be able to pass a hoop in all directions around the woman or man I have made.

This millennial dancing golem is my dream. What is real is the ongoing work of concentration, the unceasing effort to "ingather" my golem, shape it, and invest it with life. Also real are the longings, the apprehensions, and the uncertain intuitions that accompany this work—they are manifest in the sad figures that can be glimpsed in the gloomy margins of awareness. Shades are said to be spirits of the dead that refuse to depart because they still long for life. They embody our own instinctive perception that we have not yet come into being and that life is something we have yet to attain. Buddhism's hungry ghosts suffer because their huge, ravenous bellies ache under necks so thin that not even the tiniest morsel of food can pass through. Their relentless hunger is our own unsatisfied need for the being, knowing, and life that is currently denied us, and the ghosts themselves epitomize that reality-hungering unreality that is our own essence. Of all the specters that inhabit the fringes we can therefore say that they embody the needs and energies that propel our golem project. The debris and scattered heaps are all that remains of our earlier attempts, and so they are omens as well, omens rooted in our repressed suspicion that golem projects are blunders and fools' errands. It is easy to comprehend why consciousness shrinks from the fringes as from other places of abandonment, madness, and despair. For as we have seen the fringes are where we begin as a name, a question, and "nothing" else. They are the formless, dark waters from which we are struggling to emerge. To sense that we are still encompassed by those waters, to feel undercurrents drawing us back and down away from the land and light, to guess that our name, the sole sliver of reality we possess, may itself soon vanish into the depths—this is to be faced by failure, to picture ourselves drowning in total and eternal defeat.

## II. THE PARADOX

FOR CONCENTRATING CONSCIOUSNESS—for "us"—the fringes are a place of disintegration and nightmare, the Gehenna into which we fall if the golem-project we are comes to nothing. Yet we need only shift our perspective ever so slightly, we need only blink our eyes for a moment in order to cleanse them of old habits and arbitrary perspectives, and then, taking a second look at the ways we delineate the fringes and our torments there, we will be struck by their kinship with the phrases, conceptions, and images which are the most exalted we have discovered for reaching toward the bottomless and unthinkable secret of this place, that is, toward "God." How, for instance, might we attempt to describe God's being? What kind of being does God have? For Augustine God is "being itself," and for him the essence of being as opposed to becoming is an immutability which is outside time and so eternal. God, therefore, has no history, no biography, no life. Nothing "new" ever happens with God, who dwells in eternity outside both old and new. Indeed, nothing at all ever happens in God. "He" rests in a timeless present, and if he *did* change, if he began to have a history and a life, this would signal a deterioration, a dramatic "fall" in the condition of God. That God and God's measureless being cannot be distinguished and so limited as individual existence, as genus and species, as a particular this or that, but is instead the pure act of being—"altogether simple" as Aquinas writes—these are findings of traditional Christian reflection on the nature of divine being. It follows that we cannot define God and that God has no conceivable form, for all definition and form bespeak limitation. It also follows that God is neither a some-body or a some-thing, and that God has no "identity" we might conceive or English—so remote, in fact, is divine being from our golem-oriented conceptions that Aquinas asserts a person knows God best "when he realizes that he does not know him" (quoted in Maurer 1962, 170). As concentrating consciousness you and I are names seeking to acquire a story and life in time, and a definition, a body of attributes or qualities, in space. But Christianity's *via negativa* teaches that we can move toward God's storyless, unqualifiable, unimaginable reality only by pushing aside the events and the attributes—good, all-knowing, eternal, loving—which block the way. In the writings of Plotinus we find that the One is without form; it has no definition, no limit. Our best description of it "carries only the denial of particular being" (Plotinus 1952, 231). And the Vedanta teaches that the highest *brahman* is *brahman nirguṇa*, that is, "*brahman* free of characteristics." Thus our paradox is adumbrated by the fact that the glorious, inconceivable Absolute so fervently evoked by Śaṅkara, and Musil's ambiguous twentieth-century protagonist, are both "without qualities."

God—that unwavering, usually unheard monotone which contains and survives all other tones—has his being not only outside our knowing, but also outside the very words with which we pretend to name him. The use of words, names, and pronouns inevitably particularizes mystery into this and that; it gives rise to a naïve sense of familiarity, of knowing our way if ever so slightly around divine being. Plotinus therefore writes of God that "this is a principle not to be conveyed by any sound" (ibid., 231). Dionysius asserts that the Godhead "has no name," (in *CU*, 217) and Aquinas writes of God that all the names we employ "fail to express His mode of being" (quoted in Pegis 1948, 99). The use of words, names, and pronouns to refer to God tends to confuse us, for it leads us to impute golemlike being to God instead of an absolutely simple, undivided, unbounded being outside English. It leads us also to forget that God is as much "she" as "he," and as much "they" and "you" and "we" as "it," although, of course, God ultimately is none of these, for 'God' is no word, no noun, no verb, no part of speech, but rather the sound which announces an end to words and a fall out of speech and thought. Eckhart therefore tells his listeners that they should not approach God "as God." Rather they should seek him as he truly is—that is, as nameless—and they should seek him in a place free of and prior to all names (*DPT*, 198, 348).

By naming something we transform it into a "something," and so we limit and particularize its being; to name something is to enclose it, or to dream one has enclosed it, within the familiar worlds of knowing and English. To forgo naming is to acknowledge the presence of mystery—something open and untamed—dwelling beyond the confines of the clear, common light. Seeking a more systematic way to nurture their realization that the true marrow of things is beyond conception, the Buddhists have elaborated wonderfully on the term *śūnyatā*, that is, "emptiness." 'Emptiness' is a sound which, like 'God', points toward the ultimately real; it is also a method to carry us out of Sanskrit, or Chinese, or English. Emptiness functions as the latter by reminding us that the essence or "own-being" of things is precisely that they lack the named, defined, randomly individuated "own-being" they possess within our particular language. Thus, the one essential thing I need to know about what I blithely call the world is that it is not "the world." The one thing I need to know about myself is that I am not "I" or "Luther Askeland." The own-being of life is that it is not "life"; the essence of death is that it is not "death." We can see that the effect of this method is to take away the names, classifications, and definitions which lie like coverings over the unpronounceable heart of things. It is essential, of course, to apply this Emptiness method to the ultimate heart of things, Emptiness itself. Thus the one thing I can know about Emptiness, about Ultimate Reality, or about God, is that it is *not* "Emptiness," "Ultimate Reality," or "God."

The Emptiness method uses a process of negation to carry us from the verbal surface to the nonverbal heart of things. By reminding us that the one thing we can know about God's being is that it is not "being," this method brings home to us the gap separating God's being from "being" as we usually conceive it, that is, the particularized, describable, limited being we seek for ourselves in the clear, common light. In order to reinforce our awareness of this gap, it is possible to proceed one step farther and simply deny being to God. This tradition has its Western source in Plato's references to what is "beyond being." It flows through Plotinus, for whom it is a commonplace that the One has no being, and then through Dionysius, to become finally a familiar current in Christian mystical theology—thus in the passage just referred to Eckhart describes God as bared not only of all names, but of being as well. Indeed, it is possible to take even one more step to ensure that we do not confuse God's being with "being"—it is a method of reversal which attributes the very opposite of being to God. Applying this method, the Kabbalist David ben Abraham Ha-Laban calls *En-Sof*—that is, the Infinite, or God—a Nothing. He was anticipated in this by the Christian theologians Dionysius and John Scotus Eriugena, and he was a contemporary of Eckhart. Eckhart, too, calls God a "pure nothingness."

To be, but not to be anything in particular; to be empty of all form; to have no history, no life, no definition, no intelligible identity or character; not yet to have become anything, either a person or thing; to be no genuine "I," and to have none of the things which make for reality in the clear, common light; to be more like "nothing" than like "something"; to be, in one's dark, innermost reality, nameless—we can already see how these phrases connect God's being as contemplated in theological reflection with our own existence at the fringes as we picture or experience it in solitude or despair, and so we have begun to see how God's being and "fringe" being strangely coalesce. But we can achieve a more complete view of this intermingling, and so of the paradox, only after first taking a look at knowing as well. For it is with knowing and awareness as with being. That golem we seek to create and become is a magical creature in which knowing as well as being has been crystallized. My golem—that future, messianic "I"—will be a fully-formed human being from whom all shreds of nothingness have been pruned away. This realization of my "being" is an event members of both publics will observe and confirm. And corresponding to this open recognition in the clear, common light there will arise within me a perfected knowing, for it is also an essential element of my golem project that I achieve a particularized knowing and self-knowing to which no obscurities cling. This knowledge—it is obvious that it will be expressible in English—is the comprehension of my story and of where and who I am. When I finally walk and attain being, I will simultaneously reach this knowing, which thereafter will be eternally valid. This golem awareness, a perfecting of the fragmentary and often wavering knowledge I now have, contrasts sharply with that fringe awareness which can invade consciousness in conditions of floating solitude and despair. Then the slowly hardening contours of golem awareness begin to fade; all those ripening verities, our embryonic comprehension of ourselves and of this place, turn to haze; words lose their hold on us, and English begins to fall out of us and we out of it. I have said that in normal life we associate the fringes with danger, craziness, and defeat. Yet it is fringe awareness, not that concentrated golem awareness, which more closely resembles the drawings theological reflection has sketched of a knowing that might be called divine.

For Aquinas God's knowing, like his being, is altogether "simple"; indeed, the absolute simplicity of the divine means that in God being and knowing are one. It also means, as St. Thomas points out, that God's knowing is entirely divorced from succession or temporality; it is a perfectly simultaneous knowledge, changeless and eternal. All this clearly implies that Latin, English, and all other human languages, saturated as they are by multiplicity and temporality, are irrelevant to a divine knowing—God's awareness, in other words, will in no way be a verbal or linguistic awareness. Consequently, the remarkable diphthong 'I', that sound with which the voice in my head gestures so innocently toward the edgeless, largely unknown event that "I" am, has no place in divine consciousness. In God such an "I" is not used to fuse together a little ring of domesticity and intimacy which includes this particular body, the flow of words in this head, the ecstasies, sadness, and fleeting moods arising from this brain, the history and connections this little ring of intimacy has formed in time. And so in God a sliver of domesticity called "I" does not stand opposed to everything else; in a divine or perfected consciousness there will be no opposition between a supposed "I" which it is and a supposed "it" which it is not; there will be no sense of duality between I and you, subject and object, inside and outside, self and world. In the unimaginable mind of God there will be no nouns or verbs, no grammar or vocabulary, no questions, answers, or propositions. There will be no time-proof *vitas*, verbalizations of identity, self-comprehendings, or certainties about how the world is such as we seek for our golem in the clear, common light. There will only be perfect, undivided, unchanging "simplicity."

We can therefore well understand why the Yogācārins, those

Mahāyāna Buddhists who specialized in consciousness as a focal point of their meditations and reflections, should characterize a perfect knowing as *nirvikalpajñāna*, that is, "undifferentiated cognition." And since this knowing, just like divine being, is infinite, we can also understand why they would often picture it as ocean: a vast, deep, quiescent sea of mind the surface ripples of which we mistakenly identify as the main stage of awareness. Pursuing the path opened up by the Yogācārins, Zen Buddhists like Huang Po would write that Mind, the incomprehensible essence of all things, is "void, omnipresent, silent, pure" (Huang Po 1958, 35). This is not unlike Śaṅkara's interpretation of the *ātman*, the ultimate "self" of all things, as an indefinable, unchanging, shining "pure consciousness." And for that matter it is not unlike Augustine's description of God's knowing—"one eternal, immutable, and ineffable vision"—as a single, unchanging, wholly extralinguistic act.

It is becoming apparent how contrary divine awareness is to that knowing we normally seek for ourselves in the clear, common light. (The great Upanishad equatin is *brahman=ātman*.) I will formulate this antithesis provisionally in the following way. Golem knowing, just like golem being, is a product of concentration—that is, awareness is "concentrated" within that little circle of domesticity which is held together by the sound 'I'—and of complexity—that is, awareness is particularized as a structured, differentiated, verbalized, sequenced knowing. In perfect contrast to this complexity, God's knowing is undivided and unstructured; it is Aquinas' "altogether simple" and the Yogācārins' "undifferentiated cognition." And it is also the opposite of "concentrated." Just as Huang Po says Mind is omnipresent, Anselm asserts that Divine Wisdom is "wholly present" in all things. To the complexity and concentration of golem knowing, divine knowing therefore opposes utter simplicity and a boundless "dilation." God's mind, bereft of insights, questions, and English, is the simplest of "scenes." Yet it extends through and contains within itself all time and space.

Two additional points about divine knowing are important. Just as it has no connection with or need for English, so it has no connection with or need for "publicity" or the world of clear, common light. It is true that it is everywhere, but only as undifferentiated "pure awareness." Like that subjectivity which begins to engulf us near the fringes, it is therefore an extralinguistic and purely private affair, there being no currency in which it might circulate. Thus Plotinus refers to God as solitary, as "utterly unmingling." One of Eckhart's favorite themes is *Abgeschiedenheit*—"withdrawal," "apartness," or "seclusion"—and in the sermon which receives its name from this theme, he develops the notion of the "immovable seclusion" of God. It is important to note, however, that there is no sense of absence in this pure privacy. Floating in the desert of its own edgelessness, God's knowing is alone in the sense in which a blue sky, or the universe, is "alone." Resting self-complete in itself, and unsupported by anything else, it needs nothing further. It requires no recognition or confirmation. It does not need to be articulated, recorded, or memorialized in English, doesn't need to explain to itself or someone else what it is, doesn't feel a need to turn itself into something less "private," doesn't need to become part of a larger something, for God and God's knowing are already complete, indeed, unthinkably more than "complete." It is true that God is often pictured as emerging from the fullness of this perfect oblivion in order to speak, act, or create. Thus we are given, for example, the Kabbalists' grand and complex vision of *En-Sof* breaking out of its hiddenness and letting the heavenly and corporeal worlds unfold. But these actions and manifestations do not signal any kind of flaw, absence, or incompleteness in the divine condition; they don't suggest any need on God's part to become anything other or more than "altogether simple" being and knowing. Indeed, the reverse is true: we picture God's actions as manifestations of superabundance, as the *overflow* of those purely private wanderings in his desert, an exuberance coming out of his unimaginable and hidden life.

Second, the same reflections which have led theologians to deny being to God have led to a similar denial of knowing. We have already seen how theology can come to picture God's awareness as perfectly antithetical to that concentrated, particularized golem consciousness we usually think of as knowing. Since God has no being, no identity, no name, no form, and no characteristics, and since God dwells eternally outside English, how could there be self-comprehension in God in any sense of the word 'self-comprehension'? Why confuse the issue, then, by speaking both of our "knowing" and of God's? Why not verbalize them as the opposites they are? Further, why should we imagine we are doing God a favor by attributing to him something like those streams of labials, alveolars, and fricatives, and like all those slogans, dignified asseverations, and terse assessments of "life" which at one

time or another have been thrown into the general category of knowledge? And why should be assume that there take place in God events
along the lines of those micro-flows of electrical current and those faint
neuronal poppings we identify as "self-comprehension"? Indeed, if we
are going to image a divine awareness, why not do so in terms of the
highest knowing of which we are capable: the relinquishing of all those
words, images, and forms with which we have covered over God's
formless, indescribable, inconceivable essence. Why not picture a divine knowing, in other words, in terms of that immediate experience,
that *touching*, which is possible only when we break out of all comprehension and all English?

Considerations of this kind led Plotinus to believe that the One
is above knowing as well as being; consequently, it is void of any cognition and "ignorant" even of itself. Christian theologians appropri-
ated this fruitful notion of divine incomprehension. God, writes
Dionysius, "has no imagination or opinion or reason or understanding" (*CU*, 217). Eriugena teaches that Divine Wisdom is formless. Of
the Divine Nature he writes that in "the most hidden recesses of its
nature . . it is unknown even to itself, that is, it knows itself in nothing because it is infinite and supernatural [that is, above nature] and
superessential [above being] and beyond everything that can and cannot
be understood" (Eriugena 1981, III, 187). We might then picture divine knowing in the following way: it is an eternal wandering in the
divine desert, an infinitely dilating lostness in God's own unbounded
mystery. It is a divine version of "opening," of that sudden fall out into
absolute incomprehension in which for a blessed moment we are but
a hair's-breadth from a perfect, final seeing of all things.

How, then, might one sum up these various beings and knowings
as they are found in the clear, common light, on the fringes, and in
God? How might one state the paradox? I conclude that being and
knowing such as they occur on the fringes and in God stand together
in absolute contrast with their shared antithesis: golem knowing and
being. As we have seen, the latter is characterized by concentration
and particularization, that is, the "individuation" of a compact, formed,
named, defined, knowing "I." But the other two conditions manifest
a process of simplification—that is, the breaking up of all particularity—and of dilation, the very reverse of concentration. Fringe and divine
states differ only in the following way: a divine being and knowing
embodies the completion, the perfection, of the process of simplifi-

cation and dilation; but fringe existence is the process itself. As we drift out toward that personal wilderness I have called the fringes, the process of simplification and dilation begins. The magical creature we have been laboriously creating—that "human being," that sadly tenantless name we have tried to dress up in a life—begins to dissolve. The contours of its being and knowing melt. Dilating consciousness begins to drift uneasily out of individual reality, out of the world of this and that, out of English, structured knowing, and the clear, common light. It is wandering into a vast desert of pure privacy, a place in which it "is" nothing and "knows" nothing. Consciousness, once tethered so securely to that little domestic scene held together by an "I" and a name, has slipped free and now wanders ambiguously in a vast place. Divine being and knowing represents the completion of this wandering, this process of simplification and dilation. For God's state—or *brahman*'s, or a perfected Buddha's—is absolutely simple, formless, and uncontained. The absolute simplicity of divine being transcends all opposites, all categories, all this and that, all words, all images. It is outside the clear, common light, outside English, outside all knowing. It is so unlike golem being that from a golem perspective it is non-being, that is, nothing. God's knowing, too, is at once absolutely simple and unbounded. It is a divine unknowing. It is a dizzying, ecstatic dilation of pure, uncrystallized consciousness which, no longer contained by its name, roams everywhere and can slip into anything. It is a mystery which, if it *did* squeeze itself into English, would say "I" from the very center of all things.

The paradox is that the image we have of the worst possible state and the image we have of the best possible state are essentially the same image. It is that our usual picture of fringe existence—that existence we seek at all costs to avoid—and theological reflection's picture of divine existence—the most perfect and desirable of states—coalesce so remarkably. Yet we should not be surprised at the similarity of these images. They are pictures of the same continuum of life; they are as it were human and divine versions of that one "life" which contrasts so sharply with our normal golem life. From this particular perspective the paradox is as follows: we reverently contemplate in God a life which we regard as the worst fate conceivable for ourselves. I have already described the alarm with which concentrating consciousness—"we"— reacts to any threat to its golem project. Its greatest fear is that it should begin to slide out toward the fringes, out into the appalling disintegration and dispersal—that is, the simplification and dilation—of that magical human being it has been concentrating. To take the paradox one more step, and so to complete it, it only remains to point out that God finds a divinely perfect joy and delight in the fringes, that Gehenna and place of "horror." According to Aquinas God's blessedness consists in awareness of his own essence, of, that is, his absolutely simple and undifferentiated being, of what Eriugena calls his unknowable being. In both Buddhist and Hindu Tantra the ultimate, innermost essence of being and knowing is something "more" than Emptiness; it is *mahāsukha*, the "great bliss." The Vedanta teaches that we must finally experience *brahman* "without qualities," but the last three words we are permitted before passing beyond are *sat-cit-ānanda*, or "Being-Consciousness-Bliss." Eckhart, too, refers frequently to God's *Lust* and *Wonne*, that is, his spiritually voluptuous pleasure and delight; it is an "immeasurable delight" which, outside all conception, is one with the eternal flow of divine "life."

We can therefore say, paradoxically, that God has found the secret of divine being, the key to godlike awareness, and also his supreme joy out in the gloom and among the debris, shades, and hungry ghosts of those fringes we so doggedly shun. He has found divine reality hidden among the scraps, cobwebs, and dust we are always trying to sweep out into the darkness. He has achieved the plenitude of perfect being by becoming one with that "nothingness" from which we are so eager to escape, and by collecting and weaving together those tiny shreds and frayed ends of nothingness we are constantly trimming away from ourselves. Since beginningless time he has found his unimaginable lucidity in that freedom from particularity which for us is the disintegration of all knowledge, for the divine consciousness has been one, eternally, with that unchanging *om* which is the single sound of its own knowledge-transcending essence. We long to be able to say who we are, but his very inability to say who he is is God's self-knowledge. We struggle to escape the dark waters and formless mysteries of our origins; God rests in the dark waters and formless mysteries of his origins. That pure privacy we see as madness is the hidden garden of his perfect tranquillity. Final and irrevocable defeat—the disappearance even of one's name—is for him a victory, joyful release from an arbitrary and suffocating confinement. Where we are swallowed up by "nothing" he sees a place in which there is nothing to stop or limit his joy. Our nightmare is his bliss. The fringes, those waste places of pure desolation, are for him a great, holy desert in which he roams free of all division and confinement and has happily lost track of all things, even himself.

## III. AFFINITIES AND IMPLICATIONS

OF COURSE OUR HAPHAZARD, PROTEAN PICTURINGS of ourselves are largely phantasm and myth—so much more our delineations of God, our inevitably faltering attempts to put a form and face on mystery. It may be that God, who alone is "real," is actually something too simple and too near for our minds to grasp, and so even the most profound theological reflection traffics largely in the unreal. Regarded from this perspective, theology is simply the first curious, bemused sniff consciousness takes, having become alert enough to be startled by mystery. It is a word-animal's attempt to process that which cannot be processed in any way; it is an attempt to bring into one's particular world a presence which cancels out all worlds. Yet theology is the queen of the sciences. It is our deepest inhalation of the strange scent of this place, our most searching interrogation of its savor—what could be more important, and interesting, than what happens at the junction of brain and mind-breaking mystery? The images which issue from theological reflection on divine being and knowing are therefore most worthy of attention, and the images we form of our own possibilities of knowing and being are in any case of interest to *us*. But how are we to regard the paradoxical relationship *between* these two sets of images? What are we to make of this essay's paradox? I—this bit of unmeasured soul, this little ring of seemingly familiar life marked off by a name—have already said that the paradox is dangerous, liberating, a bearer of truth. But this cannot be the case if the paradox remains merely an isolated curiosity; it must be more than a quaint oxymoron drifting loose and alone, unrelated to other phenomena. To be this something "more," the paradox must connect with other forms of theological reflection and with other aspects of our perennial attempts at self-portraiture. It must suggest new perspectives on our experience. It must have implications. Let us consider three.

First, the paradox is symptomatic of a profound division in our being and consciousness, a fault, an antagonism between our most deep-seated instincts and habits on the one hand, and our most subtle intuitions on the other. For from the beginning we have been programmed to engage in the work of concentration, of creating ourselves as human beings with lives. And from day-to-day consciousness' instinctive preoccupation—so automatic, so self-evident, that ordinarily we are not even explicitly aware of it—is this particular golem project in all its detailed and never-ending complexity. Hence our unflagging attention to the care and maintenance of our golem, to the variety of performances and relationships which constitute its being, to the dangers, insults, and injuries which assault it daily in the clear, common light, to new possibilities that seem to open the way toward improvements or even completion, that is, the attainment of a final, perfect, enduring definition. Thus soul—the vast, nameless thing or event "we" are—becomes entangled in the constantly shifting task of concentration and golem-creation, of putting bones in and flesh on this name. Daily life becomes filled with the details of how I will achieve form, how I will turn myself into, or at least appear to be, this or that, how I can shape the event I am into proper and recognizable English chronicle. But at the same time there is an obscure, usually neglected presence within us—I say it is that unmeasured, nameless "soul"— which regards all form as something alien and all golem projects as bizarre digression. What strikes it about all our attempts to become something is the arbitrariness of these undertakings, the thoughtlessness, the dispatch with which some project or other swallows us up, their shoulder-shrugging and perhaps even despairing whimsicality, the obvious fact that our golem never *will* dance, the inevitable doom of this undertaking, its outcome in "nothing." And this alienation from form and from all striving for golem being and knowing is only intensified by the fact that the obscure voice within us also whispers that it and "we" have a reality outside all form and a destiny outside all particularized being and knowing, outside all definition and story, and our great blunder is that we are neglecting that reality and that destiny now, even as we have neglected them from the beginning.

It is not difficult to see how this usually repressed discord becomes manifest in the paradox. For in daily life concentrating consciousness is preoccupied by the attempt to transmute all its formlessness, pure potentiality, and "nothingness" into a golem dancing gracefully in the clear, common light. And if anything is single-minded it is concentrating consciousness. It makes use, of course, of tactical and therapeutic solitude, but there it draws the line—at all costs it avoids floating solitude, and views of the fringes, and having to listen to its own most profound intuitions. But in theological reflection, in which attention *seems* turned harmlessly toward a reality apart from daily reality, the hypnotic power of our golem-oriented visions weakens, and consciousness becomes more open to a recognition of the splendor and even divinity of what is outside all particular being and knowing and dwells in a pure privacy far removed from the clear, common light. In theological reflection, in other words, those intuitions which stand opposed to the golem-instinct and the entire cult of form are given voice, and so the great fault in consciousness, the deep fissure which bisects *us*, stands revealed.

The paradox therefore brings to light an inner duality awareness of which we usually suppress. It affords us an opportunity to dwell with and reflect on the fundamentals of our soul's condition. But it is not only in our paradox that the ominous fault within is revealed. It discloses itself as well in other more familiar phenomena, and we can better understand their significance as well by observing more closely just how they reveal the fault and how they intermingle with the paradox. The traditional golem tales themselves, for instance, are pervaded by the dismal gloom of the fringes: an aura of wrong turnings, misbegotten ventures, fiasco, and defeat. Typically this mood manifests itself most concretely and decisively in the fact that the golem project—the attempt to create a human being by means of magic—fails because of some critical flaw in the golem itself. For example, the unhappy creature may not be able to speak, or it may be prone to break out in uncontrolled destructive behavior. The consistent implication of the golem legend's numerous variations is therefore that all *human* attempts to create human beings are doomed, and that the prerogatives of creation are God's alone. These stories are at least partially an enactment, then, of theological reflection's critique of concentrating consciousness. They portray the conflict between golem-instinct and our intuitions of the divine. We find in them the elements which have led to the fissure within us and which also make up the paradox.

Tales concerning golems have traditionally circulated within Kabbalistic circles and at times have been popular within the larger Jewish community. A brief reflection soon shows, however, that they connect closely with one of the most widely familiar forms of story, of, that is, the public portrayal in the clear, common light of one or more generally significant "lives." As a form of story, tragedy has enjoyed unparalleled authority in the West, which clings more fervently than does the East to dreams of achievement and happiness within the world of form. Tragedy is so intimately connected with the golem legend—and with both our inner duality and the paradox—because the story it unfolds portrays the inevitable failure of even the grandest golem projects and so by implication *all* golem projects. Tragedy reveals that all these ventures are doomed in the end to come to "nothing," that only for a few hours or years of illusion can it seem to us that genuine accumulations of being and knowing cradle this name or indeed any name. The catharsis we find in tragedy derives therefore from our acknowledgment of the tragic story as our true story. In this recognition we gain release from all the tension and Sisyphean exertion of consciousness' daily self-deception, its repression of awareness that its own golem project is both a blunder and, even on its own terms, doomed. And the exhilaration we find in tragedy relates to the fact that we are now at least temporarily freed from concentrating consciousness, from its constant insistence that we must make ourselves into something, from its demand that we—unmeasured, nameless "soul"—must create for ourselves a life. In tragedy therefore we begin moving toward other forms of awareness. We make contact with intuition. We begin to approach that fault in consciousness which the paradox so plainly reveals.

Tragedy has its roots in religion, and in all its forms tragedy retains perhaps at least some vestiges of that origin. But within what is unmistakably the world of religion there exists a phenomenon which connects even more significantly than does tragedy to what I have said here about the fault in consciousness and the paradox. The paradox reveals a great fissure in the soul, a crack occasioned by the tension between intuition and instinct. Awareness of this fault is also powerfully manifest in that ancient religious sense of errancy and aberration—of having been, from time immemorial, in the wrong street—which has expressed itself with sad profusion in stories and images of a fall, of exile and separation, of conscious life as entanglement in a great web of primordial ignorance or illusion, of existence as we know it as the consequence of an ancient, foolhardy, perverse revolt against God. In these accounts of a fall, intuition, which we might define as the normally unheard voice of the measureless soul we are, speaks still more openly than it does in tragedy of that blunder which it takes ordinary golem-creating life to be. Indeed, we might say that traditional religious portrayals of a fall are simply ways of articulating as story the fault, the blunder, and the other elements of the paradox I have described here. The intimate connection which obtains between such myths and the paradox is shown by the fact that the aberrancy myth chronicles can also be stated succinctly in terms of the paradox, as follows: the condition we normally seek—a golem-condition of defined, crystallized, visible, self-comprehending particularity—is the reverse of a blessed and godlike condition. The direction and place toward which we are normally turned—the clear, common light—is a place of failure and certain doom, but in the opposite direction, in those fringes toward which our backs are turned, lies uncontained divine "life."

From this religious perspective, therefore, concentrating consciousness is the normal life-form of fallen consciousness, consciousness that has drifted away from God and from itself. To exist as concentrating consciousness, to be an "I" attempting to clothe its nakedness in formed being, knowing, and story, is to be turned away and moving away from divine states of being and knowing, and from a life outside all story. It is to have dismissed as undesirable and alien that uncharted wandering outside all English, comprehension, and self-comprehension in which God finds uncontained delight. It is to be diligently trimming away from ourselves that formlessness, that undifferentiated being, that "nothingness" which in reality is our true self and the secret of our kinship with God. It is not surprising, then, that something in us occasionally whispers that we are preoccupied with everything except what matters. And it is not surprising that religion, which voices our most profound intuitions and discoveries, should so frequently and so vividly hold this preoccupation up before us as a life-fixing perversity and blunder, as our "fall."

The paradox's second implication follows from the first. It draws conclusions about how consciousness can attempt to unscramble the paradox and correct the fault which has now been uncovered. Here, too, the close connection between the paradox's implications and traditional religious themes is evident—both urge us first to acknowledge the division within us, the tensions between instinct and intuition, and then to do something about it. For the paradox's second implication is what religion characteristically teaches, namely, that a God-oriented or religious life, as opposed to "normal" life, entails a radical reorientation, an about-face. This is that complete "turnaround" which is the underlying metaphor of Christianity's *metanoia*, or conversion, and of the *parāvṛtti* — "turning around" — of the Yogācārins. From the perspective of the paradox and the fault, the need for such a conversion is evident, for consciousness in its normal "blundering" state is oriented toward golem-existence and has its back turned toward God. Described in terms of the paradox, conversion therefore means that the soul turns away from the "center," that clear, common light in which golem-making takes place, and turns out toward the fringes, the regions where divine being and knowing lie hidden. Such a sweeping reorientation brings in its wake countless more specific transformations and reversals. Christian and Islamic tradition speak respectively of the death of the old Adam and of *faná*, the passing away or annihilation of the self. Eckhart refers to the *Selbstentäusserung*, that is, the self-emptying or self-disappropriation of the self, and John of Cross writes of the annihilation of will, intellect, and memory.

Put in terms of this essay, these formulations of conversion can be imaged as abandonment of the golem project, of the familiar endeavor to become something, to have a life. The first phase of conversion, the *via purgativa*, means therefore to work at dismantling our golem, to let its parts return to dust as we walk away. To begin correcting the blunder and the fault, we will now seek to turn from the world of form and crystallized, defined being—in Eckhart's terms we are leaving all images behind and moving toward union with "formless Being." We will no longer aspire to a structured understanding within that particular form of knowing we call English. Instead, breaking out into that edgeless realm which lies outside English, we will begin learning to fly shaman-like outside the word-body. Whereas we once sought to contain God and ourselves within comprehension, we will seek to "know" him and ourselves just where he and we dilate beyond all comprehension. We move away from the clear, common light and approach the fringes; we turn from the public to the purely private, from the visible and publicly accessible to the invisible and incommunicable. We will throw off our "lives" and begin reducing and simplifying ourselves into a pure, undivided attending, a Hasidic "adhesion" to God. We will slough off that name we once sought to adorn with being and a life, and will now want only to be the fire of that divine spark which Eckhart describes as "free of all names and bare of all forms." We let that "I" which once marked off a little ring of seeming intimacy break up, and we sense that old, once familiar self beginning to disperse through and take up residence in all things. We "convert" now from concentration and particularization to simplification and dilation. We give up centripetal for centrifugal life. Breaking out of the little shell of golem-focused existence, out of all form, out of all comprehension, the soul now begins to experience all horizons as simply more form and limitation, and so as horizons to be passed through; it has now entered upon the great initiation: that endless falling away of all vistas and horizons which is the soul's slow, bewildered, untellable fall out into "God."

Third, the paradox offers us an additional perspective from which we can view not only the promise, but also those complications, strains, and afflictions which are peculiar to religious—that is, "turned"—life. We have seen that the paradox brings to light the great fault in consciousness, and this recognition entails in turn the need for radical reorientation, for "conversion." But the paradox also enables us to understand with greater clarity a further paradox: the fact that the new journey toward divine being, knowing, and bliss is painfully slow, and is marked not only by inflowings of fullness and joy, but also by hesitation, conflict, and pain.

I have described consciousness as divided, as marked by a conflict between instinct, which insists on making a human being and a life, and intuition, which regards golem-making as a sad diversion from our true destiny, which is to touch and somehow participate, outside all forms and limitations, in divine "nothingness." This deep-seated conflict does not magically dissolve once the religious decision, which itself is always of course only a partial decision, has been made. Indeed, this conflict, which heretofore has been largely repressed for the sake of the golem project, becomes now for the first time truly a conscious conflict as instinct resists the attempt to turn. Just as it begins to convert, in other words, consciousness finally must confront and respond to its inner conflict, its fault. Here I will refer briefly to two familiar and important phrases—one from Indian traditions and one from Christianity—which reflect this confrontation.

The first is yoga, or "yoking," that is, the notion of a massive, deliberate, systematic, gradual program of self-transformation, of conversion. As a religious program and method yoga is the process through which consciousness is trained and harnessed to conform to the insights of intuition. There would be no need for "yoga"—under which I here include such endeavors as Christian contemplation and Buddhist meditation—if the religious life merely involved recognition of or assent to certain assertions, or if it were possible to bring about those complete, instantaneous transformations of the self such as have sometimes been imagined in both East and West. From the perspective offered by the paradox we can now see, however, that the religious life inevitably involves the great and difficult work of confronting those forces within us which created the old, habitual, "fallen," golem-obsessed life. The great difficulty arises from the fact that concentrating consciousness is powerful and clings with inflexible catlike resolution to its old ways. Left unguarded and "unyoked," this consciousness returns therefore to its habitual ways, that is, to taking note of and reacting to all the details of all the ups and downs of its golem like a broker intently watching the market. Intuition, which we might indeed see as the voice of the soul's deepest insights and longings, of its most profound "instincts," now seeks to realize those insights and longings in a reformation of consciousness, but the powerful golem-instinct resists. Intuition wants now to break out of the world of particularity and form so as to abide in the infinite; it seeks a divine being and knowing outside all English knowing. But the old self clings to particularity's seemingly familiar world. As the old self what we want is to read that letter, to consider that job-change, to ponder that odd comment she or he made, to weigh an apparent slight, to decide about Saturday and begin making plans for this summer's vacation. Our brain, that odd, unknown animal crouched in our head, is wonderfully able to scent, outside of and containing all else, the divine. At the same time these millions of years have saturated it with particularity. Hence the need, if we are to make headway in transforming consciousness, for patient effort, for a genuine, systematic program, for "yoga."

The second phrase, taken from one of the most imposing and illuminating documents of Christian mystical spirituality, is that of the soul's "dark night." Why turned life, which moves as we have seen toward divine "bliss," should nevertheless have to enter and pass through such a night is another phenomenon the paradox helps us understand. What is least dark and painful in the life-dismantling work to which I have referred is separation from those creature comforts which are easy enough to list, the "dark night of sense." Much more daunting is what John of the Cross calls the dark night of the spirit. This second night accompanies that work of eradication he describes as the total abolition of intellect and will—in terms of this essay: abandonment of the golem-dream of turning oneself into a particular self-comprehending being which has achieved and become some particular this or that. We can now understand more easily the gloomy darkness of this dark night, as well as the "aridities," "afflictions," "pains," and "deprivations" the soul now must endure. For having considered the paradox we now know that the religious life, which on the one hand is a movement away from the clear, common light out toward divine being, knowing, and bliss, is simultaneously a movement out into our worst nightmares and into regions we normally dare not contemplate. For as it approaches the fringes, converting soul is now beginning—with understandable uncertainty and trepidation—to let itself become a dilation, a slow dispersal and melting away, and it is allowing consciousness to become an obscure, uncontained, self-transcending consciousness. It is releasing itself out into that formlessness, that pure potentiality, that nothingness which is its origin. This is the nothingness from which it has continually sought to escape by becoming something, and which always lay waiting in the darkness of the fringes to swallow it again. We can therefore well understand that the soul, though on its way to God and bliss, should nevertheless feel itself to be "perishing and melting away . . . in the presence and sight of its miseries," and that the soul is now, in fact, in a "sepulchre of dark death" (*DNS*, 104). And we can also well understand that vehement alternation between "misery and torment" on the one hand, and "abundance and calm" on the other, to which John of the Cross refers. For as I approach the fringes, and as I therefore begin to break out of the shell of particularity, out of English and my life and my name, I will sometimes be filled by a boundless completeness which the sea and infinite space feebly image. But at other times I will be overcome by the golem-brain's certainty that I have marched into Gehenna. Then it will seem to me that I have voluntarily turned myself over to demons named oblivion, abandonment, craziness, and despair.

## IV. COINCIDENTIA OPPOSITORUM

NO MATTER HOW WEAK WE MAY BE, we will all someday accomplish what may now seem impossible: to pass through and leave behind, one by one, all the hours and stages of our dying. This certainty is the warrant that we will also be able to handle other lesser deaths, of which the dark night of the soul—that ordeal which lies in wait for us as we journey away from golem life and toward the fringes—is one. Soul, which now is discovering that it is not identical with any form, will therefore not be wholly swallowed up by the horrors of the dark night, just as it cannot be entirely contained within the opposite image of itself as ascending Mt. Carmel. For the centrifugal journey consciousness now undertakes is not a transfer from one place to another named place, but rather a journey out of all time, place, and name. It is an exodus from the land of form and definition, the putting aside of all context, framework, and perspective, of all those millions of maps, explanations, appraisals, and etiquettes our confident loquacity has draped over mystery. It is a shaman's journey outside English, a wandering in which soul, no longer confined within the shell of its knowing, flies uncovered out into mystery. This journey begins when I, transformed now into converting consciousness, turn away from the clear, common light and begin to move toward the fringes. But it does not end when I enter those peripheral regions in which God's majestic being strangely intersects with my own wraithlike unreality, and where God's luminous knowing coalesces with my volatilizing and seemingly empty awareness. Instead, entry into the region of paradox serves to amplify, refine, and further invigorate this movement.

One factor in particular contributes to this intensification. For as we attain greater familiarity with the seeming opposition between divine being and knowing on the one hand, and fringe being and knowing on the other, we become increasingly aware of the underlying connections and resemblances which create the paradox—we see, for instance, that God's being and fringe being can both be pictured as nothingness. The conclusion this growing awareness inevitably suggests can be summed up as follows: the contrasting images we have of divine being and knowing and of fringe being and knowing reflect two diametrically opposed ways in which we have pictured a life other than that instinctive and "normal" golem-centered life of particularity which is our daily fare. They are two radically divergent ways of representing a possible life outside particularity, English, knowing, and form, which is to say that they are two contrary versions of the same thing, the obverse and reverse of the same coin, just as the sounds 'perfect being' and 'chaos' name, or rather fail to name, the same thing. God's edgeless desert and our gloomy fringes are therefore the same place; God's being and knowing and fringe being and knowing are one, not two. The "twoness," the duality, exists within us. We can now see, in fact, that this polarity mirrors perfectly that fault or division within us which is also the ultimate source of the paradox. For when they contemplate a possible existence bereft of particularity, English, knowing, and form, our golem instincts and habits see only the gravest possible threat to that golem project they imagine we *are*, and so they see only nightmare and extinction and all the horrors of the fringes. But looking at the same possible existence, our innermost intuitions say, "That is where my true self, life, and destiny lie hidden. That is where this faint little pulsing of mystery I am can perhaps flow into and become one with the great mystery."

We are now in the presence of a phenomenon which in countless variations permeates religious experience: the coincidence, the union, of opposites. This merging of opposites is not, however, a process taking place in things, the so-called "opposites." Instead, it is an essential phase of the conversion which takes place within awareness itself. It is the perfect, if only temporary, coalescence and simplification of awareness around intuition. For, clearly, "opposites" can coincide only if they no longer *are* opposites, or, rather, only if they are no longer *experienced* as opposites. It is in English, and in all the differentiated com

prehension that is articulated in English, that there are opposites— indeed, it is by means of differentiation and opposition that language creates its variegated world. Only where there is English are there "being" and "nothingness," "knowing" and "ignorance," "bliss" and "despair"; outside English there are no named entities or qualities which might be opposed to one another or made to "unite." We can therefore picture the merging of opposites as an event in which as two things "coalesce," their hulls or coverings—that is, their names and their definitions and all the contrasting things we say and think about them—engage, and then in a powerful grinding, rasping, and flaking action are peeled and stripped away as the merger takes place. What finally remains is the "essence." And that essence is mystery, something remote from words and names, a something that has been divided only in consciousness, something that is neither "two" nor "one."

To be thus ground and peeled away, thereby creating space for edgeless, mind-breaking reality to flow in around and against us; and to be made to cancel one another out so that we, if only intermittently and imperfectly, might live in God instead of in English—that is the fate which now awaits the apparent opposites on which the paradox and this essay are based. I have described the seemingly clear, even self-evident contrast between God's perfect being and that nothingness from which we emerged, and which always lies in wait for us in the fringes. And I have noted the great gap which seems to separate God's perfectly luminous, diamondlike knowing from that dull and shapeless unknowing which sprawls though our heads as we approach the fringes. But as we have seen, these opposites, in fact, coincide. Created by concentrating consciousness and theological reflection respectively, they are images of the same thing: an un-golemlike life of simplification and dilation. Further, divine being and knowing and fringe being and knowing are simply two contrasting conditions, or dream-conditions, we have embroidered on two still more fundamental pairs of opposites, namely, the *notions* of being and nonbeing, knowledge and ignorance. But these opposites, too (that is, those irreducible categories and distinctions which provide the ultimate framework for all our pictures of being and knowing whether divine, on the fringes, or in the clear, common light) must now be made to merge, to "departicularize" one another, and thus to coincide. For in the end what are we to make of those peculiar noises—"being," "nothing," "knowing," "ignorance"—our mouths shape on the formless hum from our vocal cords?

The perspective at which we have arrived, that of the coincidence of opposites, suggests that we should no longer regard them as contraries or even as two, but rather as mysterious unities which point the way toward the one great mystery. These opposites, too, must be made to coincide; then we will be able to turn away from the categories of being and nonbeing, knowing and unknowing, and instead turn toward God, who roams free of all categories in the divine wilderness. As we bring being and nothingness into coincidence, all their contrary qualities peel one another away, and so we are left with what is neither this nor that, a "something" outside English. And as they fuse, knowing and ignorance cancel one another out; they no longer exist or are even possible. It will now seem to us that we have been using the words 'being' and 'nonbeing' for one simple reason: our minds cannot begin to imagine that single sound that is the absolutely true vocalization of this place. As for knowing and ignorance, it will now be as if they always were surrogates we used to gesture toward something whose true name we didn't know. With these two sounds we have clumsily obfuscated the singular taste and scent of this place. Even now, of course, having turned away from categories and names, we cannot pronounce the true name of this place. But it is possible that in some way we can become it, or perhaps already are it.

THE OPPOSITES I HAVE EMPHASIZED HERE—those relating to being and knowing—are only two of the countless pairs converting consciousness will encounter on its way out into uncontained mystery. It will also face, to name just a few, the dualities of bliss and despair, good and bad, ego and non-ego, matter and anti-matter, person and thing, life and death, visible and invisible, liberation and bondage, light and dark, essential and trivial. These pairs provide the framework for all our talk, thought, and inquiry, and for such activities as self-analysis, theology, cosmology, psychology, and literature, for, that is, all the picturings and comprehendings we engage in until some day that unfamiliar divine scent surprises us and then slowly begins to infiltrate, simplify, and dilate consciousness. Ultimately, of course, the many dualities used in this essay are stretched out on one overarching polarity, that of the "soul," or "I," and "God." Do these also finally coincide? On the basis of what has been said above we are in a better position to understand such phenomena as al-Hallāj's seemingly presumptuous and preposterous "I am the Real," the Buddhist identification of the world and of ourselves with the Buddha Nature, the Upanishadic "That art thou," and that persistent circling around the identity of God and the soul that characterizes Christian mystics such as Eckhart.

The fact that these declarations take place in the context of the coincidence of opposites means that we are not confronted here by "monism," "pantheism," or any other verbalized mapping of things; nor are we dealing with assertions about the positive identity of two named, distinguishable entities. Instead—as always with the coincidence of opposites—what we have here is a formula signaling the metamorphosis of awareness, soul's flight out into that divine nothingness outside words. God and I are no longer separate—that is, we now "coincide"—because neither "God" nor "I" any longer exists; there no longer *are* two even conceivably separate things.

What has changed is that the relationship between awareness and mystery is no longer linguistic. What happens no longer happens within English, and this place no longer translates into nouns and verbs; it transcends—infinitely—the patterns of the English sentence and all other patterns. The soul is no longer approaching God, to quote Eckhart, "as God." It no longer seeks a particularized God disguised under a name, but rather is approaching God as uncontained "That" beyond the dualities of form and formless, name and nameless, thinkable and unthinkable. It is no longer confusing God, the singular, unchanging taste and smell of this place, with "God." Nor does the soul experience itself as "I" separate from "God" or anything else. That little ring created by a name and the sound "I," that ring that separated this little mystery from the great mystery, now dissolves. For "I" and "God," like all pairs of opposites, belong to the particularized world of name and form. They are entries in the dictionary. They are English. What distinguishes them is that they are the last pair of opposites before flight, the last masks to remove, the last names to forget. After this culmination of simplification and dilation there no longer is an "I" or "soul" or "God." There is only a pure, perspectiveless, unformed "seeing," or Ruusbroec's "fathomless ground of simplicity" before which all "persons" must give way (Ruusbroec 1985, 152). There is only that which Eckhart glimpses as an act of divine self-begetting outside time. Or perhaps we can only say that we seem for a moment to be aware of a sliver of color or movement in the distance, or to hear a fragmentary word or tone from a dance or ceremony, a kind of ritual that is not visible to the eye, whose sequences and various gestures do not translate into anything else, and that finally is no "ritual." It is something always glimpsed momentarily, a phantomlike figure in the woods, or the recollection of a dream that, lacking all specificity, occasionally haunts the brain. But this elusive ceremony or song singles itself out in the following way: its subtle, uncanny remoteness derives somehow from its proximity and its importance. It continually eludes us precisely because it is too close for us to touch, too plain for us to see, too simple to be spoken or thought. But at the same time we occasionally know that this intimate, incommensurable something coincides with and, in fact, *is* the one true, untellable story in which we are all being told.

# IN THE MANY MANSIONS OF ECKHART'S GOD

SINCE UNITY, AS ECKHART MAINTAINED, IS TO be found in God alone, we should not be surprised to find division and complexity in everything else: in the world, in you, in me, in Meister Eckhart himself, even in Eckhart's myriad sentences *about* God. The last of these, like the others, could be explored in detail, and such a minute analysis might well lead to the conclusion that there are tens of variously described Gods, if not hundreds, in his sermons and writings. Here I shall only mention the well-known distinction in Eckhart, and in other mystical theologians, between two "Gods." One is the familiar God of Christian theology and tradition: an omniscient, omnipotent, loving but stern "He" who is the Creator, the God of Abraham, the members of the Trinity, the crucified Savior and risen Lord, the Heavenly "Father" and cynosure of eternity. Eckhart's other God, the living and life-giving center of his religious life, is that much more elusive God of the way of unknowing, the God encountered, to use Eckhart's often-quoted phrase, in the "silent desert of the divine." None of the qualities, actions, or relations listed above can be ascribed to this "divinity," for Eckhart's other God eludes all description, comprehension, conception, and reference, the sound 'God' being not really a name, but only the feeblest and most precarious of allusions. Though they share the same sacred sound, it is therefore fair to say that Eckhart's other God is wholly unrelated to the familiar Christian God, for "it"— the pronoun is much too precise, resting as it does on the odd distinction between the personal and the impersonal we have imposed on reality—is not a "person" or "thing" or "entity," and stands in no describable relation to any being or thing. As we shall see, Eckhart's other God is wholly incommensurable with our most fundamental perceptions of the world, and so it is necessary to turn aside from them in order to come into this "God's" mysterious and quickening presence.

Meister Eckhart's allegiance to this unknowable other God is grounded in a profound and apparently rare experience: a radical transformation, in adulthood, in one's most elementary and intimate sense of what constitutes the world. Most of us appear to believe—most of the time—that we understand, at least in rough outline, where we are. We tend to take it for granted that we have, and can convey to others, a generally accurate if imperfect picture of who we are and what we do, of what is happening around us, of what other people we know do and are, of what the world is "like." We formulate and communicate these pictures with language; its words, concepts, categories, and images are the vehicles used to comprehend the world. In them is embodied the peculiar supposition that we know where we are. From time to time it may well flash through consciousness that this picture is false, that the world we are living in is in fact a questionable, even a spurious world. We may sense that no human picture can even begin to mirror or even relate to reality. But such thoughts are disturbing, and if we stop to contemplate them, it is as if all reality and substance begin to drain out of our lives, posited as they are on the supposition that the world is a knowable quantity. Consequently we tend to draw back from this boundary, surrounding ourselves once again with the world, or the picture of the world, that language creates. We nestle ourselves once again in the notion that words contain and render the world, and having drawn back from that disquieting boundary, we return to the old seemingly instinctive premise that reality ends where words end, or that the limits of human thought and conception are the limits of the world. Alternatively, we recognize that there is a world beyond the limits of language and imagination, but then adopt the pose that the only reasonable and "logical" response is to turn away from it. This ostensibly straightforward and lucid stance, so threatening to spiritual impulses and so characteristic of powerful, language-centered currents within our century, is crystallized in Wittgenstein's famous statement "Whereof one cannot speak, thereof one must be silent" (Wittgenstein 1922, 189). But some individuals, Eckhart apparently being one, do not draw back. Shedding their language skins, they cross over that boundary into a new land. For those who make this cr crossing, the radical transformation referred to above can therefore be described in the following way: for them reality will no longer end where words end, but will rather begin there. For Eckhart and those who follow him, then, the limit of human thought, conception, and imagination is not at all the end of the world and of life, but rather the point at which one can cross over into a radically different life, a new reality. It will be in this other reality beyond words that Eckhart finds "God."

For Eckhart, then, the discovery of the other God is intertwined with the most profound change possible in adult life, a change in the very nature of awareness and in our perception of this strange place to which we daily awaken. It is not simply a change in one's life situation, relations with others, affections, aspirations, plans, philosophical view of the world, religious beliefs, or attitude towards life, but a change of worlds. In this unparalleled transformation the old world of words and human culture—that shared reality which human thought and words once seemed to illuminate—melts away, and another at first totally alien "reality" begins to accumulate around us. I have already suggested that we tend to shy away from the boundary at which this transformation begins to occur. At first we may also be put off by the path which Eckhart describes as the way leading towards that boundary, for it is the polar opposite of what seems to be the natural and normal response to life. Let us consider one of his most important descriptions of this journey more closely.

## ECKHART ON SPIRITUAL POVERTY

IN A WELL-KNOWN SERMON, ECKHART calls the path leading towards the other God the way of *geistige Armut*, that is, "poverty of spirit," or "inner poverty," a poverty of heart, spirit, mind, and soul (*DPT*, 303-309). As context for this we can take the fact that almost all human life appears to revolve around the accumulation, consolidation, and preservation of the most varied earthly and heavenly, external and internal treasures. In our individual lives we are limited to concentrating on just a few of these forms of "wealth," but overall their number is all but endless: money, natural and manufactured objects, land, fame, status, respect, friendship, family, romantic love, sexual pleasure, knowledge of the world, of oneself, and of "how to live," dignity, moral rectitude, the correct attitudes and behavior, artistic accomplishments, spiritual accomplishments, religious knowledge, the appropriate religious feelings and experiences, etc.

Eckhart agrees with the traditional call to turn away from the various forms of material wealth—through this renunciation one achieves what he calls "outer poverty." His emphasis, however, is on that inner poverty which is achieved when we surrender all inner riches, that is, all that we might claim to have or to be intellectually, emotionally, and spiritually. Coining a new German word that is just as alien and revealing in English, Eckhart has spoken elsewhere of the need to *entwerden,* that is, to "un-become" or "de-become" (ibid., 27) This term points towards the essence of what Eckhart means by inner poverty, just as it also probes very closely towards the tender center of our own tenuously held together lives. For though the forms of "wealth" are endlessly variegated, pursuit of that wealth manifests a universal human desire and need to "become," to incorporate and consolidate at least a few ounces of reality, to be *something* and to be acknowledged by others as being something. This need implies a disconcerting truth which may come home to us if we desist from activity and plan-making long enough to sit quietly and look inwards: we have the feeling that we are not yet real, that we only have the time between now and death to create, somehow, that reality which right now is painfully absent. Human life, therefore, is from the very first day an instinctive effort to "become," yet Eckhart urges the necessity to "un-become," that is, to reverse human life's underlying direction and goal. He calls for the abandonment of all efforts to incorporate reality, to become, and to "make something" of ourselves and our lives. On the contrary, we are to work diligently to cut away whatever reality and substance it may seem that hard work or chance has created. This reversal applies, above all, to all forms of inner and spiritual wealth. All attempts to acquire the right religious attitudes, accomplishments, and knowledge are to be abandoned. Turning aside from the goal of making something of ourselves spiritually, we must jettison whatever spiritual wealth, value, and standing we thought were ours. For in the sermon on inner poverty Eckhart speaks of a transformation into that which we were when we "still were not," that is, he calls for a deliberate return to that state of nothingness from which most human life, including most religious life, is an uneasy if not desperate flight (ibid., 304).

Just how can one un-become and so attain spiritual poverty? How, according to Eckhart, is nothingness achieved? In the sermon on poverty he defines the person who is poor in spirit as someone who doesn't want anything, know anything, or have anything (ibid., 303). Not to want or will anything is to divest oneself of all one's dreams, plans, and goals, in other words, all hope. And since he is speaking of *inner* poverty, he has in mind primarily the need to stop looking for those spiritual benefits religion traditionally promises. Here and elsewhere Eckhart makes clear the need to give up all egocentric concern for "salvation," for what will happen to *us* in the "next world." And as for this life, his words clearly imply that one will no longer desire, expect, or hope for any of the values and benefits which may once have seemed to be the very purpose of spiritual life. We must free ourselves, in other words, from all longings for grace, faith, peace of mind, a loving and unified heart, spiritual insight, and whatever else it once seemed religion "offered." In the same spirit Eckhart says that we must not have anything, meaning that we must surrender whatever goods—material, social, emotional, intellectual, and spiritual—we already possess or think we possess. Once again the last and most difficult struggle will be with the need to clear away our most cherished spiritual possessions. Eckhart's words imply the need to pass beyond: all religious knowledge; the sense of spiritual growth and wholeness; religious virtues, accomplishments, and dignity; the sense of membership in an elect from which the "non-spiritual" are excluded; the very sense of being "religious" as opposed to some other way to be.

I refer, thirdly, to Meister Eckhart's assertion that poverty of spirit also involves knowing nothing—ignorance, he says elsewhere, is humanity's "highest perfection." So-called negative theology usually concentrates almost exclusively on ignorance of God, but in the sermon on inner poverty Eckhart goes much farther—we must not pretend to know anything, he says, about God, the world, or ourselves (ibid., 306). To attain ignorance it is therefore essential to disentangle ourselves from all supposed insights into the physical world, the social world, the inner world, and the spiritual world. Consistent with his emphasis on inner poverty, Eckhart again emphasizes the last two, stressing the importance of knowing nothing about spirituality and the spiritual world, as well as the need to abandon the attempt to obtain such knowledge—it only points away from "God." To achieve the complete ignorance Eckhart describes, it seems clear that we must break free from all the assertions and affirmations with which we have pretended to understand at least some aspects of the world religion discloses, that is, we must discard all those word-pictures which supposedly illuminate spiritual reality. We could, for instance, determine what are the two or three truly primary and seemingly essential things we "know" about religion and our own spirituality, and then we could dismiss such knowledge.

At this stage it will no longer seem possible to understand, disclose, or communicate anything about God, religion, and the nature and value of the religious life by making statements about them. But the discarding of all views—whether for, against, or simply about religion—is only the first step in the process. As we free ourselves from all understanding, including spiritual understanding, and as we continue, in Eckhart's phrase, to "grow away from all light and all knowledge," our relation with the very building blocks of "knowledge" also begins to change. This second step, which often manifests itself in Eckhart as a rejection of all words, is decisive, for with the approach to that unbounded and unformed reality beyond the tiny sphere words have illuminated, or perhaps obscured, there evolves a growing remoteness from language and all its words, names, concepts, and categories. In our earliest years we all instinctively seized upon and assimilated language, letting it form awareness—words, after all, were the powers which seemed to unlock, reveal, and map the world. Now, disentangling ourselves from the supposed knowledge words made possible, we sense more and more the strangeness of the words themselves, as if they were coins of an unknown currency found gratuitously in our hands, coins whose value and use cannot even be guessed.

We once asked questions such as whether or not God exists, and what the word 'God' might mean. We once wondered, or perhaps even feigned to know, what religion is, what role it should play in human life, why we ourselves are religious, the role of compassion and loving action in religion, what religion reveals about who we are and what we should do with our lives, what can be expected from religion, and how spirituality relates to the rest of life. But as the word-mind, and with it the word-world, have dissolved, these questions have come to seem increasingly remote, like questions from another time, another life and culture, in fact from another world. And now begins the process of liberation from the very words around which all these questions turn. *God, religion, the religious life, true, good, I, ought, spirituality*—all these sounds now become markers and street signs once used for orientation far away in another place.

It is clear that the Eckhartian aim of liberation from all knowledge, including all spiritual insight, is an immense task, and so it is understandable that he returns to it so frequently. When this work is begun, moreover, it is certainly not possible to be aware of all of its ramifications. For instance, we will not at first fully understand what is involved in the need to abandon the pretense maintained both towards others and ourselves that we understand at least some things about religion and the world. It may not be understood at first that words themselves may begin to ring hollow, or that Eckhart himself cannot have "known" anything about religion either, and that one therefore must turn away from whatever supposed insights he offers. It is difficult to grasp the fact that we are leaving behind all possible tools for understanding, even in the most minimal way, just who we ourselves are, and where, and what for. Indeed, at this point it may well seem as if the path of complete ignorance is only leading into a barren and trackless wilderness, a wasteland in which we, without compass or guide, will soon be irretrievably lost. And it may well be that it will be good to have such thoughts for a time before moving on from this still very early stage of the journey. For if we think that we are "lost," and if we think that the sound 'lost' bears any relation to reality, we are still living back in the old world of words and images. We still imagine, naïvely, that it is possible to describe our condition.

I said above that Eckhart's other God is found by entering that other world which begins where all words, concepts, and thought end. I also said that according to Eckhart one can achieve this metamorphosis only by departing completely from the normal movement of human life, for it is necessary to "undo" all that one has achieved, acquired, and become up to the present moment, including all that one has and is in the spiritual realm. We have now glimpsed how to carry out this reversal: having turned away from material "wealth," we can un-become, or become inwardly poor, by striving to reach a condition of wanting nothing, knowing nothing, and having nothing. We are to want nothing, that is, our task is to identify our most profound aspirations in the social, personal, and spiritual realms, and then to abandon them. Secondly, we are to have nothing, that is, we will pare away whatever social or personal "substance" we have already acquired, especially all religious attainments, status, and definition. Finally, we are to know nothing, that is, we must leave behind us all the words and utterances which once seemed to name, map, disclose, and describe ourselves and the world—above all we must leave behind, as no longer useful, sounds like *my life, others, the way, God, the world,* and *religion.* Such words now become the quaint magic charms once idly conjured with in another life, or in a dream that once held us.

With the dissolution of all knowledge, the process of un-becoming is complete, and one is then in a position to see that Eckhart is not exaggerating when he says that to become poor in spirit is like returning to that state we were in when we "still were not." As for the personal "lives" which other people act on and talk about, lives with such and such goals, achievements, and setbacks—we will in fact no longer have such a "life," and so there can no longer be a proper "story" of one's life. As for that very "I" to which others refer, saying that "I" want this or did that or have these or am that—this "I," on our lips or just thought inwardly, will no longer refer to anything in particular, for we will now have trimmed away from "ourselves" all that we have and are. And as for that named, known, mapped world which those with lives dwell in and share—we have now drifted away from that world; it is a world now "forgotten." If I truly succeed, therefore, in becoming inwardly poor, or in un-becoming, I will find that I no longer have a life, an "I," or a world. I will be a nothingness that is nowhere.

## PICTURES FROM THE OTHER SIDE OF NOWHERE

THIS RETURN TO NOTHINGNESS IS A DEATH preceding a rebirth. The old deceptively familiar and knowable word-world must be abolished so that a much greater unbounded "something" can take its place. That something is the world of Eckhart's other God. In Eckhart that something is the world of the other God, the God beyond all names, words, and thought. For the nonbeing to which one returns is, paradoxically and miraculously, the entrance to another world. Having won back and vanished within our original nothingness, we then find ourselves in infinite being. Having eliminated everything that relates to having human "lives," we are surrounded by infinite life. Having reduced the world to a formless nowhere, we then find ourselves in "God." It is for this, and this alone, that we are to give up all we want, know, and have. But what is "this"? Eckhart points out frequently that the other God is actually "free of names" and that this "being" and the encounter with "it" are indescribable. And it is understandable why this is so. What words, concepts, or images could even begin to describe a place, or reality, or being reached only by abandoning all the words, concepts, and images, that is, all the *comprehension* which has heretofore interposed itself between us and God's immediate, indescribable, mind-breaking presence?

Because the experience is beyond description, and perhaps also because it touches the innermost self, those whose lives have become intertwined with the other God seldom even try to write about it directly. But it still remains by far the most decisive and dramatic experience of their adult lives—to repeat, it is nothing less than the exchange of one life and world for another life and world. Consequently, those who have written at all have tended in their writings to circle continually *around* that experience. Meister Eckhart, for instance, returns again and again to descriptions of the process which leads to "God." It is characteristic of his sermons that he interprets Biblical texts as allegorical descriptions of the mystical process. But when Eckhart attempts to describe soul's experience of the other God as directly as he can, he resorts to tangible images from the world of sense experience. He speaks, for example, of touching and being touched by God, of tasting God, and of dwelling in God—others, of course, have also used images of sensual love to "describe" this meeting. Thus Eckhart has recourse to the most concrete imagery available in order to evoke what is after all the most intimately and mysteriously palpable of experiences: direct "contact" with the infinite without the intervention of words or knowledge, a mystery in which the innermost self touches "God."

The extent to which such specific, tangible images come to mind can function as a possible measure of just where one stands in the attempt to leave the word-world and to enter the God-world. For example, if I still take it for granted that the world ends where words and thought end, and if I therefore equate the word-world with "reality," then the world beyond words can only seem to be a place of vacuity associated with images of desolation, sterility, and death—this could be called the "modern" perspective. But as I begin to extricate myself from the tiny sphere of the alleged "known" in order to immerse myself in the unlimited and unknown, this seeming void begins slowly to fill and is gradually suffused with a reality which cannot be categorized, but which surpasses all the equivocal and uncertain realities previously known. And as this other world beyond name and description becomes more and more the world to which I belong and in which I in fact *dwell*, these intuitions of plenitude and overflowing life may blossom into more precise and concrete images. It may seem, as it did to Eckhart, that I am touching God, or tasting God, or dwelling in God; some day for the first time, and then more or less frequently thereafter, consciousness may be invaded by the phrase: "Right now I am in one of the many mansions of God."

As suggested above, manifestations of such imagery from the world of the senses can be a measure of the extent to which one has changed worlds. As the word-world loses its self-evident reality, and as the world beyond words becomes home, that sense of immediate reality which expresses itself in tangible images is transferred from the word-world to the God-world. If therefore images of touching, seeing, and tasting now seem applicable to the experience of God, this can be seen as a sign that the transfer is taking place. If it occurs to me that I am in one of the many mansions of God, I can see this as indicating the extent to which the indescribable God-world is the world in which I now dwell, for as I "reside" more and more in that other world, how can I better express this than with imagery of dwelling and habitation? But these are only signs, and uncertain signs at that, and so they must not be taken to be authentic representations of "God" or of the encounter with "God." For to seize upon these images as a way to understand would be a retreat back into that old familiar word-world life in which I pretend to know where and who I am, what I am doing, and what is happening to me. I would therefore have and know something once again, but precisely because of this having and this knowledge I would once again have lost "God."

Is it in fact appropriate to call this other reality God? Examination of Meister Eckhart's sermons reveals that he himself is ambiguous on this point. He speaks frequently of the encounter, even the union, with God, but he also emphasizes repeatedly the need to pass beyond the notion of "God," and he even goes so far as to say that God, too, must "un-become" (ibid., 273). In response to this question I shall briefly suggest two reflections, from the points of view of the word-world and the God-world respectively. The first point, one consistent with the tradition of mystical theology, is that this other reality can be called "God" only if we have first severed all connections between this sound and 1) the known God of positive theology, and 2) all other words. Thus the sound 'God' should not suggest in any way a being who is all-powerful, omnipresent, loving, the Creator, triune, etc. As Eckhart himself says, God cannot be any "this" or "that," and so cannot in fact be "anything" at all. And since the other God completely transcends the word-world, all connections between the sound 'God' and all other words must be broken. Words derive their meaning and reference from their place in the language to which they belong; they are defined and shaped in relation to other words, by endlessly complex interconnections of similarity, opposition, etc. All such relationships define, particularize, and limit, but 'God' must remain undefined and without limit.

Before the word 'God' can be used, therefore, it must first be removed from this vast intricate network. Consequently, the word 'God' will not stand in any relation whatsoever to any other word; it will have no opposites, no synonyms, no parallels. It must not imply one part of speech more than any other. It cannot suggest the slightest hint of a "she," "he," or "it." It has no connection with either 'being' or 'non-being', with 'sacred' or 'profane', with 'good' or 'bad'; it is not more linked with 'religion' than it is with 'tragedy' or even 'comedy'. The word 'God' is to be used, therefore, only after it has first become a non-word, a word which strictly speaking is not "in our vocabulary." 'God' must become the strangest, the most anomalous of sounds, an incomprehensible, mysterious, relationless syllable which seems to break inexplicably into the little word-world from some unimaginable other place. It may be that the word 'God' can become such an anomaly—an anomaly we no more know how to respond to than we know how to respond to the unlimited itself—only if we refrain from using the word, only if, that is, it is banished from that shared talk and writing in which we feign comprehension of the world.

Secondly, to raise this question about the appropriateness of using the word 'God' and then to discuss it, acting as if there might be a plausible answer, is to dwell once again in that very world of words and feigned comprehension. It is to adopt the familiar pose of talking and acting as if we know who and where we are. It is to feign the capacity to make sense of "spiritual" life and so make appropriate and even "the right" decisions about that life. It is to return to that knowing which was supposedly abandoned when we became inwardly poor. If and when one is in the word-world, it is probably good to ask this kind of question rather than others. But what is much better than asking and especially answering such a question is to have outgrown it, that is, to have moved beyond the curious assumption, which is implicit in the very asking, that we have the tools to answer such questions and so to find our way, with at least a measure of understanding and sound judgment, through the world in general and the religious world in particular. It is better to discover instead that such questions now seem remote, relics of a former life. It is better to be in that other world which begins where questions, answers, and even words end. For the farther we are from knowing or aspiring to know anything about God or religion or our own spiritual path, and the farther we are from thinking that there *is* something like knowing about them, the closer we have drawn to "God."

## THE INVETERACY OF KNOWLEDGE

OR, AGAIN, IS IT BETTER, AND WHO IS to say that it is better or worse than the various alternatives found in this edgeless, labyrinthine place. This, too, is only more sham knowledge best left behind. For if I have been delivered from my former knowledge of God, myself, and the world, I can no longer presume to know that the path described here is *the* way, or even *the* way for me at the present time. Indeed, I cannot even categorize myself as someone who is on, or trying to be on, that way. And just on its own merits as a purely human question humanly understood, one may well ask if this way is better. For, as has been seen, Eckhart says that God is encountered only after all wealth, including all spiritual goods, has been lost. He says that we must turn around and retrace our steps, that we must un-become, undoing and unraveling our lives and our very selves. Who is prepared even to consider this venture, antithetical as it is to the seemingly universal flow of human life, including all that is usually called "spiritual" life? Who would have imagined, expectantly growing up and into the world, that one might someday contemplate the possibility of such an "non-life"? As we discovered religion and its rich promises of harmony and wholeness, who imagined that there might be a form of spirituality with no definite promises, a spirituality which in fact calls for the complete liquidation of everything that is "definite"? And as we acquired language and so gained "the world," who thought that some years later we might be asked to unlearn that language, to relinquish that world, and so to become, once again, "worldless"?

These are questions which may well arise as one wanders in the many mansions of Eckhart's God. And it may also happen, unfortunately, that it will also occur to us to try to answer them, to achieve the capacity to respond intelligibly to them, and so sadly to begin accumulating inner wealth once again. Up to this point I have, I believe, been faithful in this essay to the spirit of Eckhart, or at least to the spirit of one of the numerous Eckharts mentioned in the opening paragraph. Concentrating on just a few of his important thoughts and formulations, I have attempted to draw out of them as clearly as I can what is already implicit within them. Now, however, in connection with this new temptation to comprehend I would like to introduce a point which is more my own, though it can also be seen as an extension of Meister Eckhart's perspective. It is the explicit recognition that after entering the God-world we have a powerful tendency to begin making all over again the same basic mistakes which were characteristic of the old word-world life. Specifically, the chronic habit of pretending to ourselves and others that we know who and where we are and what we are doing tends even here to reassert itself with great tenacity and so threatens to interject knowledge once again between God-awareness and God. Even while dwelling in God's many mansions we often display, in other words, the same remarkable naïvete about our grasp of reality which defines the human pose in the word-world. I have said that the old self must un-become, or die, before it can be reborn in the God-world. But just having been reborn into the God-world, we often begin acting as if we had been reborn as mature adults instead of as the infants we so obviously are. We look around us as if this were something quite easily taken in. Having just opened those infant eyes, we actually believe we can comprehend God's house.

The concepts and perspectives of traditional religion are often of decisive importance in shaping this imaginary comprehension of the unknowable God-world. As was mentioned earlier, the work of inner poverty includes the need to put aside all concern for religion's traditional promises and benefits. But these very preoccupations with achieving a condition of perfection, wholeness, and harmony tend to spring back to life and even to dominate those pictures of God's house which, even after "rebirth," chronically reappear. Among followers of the way of unknowing there is a widespread tendency, in other words, to smuggle back into their spirituality those promises and rewards which traditional religion offers so straightforwardly. Zen Buddhism, for instance, involves immersion in a new life beyond words, concepts, and images, but on the other hand the familiar classical accounts of the Zen Master convey a definite if subtly drawn picture of that new life, and this picture corresponds recognizably to familiar religious conceptions of the perfected life: the Master acts with miraculously untroubled spontaneity, but always "correctly," and his inner life is pure lucidity, harmony, and serenity.

Eckhart, too, yields at times to the temptation to comprehend, and thus diminish, the new life. In a manner reminiscent of Zen he portrays an ideal condition in which a perfectly harmonious life flows within and then expresses itself outwardly in spontaneous, and always "good," actions. All this happens, moreover, *ohne Warum*, that is, "without a why" (ibid., 371). Subtle and initially appealing as they may be, these *pictures* mark a return to descriptions, to knowledge, and to the familiar and limiting pairs of opposites, this time applied not to the old world, but to life in the God-world itself. Perfection, harmony, wholeness, and spontaneity are after all opposed to and limited by imperfection, disharmony, fragmentedness, and awkward hesitation. Why must the latter be excluded from the new life? And aren't all of these limited human conceptions and distinctions swallowed up in the vastness and complexity of the relationship with that indefinable and unlimited "God"? For let us recognize once again: *perfection, wholeness, harmony, peace, centeredness*, and all sounds like them are just words and concepts opposed to and limited by other words and concepts. Their home is the finite, equivocal, even chimerical world of human knowledge. These youthful fantasies must be left behind if our goal is to touch "God."

We are predisposed, then, to bring into the new world of God's many mansions that knowing air we once maintained with such astonishing aplomb in the old world. Forgetting the inner poverty which made rebirth possible, we rapidly begin accumulating new wealth. Having just been reborn in God's endless mansions, we begin describing to ourselves and even to others the plan of the house. Since these instincts of accumulation, re-becoming, and imagined comprehension are so powerful, it will clearly be necessary to work to maintain that inner poverty already achieved. We need the constant recollection that our status in the many mansions of the other God is that of infants who are just beginning to find their way about one or two tiny compartments of an infinite place. For God, God's many mansions, and the life that can be lived there are unlimited—they are impervious to and not even touched by all attempts to grasp, encompass, and comprehend them. Earlier I discussed how one can achieve the ignorance which is such an important attribute of inner poverty. How, having been reborn in the God-world, can one then retain that ignorance? How can awareness that we are infants in God's infinite house be maintained?

One can begin by noting the impossibility of comprehending something so relatively "simple" as individual spiritual life. At the present moment, for instance, and as I write this essay, I am approaching God from within the context of the specific experiences, activities, emotions, thoughts, and physical condition which presently shape my life and which could of course change radically in a single moment, thus changing me and my experience of God as well. This means that at the present moment I am, so to speak, in just one of the rooms of God's many mansions, though I tend to form an impression of the entire house—one that obviously is far from adequate—from the few things I take in about the room I am in. For in spite of memory and anticipation I am largely a creature of the present moment, and I cannot begin to encompass or even bring into awareness all that I have experienced in God's house during the past days, or months, not to mention years, and of course nothing can be known of the experiences I shall have and the rooms and mansions yet to be passed through in the future.

One can note, further, that this life has been and will be infinitely varied. There have been and will be "mansions" which must be called mansions of desolation and of God's absence; in God's house there are places of discouragement, frustrated expectation, and weariness, as well as places of joy and gratitude. I mention this now just to make the following point: as shadowy and ephemeral as it may be, one's own actual life in the many mansions of God surpasses, absolutely, all the pictures, statements, and words one may use in the vain attempt to comprehend that life, just as scholars, to broaden the example, may spend their adult lives wandering in the great labyrinth of Meister Eckhart's words about God.

In order to retain awareness of that permanent infant status I can then note this further point: any individual's immeasurable life in the many mansions of God vanishes in turn within the collective human experience of that other world. For the more I discover about the extent and variety of human experience in that place beyond conception, the more I can see this collective human experience as being itself an image of that divine infinity which transcends all experience and awareness. Many Christians have discovered that world, as have Jews, Muslims, Taoists, Hindus, Buddhists, and others—all these traditions have their names, such as the Tao, Suchness, the Tetragrammaton, and "*brahman* without qualities" for the "nameless." Of the countless individuals who have lived in these many mansions, only a few have left behind any record, and in his or her own brief lifetime any one individual can explore, inadequately, only a few of these testimonies. In one of the innumerable rooms it may someday happen that I shall notice and for a short while contemplate some small object or architectural detail no one has noticed before, but for the most part, of course, I pass through the same rooms and reenact, with but slight variations, the discoveries and experiences of those who have already been in this place. And this is only to be expected, for those records which have fallen into my hands—Meister Eckhart's, for example—also serve as guidebooks. It is from them that I have obtained most of the images and viewpoints which constitute my particular understanding, or misunderstanding, of God's house.

I have said that my own complex and constantly changing life in the many mansions of the other God transcends at all times my meager ability to comprehend that life. In turn that vast individual life all but vanishes in the sea formed by the collective human experience of these rooms. Further, all that we human beings have experienced of the other God until now is dwarfed by the total collective experience of which we, given the time, are capable—until now, as it were, human beings have succeeded collectively only in casting just a few hurried, dazzled glances out into just one or two of the rooms of God's unmeasured house. The way in which my own understanding is dwarfed by my own experience of God, which in turn disappears within the collective experience, and this, in turn, in humanity's *potential* collective experience, suggests two perspectives which can help illuminate our status in God's many mansions.

The first is that it would be very naïve to suppose that any human being might be an expert, a master, or even just somewhat "well-informed" about the God-world—this is a pose, after all, which was not even justified in the old word-world. Since we are all dwarfed by this place, and just by the collective human experience of this place, all human beings, including all the so-called masters, are in fact like infants who have just opened their eyes, or just taken a few awkward, uncertain steps in one of the untold mansions of the other God. Indeed, it is precisely this infant condition to which our own century with its word-world orientation is blind when it complacently imagines that there *is* a logical response to the unsayability of the world, as Wittgenstein suggests in his *Tractatus*. Faced by the wordless, Wittgenstein still purports to know—and to be able to reveal in one or two gnomic utterances—how one can best respond to it. He retains the word-world pose of orientation and comprehension. By contrast, the Eckhartian perspective suggests that an alert if still embryonic awareness of where and who we are arises only after the pose of comprehension has been abandoned, and our infant status in the God-world has been recognized and accepted. This acceptance includes the recognition of how incongruous it is to pretend to know how to respond to the inexpressible and unknowable. Consequently, one will no longer be entangled in the possible view that silence is better than speech, or vice versa, or that quietude is better than action, or vice versa. Instead one is freed to the richness and mystery of Eckhart's images and the Buddha's silence, the yogin's immobility, the dervish's dance, and the shouts, weed-pulling, and nose-pulling of the Zen Master.

The second perspective is that the unimaginable vastness which is humanity's potential collective experience of God is in turn as nothing compared with God's own unboundedness. It can be tempting to lose oneself completely in the security and immensity of the reports of others, in the words of "masters," in the traditions, and in one's own experiences and the words used to transcribe them. But all these human experiences, which swallow up all "knowledge," are themselves ambiguous: they point towards God, but they can also cover up God. And ultimately they are not what we seek. Ultimately they belong with that inner wealth which is to be discarded, for they are, finally, tiny, weak flames which must be extinguished totally so that we can dwell in that infinite sea of light which is "God."

## THE ONENESS OF THE REAL

I BEGAN THIS ESSAY BY POINTING TOWARDS the profound change in awareness and in experience, a change of worlds, which is inseparable from the discovery of Eckhart's other God. I then referred to the work of inner poverty, or un-becoming, which Meister Eckhart describes as a way leading to this transformation, and then explored his definition of inner poverty as a condition of wanting, knowing, and having nothing. I attempted to point towards the new world which begins to manifest itself as the old word-world dissolves, referred to the namelessness and indescribability of this "God-world," and suggested that images of touching, tasting, and indwelling can serve as very approximate measures, but not as descriptions, of participation in that world. Having asked whether it is appropriate to call the central reality of that other world "God," I described the conditions under which such a sound might be appropriate. Having asked whether life in the many mansions of Eckhart's God is to be preferred to life in the familiar word-world, I suggested that we cannot and should not answer or pretend to be able to answer this question. Noting our chronic propensity to ask and even answer such questions, I proposed the following generalization: we often carry over into the God-world, wholly inappropriately, that old pose of comprehension which was unwarranted even in the old word-world, for we have always, *at best,* just been reborn, and we are always, *at best,* just infants in the many mansions of God. Finally, I sketched some perspectives which can help sustain awareness of that so easily forgotten infant status.

In conclusion I would like to add briefly two final points, one relating to Meister Eckhart's account of the way leading to the God-world, the other to the "location" of that world. The first is simply to iterate the absolute simplicity and seriousness of the Eckhartian demand of inner poverty. In order to be reborn to another life, it is not enough to be sick or wounded—first one must die to what has been "life" until now. Eckhart also expresses this thought in terms of the need to become *bloss,* that is, "bare," "uncovered," or even "naked" (ibid., 433). This nakedness is a tangible image of inner poverty: we must put aside all the protective plans, hopes, convictions, and connections which provide strength to face life, shield against the infinite, and create warmth in these seemingly cold, dark spaces. For the operative law here is that God will hold us up only if we have first left behind all other support, including, as was suggested above, the support that often comes from "religion." We must first become entirely naked; then, Eckhart suggests, we will be clothed by God. We must first experience absolute "homelessness"; only then will we awaken to the many mansions of God.

The second point, one which brings home perhaps more forcefully than anything else how unmappable the God-world is, expresses itself in the following paradox: the "many mansions of God" are not somewhere else, but are, bewilderingly, the usually hidden innermost reality of this very place. I have suggested that the contours of the small, familiar, word-world are the creation of language, which maps that world and establishes the limits of thought and conception. In drawing its lines around awareness, and so around "being," language covers up the infinite other God, thereby making it all too easy to pass through life with only the most fleeting intimations, if even that, of the mystery which transcends human thought. If and when we begin to break out of that bubble and to discover the unimaginable and edgeless God-world, we are naturally led, as I have been led here, and indeed perhaps even forced, to differentiate between the "word-world" and the "God-world" as if they were two distinct realms or places. But God cannot be contained; no barrier can possibly keep out the infinite. There can only be one "reality," and it is absolutely singular, undivided, and unmeasured. What this means is that we are in, and always have been in, the "God-world." The God-world is this very place, no longer buried under our feigned comprehension of it. Right now, in other words, we are in the many mansions of God. *The world, the universe, reality*—these are just some of the sounds we have used to reduce God's unknowable house to the shrunken, diminished world we usually tolerate as home.

In suggesting that the God-world is not located somewhere else, but is in fact the hidden reality of this very moment and place, I am only glancing in at a room which Eckhart passed through and spoke of frequently. He often stresses, for instance, that the "birth of the Son," a primary image for him of rebirth, is not something which occurred once, but rather an event which takes place in "eternity," that is, in an ever-present "now." And in consonance with the traditional expression that God is closer to us than we are to ourselves, Eckhart says that "the creature is outside itself. God is within and in the innermost parts of the creature" (ibid., 181). After it is noted that by "creatures" Eckhart means all created things, and as one contemplates the mysterious

oneness of the two "worlds," two reflections engendered by that ultimate paradox may well arise. The first is that even the most familiar,
seemingly negligible things are "divine" not only because they are in
fact infinitely more than negligible. Since they exist in the many mansions of God, they transcend, absolutely, all distinctions between the
ordinary and the divine, the profane and the sacred. They themselves
are beyond description and "free of names," even transcending, for
that matter, such hopelessly inadequate sounds as "God-world" and
"the many mansions of God." Consequently, even the most commonplace things and events are worthy of an eternal meditation. My own
breathing, which seems to lead an unknown life of its own; the unseen web-building of the equally unseen spider behind the stove; the
trees outside swaying in the wind in the middle of the night while I
sleep; the back of the hand and the earliest memory of the person who
is simultaneously living and dying beside me—all these are permanent residents, in fact "angels," in the many mansions of God.

The other reflection is the following: the recognition that this very
place is the many mansions of God becomes even more of a mystery
when related to our sense of the present time. We must be careful, of
course, not to single the present out as a special case. The "times" have
almost always been bad, with cruelty and folly always on the loose,
accompanied by the sad wasting of lives. The present age is typically
the "last" one, and the end—which anthropocentrically tends to mean
the human end—has often been said to be near. As the great church
which virtually constituted his world turned on him in his final years,
Eckhart himself must have sometimes felt that the world—the human
world—was not right, that it was in fact grotesquely twisted in its very
core. Though it is evident, therefore, that our more bleak assessments
of the times and fears for the future are certainly not unique, we are
often vividly aware, in any case, that there is immeasurably more suffering and misery in this place than we can cure, respond to, or even
fittingly acknowledge. And we are also all too frequently reminded that
our collective life on this planet *could* end, just as our individual lives
certainly will. The experience of the world towards which Eckhart points
is of fundamental importance for these dimensions of social, political, and ecological awareness in contemporary spirituality. For the
ultimate context framing recognition of the immeasurable value of the
world, of the pain which exists within it, and of the dangers which
threaten it, is the sense that this place is after all the "earth room," one

of the compartments in the indescribable house of God.

The last "room" in this essay has been the mystery that the God-world, the indescribable world beyond words and conception, is in fact this very place. It is a mystery, one we shall never penetrate, that the unknown is precisely where we have been all along. It is a mystery that this place exists at all. It is a mystery that some of these mansions are places of uncomforted suffering. And it is a mystery that there should be more overflowing fullness, more possible joy, more "divinity" in a house sparrow than there is in God if we know anything at all about God. We are infants who have just begun to open our eyes; to expect that we might comprehend or know how to respond to these enigmas bespeaks a profound confusion. Indeed, the very articulation of this inexhaustible mystery, at least as I am laboriously putting it into words right now, is of course much more wrong than it is right. The affirmation that this very place is the many mansions of God is at best an error that can be used to push aside other errors; yet it can all too easily ingratiate itself into awareness as knowledge. It, too, threatens to become wealth, something to know and have. We shall have to discard it as well before we can touch God.

# PART III
# WAYS IN MYSTERY

# OUT OF AN AGE OF IRON

*Then will the clear become dull,*
*. . . the lands will fall into confusion.*
Ancient Babylonian Text

THAT HISTORY, LIKE THE DAY, SEPARATES INTO
a handful of readily distinguishable segments, and that as these great
spans then succeed one another, human beings become shallower, less
just, shorter-lived, duller, unhappier, less "human"—such thoughts
have been ventured by Hesiod, by Plato and neo-Pythagoreans and
Ovid, by Lactantius and the Christian chiliasts, by Rousseau, by the
ancient Iranians, Scandinavians, and Chinese, by India. It may indeed
*be* true, as Borges already intimated, that the present age is always the
worst: the Indian Kali Yuga, or Dark Time, the Greek and Mazdean
Age of Iron, the ancient Scandinavian Days of the Wolf.

Certain, at the very least, is that the seemingly sophistic and self-
contradictory character of this latter proposition, like so much else,
is mere surface appearance. The mirage vanishes as soon as we take
time to consider some elementary implications of the general theory
of decline. For if it is in fact true that our powers are continually de-

clining, our stature diminishing, our humanity eroding, our horizons shrinking, and our alertness waning, and if as one after another the centuries fall away behind us into the bottomless past, we aspire to less and less, and venture less and less, for our innermost, least expressible, all else determining sense of what we ourselves are, and of what *This* is, is each day more circumscribed, more impoverished, one day closer to nothing, then it follows that each successive age *is* the worst. As for the insightful penetration, the "wisdom," of this seemingly gloomy hypothesis—which, in its two primary variants, may see the process as occurring just once, or as repeating itself infinitely in horizonless time—I propose that we prepare to assess it in the following ways. Let us recall that *all* things which appear inside those mysterious apartments we call space/time are destined to decline and then vanish. Let us survey those verbal creations we have subdivided, with such charming naïveté, into "myth," "legend," and "history"—this will enable us to examine humanity's accumulated experience and perception of its own collective movement through time. Let us turn inward and contemplate our own individual intuition, crystallized slowly by time and experience, of our present condition and direction. Let us observe how the very old—how you and I, soon—having long since relinquished the barren, eternally unreal future, and then having yielded up with greater difficulty the ever less substantial, the increasingly irrelevant, inaudible, unreal present, cling so much more fervently to the one enduring repository of truth and worth: the past, that which was, and now more and more just *is*. I conclude that few perceptions speak so persuasively to us as does the perception—the intimate and, with each year's gestation, ever more compelling dream—that our kind's collective life in time traces a descending movement, a sudden and dramatic fall in the very first moments perhaps, or at the other extreme a slow, infinitely graduated descent, a stately and grotesquely magisterial largo soul need not—and usually does not—seem to hear as it dances its way with blind nature's perfectly timed and calibrated movements through all the soul-stages and outward manifestations of ruin.

Right now it is as if this great spectacle—a Platonic vision or dream of this great spectacle—permits me to glimpse, one by one, its most dramatic and momentous scenes. Above all I see its first moment, *our* first moment, the inexplicable sudden appearance, where such subtlety and intimacy had never before been, of that mysterious presence, of that most delicate and precious wildly undulating phosphorescence we clumsily grasp, or perhaps altogether miss, when we emit or inwardly contemplate the crude sounds *human consciousness, human awareness*. The traditional Four Ages view of history dictates that it will have been a moment of perfection. To me this means: a moment of unbounded opening; a luminous and flawless transparency; unthinkable, because all-inclusive and indivisible, unity. It means wholeness prior to all limitation and differentiation, an unbrokenness prior to one and two. In that moment of uncontained, godlike lucidity, awareness had not yet narrowed itself, had not yet pared away from itself most of itself, and so *lost* itself, as it came to be fixed on just this or that particular scene, event, thing, necessity, threat, or desire. It was not yet entangled in habits, certainties, and puzzlements of its own making. It had not yet hollowed out, by repeated use, the tunnels, the gloomy pathways it would be doomed, later, to traverse again and again. At that time consciousness still had not chosen or been driven to identify itself with one tiny fragment of its infinitude, had not let itself shrink into this or that particular, gratuitous, parochial, minuscule shape, for just like God it transcended all form. It was not trapped in particular views, knowings, questions, or doubts. In its perfection it was undoubtedly aware of tastes, smells, touchings, sounds, sights, words, and interrogative and declarative sentences, but it was not contained within them or shaped by them, and so its awareness did not depend on them. This first "moment" was a moment prior to all particularity and change, prior, that is, to time; therefore it was, or is, neither long nor short, for it has nothing to do with duration.

It follows from all this that our primordial lucidity, that mystical knowing which was omniscience because in it not one thing was lacking, has no resemblance to the "knowing" we in our fallen or falling state associate with particular, constantly shifting musterings of verbal signs, Spanish, say, or Urdu, or Gã. In that moment we knew all, our knowing was something wholly unlike "knowledge." It was not the product of what we in the Age of Iron call "human thought." Since no particular thing contained or limited our awareness in any way, and since this undivided, unfixed awareness was free of all particular signs, we were aware of, and knew also that we were somehow enfolded within, just one "thing": the uncontained, the unspecifiable, the unbroken, the signless, the supreme opening, that is, "God," that is, "*This*." For what is God if God is not that supreme, unlimited, unspecifiable oneness—closer than all thought and more certain, more real in its unsayability than any signified thing—which liberated or awakened soul *touches*? And what is the use and meaning of the demonstrative pronoun 'this', if not to motion, no matter how ineptly, towards the singular and unclassifiable place, the event, the reality within which we find ourselves, even if such reality is something wholly other than and beyond that tenuous, constantly revised fabrication—"the world"—which desire, unseen neurons, and chance, operating our handfuls of verbal signs, construct?

Yet we are animals—we dream ourselves "animals"—born here under the moon and within its kingdom. The moon's sign, the law of its realm, is change. What is perfect, however, can only change into the flawed, infinity into finitude, oneness into separation, bliss into confusion, despair, necessity, hesitation, fear, waiting, or hope. I have described one moment. The sequel—history—is our loss or scandalous letting go of that moment, is the slow weathering away of the residue of that moment in the cruel siroccos of time. This story is one of diminution and specification, of ever smaller horizons, of the ongoing fixing and contraction of awareness in order to focus on this or that seeming need, danger, enjoyment, or fact. To put in one sentence the process of transformation which history is: it is the increasing ascendancy and ultimate triumph of signs, and in particular of verbal signs. When we were perfect, our unbroken awareness touched the real—the unnameable—and was contained just by the uncontained. It inhabited horizonless opening. Signs drifted through *it*, as clouds or birds through edgeless sky. They depended on it, not it on them.

More than anything else, history is the process of transformation during which consciousness, during which *we* are gradually taken over by the signs which should be our servants and instruments. Nature shows many strange reversals, predations, and usurpations, but surely none so uncanny and dramatic as this. Some of its primary manifestations, phases, and consequences are: the inevitable diminution of awareness as it is captured by and enclosed within the particular signs of a particular language, as it assumes the shape of that language's signs and is henceforth able to move along only within the limitations of that language's possible sentences; the displacement of undivided sign-free awareness by verbal intelligence and comprehension, by "knowledge," doubts and certainties, by the search for the "true" sentence; a gradual loss of contact with reality—uncontained, immeasurable, unsignifiable—as the takeover of consciousness by its own signs progresses; the sad fading away of the very memory of reality, even as reality endures, unchanging and tranquil, remote from all signs; the replacement of unsayable reality—the one certain thing, the rock—by that spectral, constantly shifting, ever more solid seeming dream-reality, the verbal field or "world" of space and time, which is formed and sustained by the stream of words just as the quickly rotated torch creates the fiery circle. History is therefore a *losing* of consciousness, a clouding over, a forgetting. History is the withering of our finest nerve, of that primary nerve, our special birthright, which, always, should run along—should *be*—the defining center of consciousness. To contemplate history is to watch us sleepwalk down narrow passageways, each narrower and more unreal than the last. The bizarre, dreamlike culmination of this process is easily identified, for it always displays one telltale mark, one absolutely unmistakable symptom: it no longer even *occurs* to human beings that there might be a difference between reality and their signs.

That we are well into the Age of Iron is demonstrated by the fact that this confusion is now nearly complete. I switch on a radio or TV; I browse a newspaper, magazine, or journal; I attend a meeting or lecture; I talk to friends, neighbors, and colleagues, and overhear fragments of other conversations. There is of course nothing odd about the superabundance here of those orthographic symbols, voiced exhalations, and accompanying taps, stops, and puffs we call English. But this is odd: the absence, in this great, constantly swelling swarm of verbal signs, of any acknowledgment or apparent awareness of that other realm —unbounded and indivisible reality—which encloses English and which, just because of its unboundedness and unbrokenness, cannot be contained, disclosed, or distinguished by any sign. For as I attend to these news reports, interviews, background reports, conversations, explanations, stories, personal experiences, and justifications, I note that there never is reference to the uncontained, the signless, the inconceivable. It is as if *This*, most intimate and yet wholly ungraspable, didn't "exist," as if *God*, the one unsayable certainty pervading all these ambiguous and enigmatic sign-perceptions, did not "exist."

Further, as one attends both to the usages and curious omissions which characterize English at the present time, it gradually becomes clear that all this talking, writing, and thinking rests, none too securely, on one astonishing axiom. It is the now seemingly universal belief, the mad fantasy which, adopted by all, becomes self-evident truth, that reality—that is, the world, this place, *This*—consists just of the sky, the earth, human beings, you, I, Africa, interest rates, medicine, stars, literature, schools, ozone, etc.—that is, just the very things for which we are fortunate enough to have nouns in English. Our spontaneous and unconscious adoption of this axiom—the fact that we take a list of English words at face value as an inventory of reality—betrays a complex dullness and forgetfulness. For we are oblivious to the fact— we have forgotten—that the "world" of twentieth century Americans, just like the "worlds" of first century Americans, and of Dharmakīrti and Swedenborg, of dreams and whales, of the optic nerve of a bee, and of Hamlet, *Hamlet*, and the Olympians, is not a key which unlocks and discloses reality, but one more event *within* reality, not an explanation of mystery, but more mystery. Nearing the culmination of the enclosure of consciousness by its signs, we have lost the perspective, the infinite perspective, which enables us to observe the following about any English dictionary: it is not a roll-call of reality, of *This,* but a cryptology, a wonderfully subtle and arcane trail left by particular human brains in a particular place and time. We have forgotten that "the universe" belongs to the subject matter of psychology. It no longer even occurs to us that the world, or reality, might rest—peaceful, motionless, boundless, unimaginable, undivided, unchanging—just on the other side of, just *through* that flimsy wall made of every particular thing we might think, dream, or wonder about "the world," so that of the world the one thing we can count on is this: it is utterly unlike everything we might think of as "the world." And so we have also forgotten that awareness can touch and dwell within that boundlessness and unbrokenness, that rest, only when it abides outside all signs, only when its signs are once again in it, not it in its signs.

The theory—the myth—of the Four Ages assures us that it has not always been so. It is true that the creators of the Rig-Veda are outside and already far from our first moment. Their perceptions, preoccupations, and limitations, like ours, bear the marks of sublunar life. In their verses we find, insistent and already fully formed, what we might call the operative fantasy, the life-sustaining myth of existence within this realm of multiplicity, change, and signs. It is the notion that the implementation of certain specific actions or the bringing about of certain specific events or conditions—a properly executed sacrifice, say, or fervent austerities or belief, or a crusade, acclaim, prosperity, health, or the yielding of this or that particular person to my particular wish—will at last bring the act's performer into a state of well-being secured against all further change. Yet there are passages in the Rg Veda in which our first moment survives, or is most ecstatically recovered. The very word *muni* suggests silence, a life outside words. The Veda's long-haired *munis*, naked or in red rags, are drunk on soma and silence. Having passed beyond normal sublunar consciousness—for they have resisted enclosure, and in them awareness has broken through the encircling signs and become, once again, infinite —they mount the wind and course all-seeing through the sky. The Upanishads, the Buddhist Sutras of the Perfection of Wisdom, and Christianity's mystical theology belong to a later age. Their ecstasies are more domesticated, more controlled, more deliberate, more limited by accumulated tradition. Now the metaphors are more metaphorical. Yet the *munis'* shaman-like flight out of verbal signs into wordless reality survives. Dionysius urges his reader therefore to pass beyond everything that can be known "by the normal processes of mind"—such processes include, for instance, the usage of nouns and adjectives. Having done so, one attains to the nameless divinity "beyond thought" (*CU*, 209, 212).

Then at a certain point these magnificent explorations of the long, arduous passage from signs and "knowing" to unsayable reality are no longer being composed. At a later time they are no longer even understood—now the brain registers nothing when confronted by a Dionysian phrase like "supreme and dazzling darkness," that is, the unsayable, unthinkable essence of supreme reality, of the hidden and ultimate truth of *This*. At such a time our first moment survives just as fragmentary glimpses, ephemeral half-intuitions, unsettling and unidentifiable pulsings of recollection. Then even religious consciousness is being rapidly enclosed within verbal signs.

That is how I see the condition of my forbears three hundred years ago. Usually they confused signs and *This*, just as we do. Almost always, therefore, they perceived with the unequivocal certainty of dream that where they were was: among sky, pasture, cattle, mountains, clouds, and rain; among children and the old, the table, the barn, the stubborn darkness of winter, bread, spring's green and blue, the suddenly irresistible eyes and smell of a man or woman. But then—perhaps just because they were closer to the first moment than we, or because they were much better equipped than we to experience words and statements as events in nature, frail and secretive like all sublunar events, or because they, unlike us, were still familiars of silence, and so could at least obscurely intuit, when they were immersed in and invaded by that muni-intoxicating element, the quickly reached limits of words and an unlimited something beyond words—if they encountered a mad woman or man, a lunatic savaged by and unfit for life under the moon, it might occur to them that the ravings of this woman or man carried and expressed, in garbled form, truths greater than any they had heard, and it could occur to them that the very derangement itself was just the outward sign that Mad Hans or Crazy Dorothea had seen God. Or likelier still: sometimes as the minister gave them to eat and drink what he said was God's body and blood, they knew for a moment— and perhaps the minister knew it, too, though no one would mention anything, for there was no longer an acknowledged occasion and way to say or even allude to it—that as to the question what was happening at that very moment, and who in fact they were, and just *where* they were, no one, absolutely no one, could say, and so it would be better to say nothing and *imagine* nothing, for anything anyone said or thought and any image they pictured would make this event, and they themselves, and *This* out to be something less, indeed infinitely less, than what it secretly, silently, and unthinkably is.

Now such moments of dilation—the beginnings of an awakening, the first stirrings of a muni-like flight out of the word-body—are even more blurred and rudimentary. History, the overthrow and enclosure of consciousness by its own signs, is now nearing completion. Soon there will no longer remain the tiniest crack through which awareness might gaze or slip out past the multiple, constantly shifting phantasmagoria of signs into the solid, irreducible, unencompassable, unthinkable world. Never before have our nerves been so dull, our link to reality so tenuous, our horizons so small. Never before have we registered so little, or been so out of touch with and unresponsive to our actual surroundings, to *This*. Nature, life, death, human beings, you, I, words themselves—none of these mysteries has ever loomed so dwarfishly as they now loom in our undiscerning thought and speech. I have already suggested that someone schooled just by attending to what we now say and write to one another would remain entirely oblivious to uncontained, immeasurable, unspecifiable reality. He would dwell just in signs and their ghostly doubles, the "things". These two together would constitute "the world." To that general observation I shall append just one specific illustration from enclosure's last days.

Each action, movement, or gesture participates in and, for a consciousness which has passed out of time, is indistinguishable from the supreme creative event: the ungraspable coming into being, or just the fact of the being, of *This*—as your hand turns these pages, for example, it *is* that event. A century ago this was already largely forgotten, yet in some of the actions of a few individuals, the "creative," something even divinely creative could still be discerned. We notice this when we read nineteenth century accounts of encounters with venerated writers and composers. For the writers of these descriptions, it is as if they have come into the presence of a special being, a shaman or muni who sees and feels what mere mortals cannot—indeed, the predictable, formulaic solemnity of these accounts suggests that we are dealing here with a kind of ritual encounter with the sacred, probably the last in this cycle. In these "seers" links with the past, with the munis' silence and edgeless sky, even with the first moment, tenuously survive. The poets and composers themselves can therefore speak in their work of being drawn towards *das Unendliche*. They allude to *l'innommable*. Music is said to be the supreme art because it discloses a realm—the very heart of the world—which is inaccessible to words.

Now, however, such notions are dated, that is, they are the remnants of a time when consciousness was more alert, more spacious, more adventurous. Now art, too, the last enclave of the boundless and unsayable, faces or in its final decay even appears to welcome enclosure. The work of art or craft, which once seemed to come to us from a place outside our usual capacities and comprehendings, and to speak to us in a special way of something incommensurable which could not be gathered entirely into words, color, sound, or form—for the work itself, even as we gazed upon it, listened to it, or reached out towards it, still gave off and was pervaded by the smell and taste of unsayable reality—is now just like everything else an effect to be discussed, assessed, and comprehended. It is now, just like everything else, defenseless against the swarming signs. Now the artist is like everyone else, not because we have recovered the truth that all acts reenact or just are the mystery of creation, but because our failing central nerve no longer responds to or even discerns the mystery of creation. More important than the work is what the artist, critic, or spectator has to say about it, for the work of art is more and more just this: a cue which makes it possible for us to begin talking about works of art; a device which entitles the artist to begin explaining herself and her art. Somewhere within all this explaining, legitimating, and promulgating, the last refuge of silence, of our first moment, has been swallowed up. The muni is extinct. *L'innommable, das Unendliche*, reality, *This* is forgotten. And consciousness is now everywhere overrun, is now nothing but those swarming and triumphant signs.

The seemingly grim and nonsensical designation of each age as the worst is, like all declarative sentences—like all that is —an occasion for unending reflection. Only after long and arduous effort does it begin to disclose to such reflection its secret essence. It is, like your existence and my life and these lines and all questions and the world, a great koan, an apparently solid wall which, diligently questioned and contemplated, becomes at last a mysterious opening through which we can glimpse and even enter boundless, unsayable reality—just in these past few *minutes* we have been able to glimpse, if only obscurely and most tentatively, that infinite prospect. Nor are the various myths of successive ages expressions of despair or gloom. The particular version I have told here affirms the supreme reality and importance of that boundless, incommensurable, undivided, unchanging, inconceivable, incomparably intimate something towards which consciousness thrusts itself, most ineptly and ponderously, as it pronounces the great mystic syllable 'God'. Further, it asserts that a condition of supreme awareness, infinitely alive to God, to reality, to *This*, has already been achieved and therefore has long since been entered within the category of what can be, rather than in the categories of what cannot be or what perhaps can be. In contrast, the myth of progress always implies—wherever and whenever it is maintained—the dire truth that perfection does not exist and in the beginningless infinities of the past never has. Yet we are invited to commit our hopes, acts, and even our lives to the expectation that some day it shall.

Still further: the fugacious seeings and dreamings I have transcribed here actually suggest that God, supreme reality, and our original perfection are always less than a hair's-breadth away. Born in the Age of Iron, we instinctively take ourselves to be small and weak, and so we picture ourselves as trapped in history, as engulfed and carried along by time. But we are neither "small" nor "great." We are a mystery prior to and beyond all words, and we first begin to comprehend and recite our life story the moment there are no words in our mouth. As for 'history', it is a short, complexly voiced, three-stage exhalation. Just as the fleeting sonic and mental events they are, the sound 'history' and the dream 'history', like a falling leaf or muons or a sudden middle C—are perfect and complete in themselves. They are small, self-contained miracles, but here in unsayable reality they do not stand in relation to some other great all-consuming beast and juggernaut — history—which they supposedly name or duplicate. And time, like space, is a part of "history," of the social, psychological, intellectual, and neuronal "history of ideas." 'Time' and 'history'—and for that matter 'signs'—are signs. They belong to the marvelous and random dream we dream *within* this, not to *This*. They share in all the limitation, unreality, greatness, loveliness, and horror of that dream. They are in us, not we in them.

It follows that at this very moment, nothing of substance —nothing "real"—separates us from uncontained and unsayable reality, from God. In the Iron Age oblivion of our sleep, we have become like speechless animals confounding signs and reality, *This* and "the world"; and so as we begin to awaken, we confusedly think that God, who is not "the world," must be somewhere else. But God is closer to us than all things and all signs, closer even than the mesmeric English sign 'I', for how can anything be closer than all-pervading truth and reality, closer than *This?* How can anything be more intimately and overwhelmingly present than signless, undivided, uncontained presence? Therefore no journey is required. There is no wall—not even the thinnest, most dreamlike of membranes—through which one must pass. There is no opening one must negotiate so as to arrive somewhere else. At this very moment, nothing of substance—nothing "real"—prevents the arising in us of a perfect, seamless, infinitely alert detecting and registering of *This*. Nothing stands between us and that first moment. Nothing prevents us from dwelling right now within it. It is as if awareness only needs shed its now loose and outgrown outer skin, as if I only need awaken from the arbitrary and marvelous world —from that dream of the arbitrary and marvelous world I have been—and I shall once again be, shall never have been anything other than original perfection, as if the moment I awaken from this particular thought, this one last sentence and word-dream, there will just be—undivided and boundless—the real.

# AVIGNON

FOR MUCH OF ITS TWENTY CENTURIES CHRIS-
tianity has held forth to our view—perhaps all too monolithically—
a suffering Christ. But what single, similarly unequivocal image would
be truer, more salutary, more urgently required? This complex and far-
flung perception, which the first Buddhists, less iconic, transposed just
as monolithically into the four syllables which formulate their first Noble
Truth *sarvam du≠kham*— "All is suffering"—is the very image we need
when we ourselves suffer. Suffering is inevitable, for in the constantly
shifting world of duality we all too steadily inhabit, the pairs up and
down, life and death, good and bad, joy and suffering move in incessant, ubiquitous alternation. If not now, you and I have been familiars of pain and anguish, or will be. During this very day and the night
which is its mate, hundreds of thousands of human beings, not to
mention other creatures, are to die. It is true that suffering often
strengthens and tightens the bonds which connect us with those closest

to us. But even as that coming together takes place, suffering, which is what defines us at that moment, also sets us apart and isolates us from those loved ones—they are not suffering, as we are. And so we are comforted by, and feel that outside the little world of space and time we are somehow even together with, some extraordinary or even divine figure whose clearly and vividly perceived destiny coincides in that very moment with our own.

For similar and equally urgent reasons, I know of myself that I sometimes require, and may then spontaneously conjure up, an image of tranquillity and strength, someone who seems to move through decisions, events, and time as effortlessly as a fish coasts, after one casual sweep of its tail, through the water. For me—even at fifty-three—that image is the image of my father, eirenic and, except for his own seemingly few moments of Christlike suffering, an inhabitant in Lutheran fashion of that less specifiable, but more substantial and enduring world beyond duality; and at other times it is the image of Irvin, fiddler and ginseng hunter, now twelve years gone of liver cancer, who once about ten years ago seemed to be present here most plainly, if not bodily, and just by his steady and untroubled presence enabled me to pass clear of craziness into which I otherwise would have been drawn. Lastly, and perhaps just for other, happier moments, we possess images which do not incarnate suffering, or the strength which helps us endure and overcome it, but which instead show forth suffering's great opposites: peace, perfect bliss, infinite and astonished joy. Having turned from or even temporarily forgotten suffering gods and heroes, we then contemplate the boundless good cheer of a god who has just created the inexhaustible world, or the blissful, all-containing serenity of a Buddha whose diamond-like consciousness has "gone beyond, gone altogether beyond," or the undivided joy of Shiva and Shakti—more than anything else from this world of fragmentary and opposing images, their embrace hints at that greater ecstasy which flows when particularity mingles with the One, dream with reality, word-made consciousness with the unsayable and uncontained.

Just a few centuries ago, the moment's most powerful men in Rome and in the courts of various Protestant princes and kings legislated for their unknown subjects the great symbols and truths—at that time the suffering Christ was *the* image of suffering for most Europeans. Now such hegemony is not even attempted. In Europe, the Americas, and elsewhere, we choose, or are perhaps captured by, one or a hand-

ful of the variegated and discordant symbols which offer themselves
to us. As a result of processes so elusive, complex, and many-layered
as to seem pure chance, a so-called head of state may all at once find
herself announcing a state of war, just as a man, entering a quiet hall-
way near the end of his sixtieth birthday party, may for the first time
be astonished and overwhelmed by the realization - the uncanny,
unfathomable mystery—that he *exists*. Born in 1941 in North America,
I have arrived by similar haphazards at my own images of suffering.
Similarly unnamed and inscrutable forces have made of me an atavism—I spontaneously assent, for example, to Aristotle's assertion that
contemplative participation in supreme truth and reality is our highest, our most worthy and desirable, activity. It is therefore no surprise
that my paradigms, including my three images of suffering, come from
earlier times, or are themselves atavisms, and share that Aristotelian
notion, which of course is Plato's as well. All three are overtaken by
great suffering, and two of them reach—seem to reach—their life's
end engulfed in great suffering. Perhaps this latter fact merely con-
firms our inevitable and enduring need for such images, merely reaf-
firms the truth of that first Noble Truth.

THE ATAVISM—THE GREAT, COMPLEX, tragic throwback—is Nietzsche.
Scornful, like Schopenhauer, of the academic philosopher's *bürgerliche*
way of life and dependent subservience to the state, and desiring to
form with others a "new Greek Academy," Nietzsche wants to be a
philosopher just in the very way the ancient Greeks—just as Heraclitus
and Parmenides—had been philosophers. He aspires with equal intensity to the life of the monk and the ascetic, for the man who can
sign a letter "Frater Fredericus" also dreams the new Academy as a
monastery—here those like-minded souls who "want nothing more
to do with the world" will live in the "greatest simplicity," having given
up all else for the sake of supreme truth (Ross 1980, 217, 379-80, 483).
And Nietzsche is our last, our last would-be, mystical theologian and
ecstatic. That is why Lou Salomé, who perhaps knows him best, can
call this so-called atheist "the God-seeker Nietzsche"; and it is why at
the end the insane philosopher will then sign himself "the Crucified
One." Like any theologian he seeks above all to affirm, to say "Yes!"
unreservedly to that unfathomable mystery towards which we toss our

tenuous and easily windblown syllables *life, reality, the world.* And like any previous mystical theologian of the Middle East and Europe, like Dionysius and Eckhart and Juan de la Cruz, he senses that reality—that *This* —infinitely exceeds all words and all human knowledge, so that we enter most fully into supreme reality, and touch it most keenly only if, as we entered, we left all our knowledge and all our words behind. For Nietzsche all these aspirations come together and are joyfully realized in the Swiss Engadine in the summer of 1881, just as, a few years later, an ecstatic Zarathustra attains them in the climactic "Ja- und Amen Lied." Here Nietzsche/Zarathustra has left behind all connections with earthly things, with human love, words, earthly knowledge. He seeks the highest, most dizzying affirmation we can imagine: to desire—without the slightest hesitation or reservation—just that this very moment, with all it contains, together with every single moment and experience which up to now have constituted my life, might be repeated over and over, without end. And just like that other ascetic-ecstatic-mystical theologian, Juan de la Cruz, he portrays his experience of union with supreme reality in boldly erotic terms—"eternity" is the woman Nietzsche/Zarathustra now marries, just as "God" is the beloved for whom, in the Carmelite's writings, soul languishes, or with whom it is united in indescribable joy.

That first summer at mountainous Sils Maria, where he is "6000 feet beyond humanity and time," (*Z*, 370) and the rapturous passages which end *Zarathustra*, Part III, are the highest flights of Nietzsche's imperfectly realized dream of affirmation and joy. Looked at as a whole, his life and work convey a very different picture, for we can see, almost everywhere, the seeds of his escalating despair, his relentlessly gestating collapse, his great suffering of body and spirit. Through all his years Nietzsche remains keenly aware of the fact that his father's fragile nervous system had endured a mere forty-two years, and so he fears—continually, feverishly, rightly—that disintegration has already occupied and now quietly spreads through his brain. He commits himself unreservedly to his work—to his thought and his writing—but no one listens, and so the author of *Birth of Tragedy, Daybreak, Joyful Wisdom,* and *Zarathustra*, I-III, must himself finance the printing and publication of *Zarathustra*'s concluding fourth part.

His mind, Europe's best, is being undermined from within, and his "career"—his relations with the human world—is a fiasco. Yet these two elements of his suffering are not as intimate or relentless as the third: the hopeless contradiction, the self-negating venture and "task" which he himself is. For Nietzsche shares the traditional recognition—indeed, it helps make of him a mystical theologian—that our words and human comprehendings finally avail little, that they are nature and biology—shadowy and mysterious events like a bat's auditory "seeing," like the conversations of bees. He knows that we become better philosophers and theologians, that our nerves are bared most keenly to reality—to "God," to "eternity"—just when we have passed beyond those words and knowings. But at the same time he has also been captured by the fantastic dream—which had also dazzled Kant, Schelling, and Hegel, and would later seize the young Wittgenstein—that a philosopher—perhaps "I"—is destined to spell out definitively, and in words, just "how things are." Nietzsche's despair, his inevitable disintegration, consequently derives first of all from this: whenever he looks within, what he sees—as self-evident and inescapable as Descartes' *cogito*—is the certainty that he Friedrich Nietzsche is an attempt to do what cannot be done.

Nietzsche's sufferings come from without and from the past, but even more from within. His "failure" as a writer, which with time is only becoming more painfully apparent; the disease undermining his brain; the unresolvable contradiction at the center of his thought and work—all accumulate year by year until, in 1889, his mind definitively gives way. The other images of suffering I contemplate at least *seem* less complex, less inward, briefer, but perhaps during their shorter span more intense. In December of 1577, the thirty-five year old Juan de la Cruz—the most fervent, natural, and gifted of contemplatives, mystical spirituality's Mozart—is kidnapped by "shod," or Calced, Carmelite monks hostile to the order of "Discalced" Carmelites to which he belongs, and kept prisoner in their monastery in Toledo. His windowless cell, a "closet," is unbearably cold, then suffocatingly hot as spring heats up to summer. Thrice weekly he is led to the middle of the refectory at the time of the evening meal. Observed and taunted by the monks, he eats his bread and sardines off the floor, like a dog. When his Calced brothers have finished eating, each one strikes him with a lash. To quote Kavanaugh: "This scourging lasted for the time it takes to recite the Psalm *Miserere*" (*CW*, 22). Such is the fervor of these ministrations that Fray Juan's wounds will not heal for years.

Let us try to imagine a few moments and a few strands of the formless agony-mass these sentences casually pass by. The relentless cold which occupies your body—it lets go of you only in the rare moments of sound sleep it permits. The sharp, slowly ebbing pain of the whip, aggravated by its predictability and familiarity, above all by the repetition of lash upon lash on wounds which already burn. To the pure animal pain of limb, skin, and flesh, add the varieties of inner torment: his humiliation, his self-doubt, his fear, his traumatized shock, his impotent anger. And then still worse—for they tempt him to give up all he is and represents and aspires to be; they tempt him to become something much less than that dog—are two abysses which yawn before him whenever he begins to reflect. One is the spirit-corroding recognition that his cruel, even demonic torturers are fellow human beings, fellow Christians, fellow monks, fellow Carmelites. They are all—intimately, devastatingly—*he*. The other, closely related to the first, derives from the fact that up to now his entire life *has* been the life of soul—that divine mystery—wedded to and living for the institution which is the divine's proxy and messenger upon earth. What is he to make of this life, this place, what is he to make of "God" now that the Church has taken on the form of his jailer, his torturer, the proprietor and master of this hell?

---

OUR CONSIDERABLE KNOWLEDGE of the ways in which Nietzsche and Juan de la Cruz *react* to suffering—here our view becomes broader, more comprehensive—enables us to see both as images not only of suffering, but also of strength. The only son of Pastor K. L. and Frau Franziska Nietzsche of Röcken, triply afflicted and doomed, becomes a paradigm of courage and strength in the one way he can: he endures, he works, for as long as he can he struggles to maintain life, form, and balance in his scattering and entropic brain. This is the central action and meaning of his mature life, which begins in 1879 with his departure from Basel and academic life, and ends ten years later as he collapses in a Turin street. He thinks while walking, or on winter evenings while lying in bed, the only warm place in his stoveless room. He moves back and forth among the *pensiones* which suit his own meager pension, almost always taking a room on the cheaper northerly side. Waiting for the day, or just a few hours, when his body and mind will permit him to write, he endures days, or many consecutive days, of violent nausea and piercing headache. He sends his books out into the world; even worse than the nearly universal silence are the few incomprehending letters of support and praise he receives *poste restante*. He consults various doctors, and in unremitting pursuit of that most precious and unattainable thing—health—he tries every regime he hears of or concocts. He lets himself envision the posthumous fame which a century later will in fact be his (for with regard both to his future madness and to his future fame, he is equally, and preternaturally, prophetic). By moving continually from place to place, he is able to give himself the relief of hope for imminent dramatic change. So that he can avoid contemplating the madness and tragedy which are spreading within, he clings to his desperate and already half-mad belief that everything —"recovery," health, happiness, great discoveries, great accomplishments, great "philosopher-deeds"—hinges on finding just one divinely immutable *external* thing: that one necessary Edenlike place, somewhere in Switzerland, or perhaps Italy, where clouds never appear, where there never will be anything but the lucid and inexhaustible midsummer sky of Zarathustra's eternally ecstatic "Yes!"

Nietzsche's exemplary strength is strength unavailingly deployed against the inevitable, against the breakdown in Turin, the months in the psychiatric clinic in Jena, the decade as a passive child in the care of his mother, and then his sister. But Fray Juan's is strength which triumphs. His situation in Toledo differs from that of Frater Fredericus in one important respect. He has a real chance to come out on the other side of his suffering, to save the body, so that soul can recover its life and work. From a worldly perspective, the prisoner can have but one aim: to escape his prison. Like Nietzsche, Juan de la Cruz gathers all his resources, concentrating them all on that one aim. Patiently, shrewdly, cunningly, he plans and prepares, and then in August skillfully achieves his escape. After finding temporary refuge in a Discalced convent in Toledo, he journeys south to El Calvario to recover his health, his life, his true being. Just two months later he is elected Prior of the monastery there.

From a worldly perspective, as from that of those *The Cloud*'s author calls "actives," Fray Juan's strength is the strength of his escape, of that masterful, splendidly successful *act*, but from a contemplative perspective there is more. Warriors display their strength and daring in battle, explorers in journeys into the trackless unknown. But contemplatives, ascetics, and ecstatics—those mysteries we imagine we have identi-

fied when we make the sounds *contemplatives, ascetics, ecstatics* —
undertake much more, and on that much greater field: the edgeless
expanse which lies within, which *is*, consciousness. For Peary, Scott,
and Amundsen, two easy syllables—"the Pole"—spell out and even
exhaust their destination. As they set out, they know that the journey's
conclusion and outcome—"triumph," "failure"—are just a few months
distant. But for the seventh century Buddhist writer and contemplative Śāntideva, it is essential to realize that the supreme goal called
*bodhi*—that is, "awakening," "enlightenment"—neither is nor is not;
the one goal for which he is to sacrifice all else is, illogically and im-
possibly, to have no goal, to seek "nothing." Bodhi is freedom from
ignorance and illusion, especially the illusion of the self, the "I." To
combat that greatest, most fatal of errors, Śāntideva conceives a journey
more arduous and hazardous than Peary's. Though he realizes that
completion will require, not three months, but rather untold millions
of rebirths, he sets out to perceive and to *experience* the "you" as "I,"
the other as himself. The strength—that is, the daring, the freedom,
the disregard for trivial and irrelevant limitations, the unhesitant doing
of what is to be done—of the inner explorer shows itself most simply
and vividly in the figure of the Christian ascetic who undertakes to
live, henceforth, in a shallow cave or hollow tree; there her one contact, comfort, and resource—will it be sufficient?—will be "God." More
subtly, but just as audaciously, Chinese Zen adepts have reasoned that
nothing is more difficult—and so more intriguing, more compelling—
than to become and be a Buddha, an "awakened" one, while living just
as everyone else lives. Their aim, then—as they beg in unmonkish rags,
or sell fish, or generate new human life—is at all times to be, inwardly,
just that unbounded, transparent, tranquil, undivided Buddha-mind,
and to remain unconfused, "unobstructed," "unhindered," by any action.

During and after his imprisonment, Juan de la Cruz comes to see
an analogous opportunity in suffering. His goal—the climax of soul's
"ascent"—is, always, to dwell in God rather than the world, to "exchange the mutable and comprehensible for the Immutable and Incomprehensible" (*CW*, 223). Suffering, especially that inner suffering
he calls the dark night of the spirit, conduces to the relinquishing of
the mutable and comprehensible. It is inevitable in any case. The
unlearning of familiar desirings, perceivings, habits, expectations, and
ways; the necessary "annihilation" of will, memory, and intellect; soul's
slow transformation from a terrestrial and human condition to one

that is celestial and divine—this death and rebirth, this astonishing metamorphosis, necessarily involves pain. By describing that pain in his great work, by proclaiming its necessity and great usefulness, by encouraging us to seek it out, by portraying it as a significant and *given* part of the ascent, the means to a much greater end, he makes us freer, stronger, bolder. He delivers us from the shackles of apprehension, the prison of fear. As for his own life, he displays to the end the liberating strength of the ascetic, and as in Toledo he gets his way as well. His subsequent life is service, devotion, and contemplation within his chosen Order, his chosen life. In that life there inevitably are additional sufferings: hostility, new "persecutions," painful physical afflictions. At the end—the year is 1591—he is given what he has described as the most desirable death: "Not to die as a superior; to die in a place where he was unknown; and to die having suffered much" (*CW*, 26).

<hr />

THOUGH FROM A DISTANCE, AND DIMLY, we can follow the painful struggles of Nietzsche and Juan de la Cruz from their beginning to their sharply contrasting ends. Of Eckhart's we can, for the most part, just speculate. We know that in 1326, Heinrich von Virneburg, the Franciscan archbishop of Cologne, charges Meister Eckhart with heresy before the Inquisition, that Eckhart responds in Latin with his so-called "Defense," that the matter drags on, and that Eckhart submits an appeal to the pope in Avignon. We know—the precise circumstances and reasons are not clear—that the renowned Dominican master subsequently journeys to Avignon, where a papal commission reviews the case. The commission's identification of seventeen heretical propositions in Eckhart's writings, and of still others which are "suspicious" or "evil-sounding," is spelled out in the papal bull "*In agro dominico*" from March, 1329. The bull refers to Eckhart as dead and adds that before dying, the victim and instrument of the "father of lies" retracted his erroneous and heretical views.

We can understand Eckhart's spirited and well-argued Defense as the fruit of his initial reaction to Virneburg's attack. It is the natural and human response of a celebrated preacher, teacher, intellectual, and theologian, a man of high rank in the Dominican order. But of what follows the Defense—and that piece of writing quite clearly fails to avert or delay the ensuing catastrophe—we know, we understand, very little. What personal decision, letter, or papal command brings Eckhart to Avignon, and what happens there? Above all, what happens *within* Eckhart in Avignon? It can take years to digest the meaning—and appreciate the sheer *fact*—of a loved one's death. In an entire lifetime we do not even begin to absorb or comprehend—or even turn towards—the equally certain fact of our own. In Avignon, I speculate, Eckhart finds himself all too clearly being engulfed by a similarly momentous and inexorable proceeding, a nightmare as it were designed just for him, and which requires all his moments and abilities just to perceive, or even just to name.

What easily misleads us here is the absence—so far as we know—of crude and terrible torture, of physical pain, of the most vivid forms of psychological affliction and abuse. If only by the horrors of the lash, or of the eternally chilled or retching or migrained body, or of cruel humiliation or oncoming madness, Nietzsche's and Fray Juan's attention is often turned away from that most devastating of inner perceptions: the perception that hope and resistance and efforts to get beyond this suffering are futile and foolish, that—henceforth, for me—this suffering *is the world.* In Avignon nothing diverts Eckhart from his continual contemplation and vain processing of the nightmare his life has become. Nothing displaces or diminishes that perception which, more than any other, inclines human beings to stop trying, to let go of their dearest possession, that "Yes!" Unlike the writings of Nietzsche and Juan de la Cruz, Eckhart's are consistently written from within that "Yes!"; are all, as it were, composed under that cheerful and "halcyon" sky the restlessly searching Fredericus never found. Eckhart is—he at least *seems*—the most unswervingly harmonious and joyful of ascetic-ecstatics. Then towards the very end of his life, and above all in Avignon, we see him engulfed and carried away by the most unforeseen, extreme, and shattering of peripeteias. For Meister Eckhart, God is beyond all descriptions and names. To the extent, therefore, that Eckhart can name and describe his life and the meaning of his life, he need use only one word: the 'Church'; it is as a member of that greater *body* that Eckhart has studied, taught, journeyed, preached, and prayed in France and throughout Germany. The Church has been the scene and meaning of his describable life. It is the visible chamber which is also a gateway into the invisible and unnameable. Now—suddenly, unbelievably, undeniably—the Church is denouncing him and casting him out. He is now being told that his life has been a sowing of "thorns and thistles," that he himself has all along been an instrument of the devil. Each waking moment—and now few of his moments are not weary, blear-eyed "waking" moments—Eckhart can do nothing but stare undiverted and in full consciousness at one momentous fact: that he is "lost," that he can say or think nothing which lessens or calls into question the shattering perception that he is completely, irrevocably lost.

From now on this one perception will constitute Eckhart's *specifiable* world. Here, too, comparison underlines the unanimous nature of his inner dark night. To the end, Nietzsche will always be supported by his admiring composer friend Gast, and by Franz Overbeck, his one-time colleague in Basel. Juan de la Cruz is ridiculed and abused by all the monks of the monastery, but that one monastery in Toledo is not Christendom. In Avignon, however, Eckhart has no friends. He is repudiated and cast out by the supreme tribunal, by that papal court which speaks and legislates truth for "the world." Fray Juan can hope for and plan his escape. Nietzsche always hopes he will find the right doctor or regimen, and to the end dreams of being heard. Indeed, he experiences —exuberantly—the germination of his renown during that euphoric, strangely incandescent flare-up of mixed madness and lucidity which marks his final months in Turin. When Nietzsche leaves Basel in 1879, he is thirty-five. When Juan de la Cruz is seized by the Calced Carmelites of Toledo, he, too, is thirty-five. At thirty-five, hope remains. At thirty-five, the nervous system is still actively producing hope; it can still emanate and sustain that most bewitching mirage: the future. But as Eckhart begins in Avignon to grasp the reversal which has descended upon him—as he starts adding up the appalling sums and magnitudes of his ruin—he is nearly seventy, the age, for those still living, of honor and rest. But now for him there is just the perception that as far as the eye can see, he is cast out and alone. What can he do other than let himself by swallowed up by the fact—the Eckhart-defining fact—that he is lost?

⁓⁓⁓

I HAVE PUT ON PAPER SOMETHING of the circumstances and the psychology, but not yet even alluded to that singular deprivation which forms the desolate center and explains the special character of the sufferings of Nietzsche, Eckhart, and the man born Juan de Yepes. For the three share a susceptibility to a particular anguish; that center is a unique experience—the ecstatic's unique experience—of loss and aban-

184 ⑨ *Ways in Mystery*

donment. To approach it, we must first understand what up to now has sustained, nourished, and quickened these "ascetics." We must know what they—what their spirits—have lived on. For all three, that life-giving sustenance has been the same thing. It is nothing in "the world," nothing they can comprehend or seem to name as they seemingly name other things. It has been, rather, the experience—the *mystery*—which is enacted when boundless and unsayable reality, unmediated by any figure, symbol, or form, directly touches or just brushes against that most subtle and complex nerve-end we call consciousness. That supreme reality contains within itself unlimited energy, unfathomable calm, infinite life. Consciousness' immediate contact with it—that nerve-firing, that inflaming "touch"—has, "in the world," one great likeness and hieroglyph: the first intoxicating scent interminglings, the first touch, of lovers. For the timeless instant during which bare consciousness directly touches boundless and unsayable reality always seems like that very first unrepeatable touch. It is—always—an ecstatic touching of something unlimited, something inexhaustible, something infinitely desirable and infinitely unknown.

For Eckhart and Juan de Yepes, the most characteristic syllables they will use to gesture towards that name-transcending reality—*deus, Gott, die Gottheit, Dios*—are a given, yet such is their alertness to the distinction between reality and words that their use of these terms is never as purely habitual, as oblivious, as our sleepy use of the syllables *you* and *I*, of the mysterious syllables *English*. For Nietzsche, who settles on *die Ewigkeit* ("eternity") as he attempts to put into words his ecstatic encounter of 1881, the selection is more deliberate, but for all that not necessarily less arbitrary. In spite of such verbal differences, all three agree—monkishly, ascetically—on the conditions which make that indispensable quickening touch possible. One must have severed all ties and turned away from the world in Eckhartian *Abgeschiedenheit*—that is, withdrawnness, or separatedness—or climbed "6000 Fuss" above that world, or deeming everything in the world as "finished," one must attend just to "holy solitude" (*CW*, 664, 673). When a state of aloneness has been achieved, the self must then itself be emptied of whatever worldly contents remain. Eckhart writes that soul must become bare, or just "nothing," Juan de la Cruz that all soul's "natural activity" must be halted. The latter's wonderful image for this cessation is the "stilled" house evoked at the beginning of his most famous poem.

The stilling of one's house requires the quiescence of the "sensory part," of the memory—that is, any particular awareness of events, persons, and things both "worldly" and religious—and of the will. It requires as well the arrest of the "intellect," particularly the liberation of consciousness from its confinement within all those dominant conceptual and metaphorical verbal perceivings which seem to disclose to us "where we are" and "how things are." For those crucial sentences—those verbal specifyings—divide, limit, parcel out, diminish, and falsify boundless and unsayable reality. By their mere presence —by covering, by clothing, both consciousness and reality—they prevent direct contact, the touch. "While the intellect is understanding," writes Juan de Yepes, "it is not approaching God, but withdrawing from Him." To reach Him, it consequently must be empty of both "natural" and "spiritual" knowledge" (*CW*, 628). Eckhart writes that one must know nothing "either about God, or the created world, or oneself" (*DPT*, 306). To reach the heights and that glorious, shadowless meridian hour, Zarathustra has had to climb above the zone of words and conventional knowledge. Henceforth he will not speak, for all words lie, but rather sing out the "bird-wisdom" of his ecstatic flight (*Z*, 257).

After one's house is stilled, and then perhaps also after a time of waiting in "holy idleness," a miraculous event or transformation—or rather something simply indescribable—takes place. Juan de la Cruz writes that soul no longer experiences things "after a human and natural manner," and that it passes from being "human" to being "Divine," Eckhart that one is no longer in the "before and after" of moving, segmented time. The ecstatic Frater Fredericus of August 1881—"6000 feet beyond humanity and time"—combines both great transcendings. More vividly: that event is the marriage—the touch, the mating—of soul and God, of naked consciousness and naked reality. The poems and commentaries of Juan de Yepes lovingly unfold the evolving particulars of this rapturous, painfully awaited union. The climax of Nietzsche's most famous work is Zarathustra's fervid declaration of love to eternity, a declaration made all the more moving by its directness and unembarrassed simplicity. Eckhart's favorite image is not the generative act which begins, but rather the parturition which completes, the mystery of creation. For when the "I" which inhabits space and time is dissolved, all that remains is unsayable, undivided, uncontained reality, that is, "God," and God's timeless "work" is: to give birth to the Son, to create the world. So it is that the unknown something which no longer is "Eckhart" can say, having reappropriated that old pronoun, that "I" act together with God in all his works, that the soul gives birth to God, and that "I" am "the cause of myself and of all things" —"if I were not, neither would 'God' be" (*DPT*, 402, 399, 308).

At less rapturous times—when Zarathustra's shadowless high noon has been succeeded by Fray Juan's dark night—what is then the "particular anguish" of these three ascetics? They have struck off on that narrow path where one gives up everything else for one compelling goal: to perceive, experience, and abide in the truly real. And it has been granted them to experience the bare touch of unsayable reality— of *This*—in that partial and fleeting way which is all that is possible. Since the touch is outside time, description, and specification, it cannot be recalled, but it is the divine food, the manna, which quickens soul, providing energy for the new life of contemplation, devotion, and action which grows up around that touch. The attainment of that touch and that life is difficult in the best of circumstances. It requires the stilled house, a stilled world, the most carefully prepared consciousness, a patient waiting, "holy idleness." From all the perspectives of common sense, reason, and common experience, the following must be clear: nothing is as destructive of the touch and that new life forming around it—nothing drags consciousness back into time and "the world," nothing compels us so immediately and irresistibly to become, once again, merely "human"—as the sufferings of both flesh and spirit.

As a result, when suffering overtakes them, the three monks are doubly bereft, doubly mere wilderness. For on the one hand they have discarded all the connections and supports to which others can turn when they suffer. In times of suffering the non-ascetic finds comfort with family and friends, and in familiar activities. We "naturally" redirect will and intellect towards overcoming the suffering. We who have not "gone beyond" words can take refuge in verbal perceptions of all kinds: sentences which assure us that our suffering will soon pass, or that we are "right" or being unjustly treated; autobiographical sentences which make it clear that we should in fact be content, even pleased, with our situation and ourselves; theological and philosophical sentences which place our suddenly less significant sufferings within a greater and on the whole gratifying picture of life and the world, of "how things are." But as an essential element of their program, these ascetics have broken their connections with the world —Nietzsche and

Juan de Yepes in particular often evoke this isolation, this very personal *Abgeschiedenheit*. And what is perhaps even more hazardous: they have "broken" with words, with the old life's comprehendings by means of verbal signs. In their new lucidity, they are far from all verbal "support." They no longer have any specifiable verbal or conceptual place where they might stand, and they can no longer shelter consciousness within humankind's handy, quickly assembled word-shelters and refuges, our never-ending justifications, defenses, excuses, and rationales. As a result, consciousness in them is now exposed, naked, to suffering as it was once exposed, voluptuously, to *Ewigkeit*, or to "God."

And on the other hand: having been dragged back into their "humanity" by suffering, they have been uprooted—have been torn—from that touch and new life for which they have abandoned all else. For where is the "beloved" now, where just the slightest *sign* of the beloved? As he awaits the next bite of the whip, how oblivious is Juan de la Cruz to the "sensory part"? And how can his house be "stilled" now that his situation clearly demands the exact opposite: that he exert all his faculties—his entire "human" repertoire—to endure his suffering and achieve, if possible, his escape? After days of wrenching nausea and migraine, how can Frater Fredericus pretend to be far above "humanity and time"? As in Avignon the bare outline of the cataclysmic reversal which is overwhelming him begins to disclose itself—as he sees, more and more, just an old man being swept aside by suddenly monstrous great powers—how can Eckhart persist in the unavailing and outlandish fantasy that in him, timelessly, God is making the world?

So that he might find and at last disappear into God, the Indian *sādhu* renounces all worldly reality, identity, and function; henceforth, he will have no caste, family, home, or possessions, and from a legal perspective he will be "dead." Varenne writes that for the most part these *sādhus* wander about "wretched and half-starved," and that "the vast majority of them succumb to malnutrition and disease in a very short time" (Varenne 1976, 96). That mystery we call fate, or God, or character—or shall we just say their own abysmal blunder?—brings them at last to a desolate dying-place by the roadside. As for the three ascetics of whom I write, suffering drags them back into a place which, figuratively and spiritually, is just as desolate: "the world." Their peculiar helplessness is the helplessness of one who has renounced worldly support and functions, but worse still it is the appalling and seemingly irremediable desolation which all day fills that room in Toledo, in Genoa, in Avignon. That desolation is the absence of "the beloved," indeed the seeming *non-existence* of that beloved. For as we have seen: suffering, by throwing one's "house" into chaos, prevents the touch, and so dissolves that new life which emerges from it as animal life emerges from food. And as we also have seen: the touch, which even as it is experienced cannot be "fixed" in words or images, clearly cannot be "retained" or "recalled" by memory. In those rooms, the other world of God and eternity—of "the Immutable and the Incomprehensible"—no longer exists. All that *is* is the world grasped by the senses and by words, the world of pain. For that mere "human being" they now once again are, there is no "beloved." They have nothing which shows that a "beloved" has ever *been*.

Drawn back into the world and time, they react as the individuals they once again have become. Fray Juan's response is to resuscitate as best he can that old "human nature" whose death he had sought. By returning to the ways of his former, and now insipid, life, by re-animating will, memory, and intellect, by committing himself unconditionally to hope and desire, and to observing, considering, calculating, deciding, planning, and acting as shrewdly and capably as he can, he is doing the one thing which might enable him to return to the life of annihilating the intellect and will, the life free of calculation, decision, and shrewdness. He unreservedly takes on the particular person and human life of Juan de Yepes so that he might soon cast them off again and just be "soul." He backtracks from God—he descends and dismounts the "ladder"—so that he might someday reascend to God. In all this, wonderfully, he will succeed, but Nietzsche, on the other hand, is doomed; time, inexorably, is against him. After 1881, his threefold disintegration continues, and the quickening effect of that year's experience, seldom if ever repeated, inevitably fades. The urgency of his great and unrealizable mission—to definitively fix *This* in words, to formulate "Zarathustra's" philosophy-completing philosophy—confines him within words and sentences he knows cannot disclose the fullness of the world. He works—he holds out, he endures —comforting himself more and more, as the memories of his and Zarathustra's high-noons outside time dissolve, with fantasies about his role in those peculiar, all-too-temporal, and still more evanescent nineteenth century dreams: "the future," "history."

Unlike John of the Cross, Eckhart in Avignon has no conceivable future—to what escape, what returns, what new life, might he now

aspire? Unlike Nietzsche, he does not even see beckoning the sometimes alluring false-sunrise of madness, for Avignon is a place—such
is the roadside to which fate has brought this pitiable *sādhu*—of unwavering, undiverted, terrible lucidity. Like any *sādhu*, Eckhart has
renounced all worldly identity and reality, having ceded everything—
livelihood, will, status, the form and contents of his days and nights—
to the Church which now is casting him out. The exigencies of his
"defense" have dragged him back into the world of will, memory, and
intellect, of desire and words. He is no longer in the "still desert of
the Godhead." He has no clear recollection of ever *being* there, no
experience or even specific recollection of "contact." All he perceives
is that he is in "Avignon," that there is no escape or remedy to either
desire or plan, that he can do nothing to avert or even affect the bitter
casting out which now is taking place. Sheltered within the splendid,
intolerable privacy of madness, Nietzsche experiences at the end the
parodistic fulfillment of all his wishes. In Turin he, like Fray Juan's
perfected soul, becomes "divine." When he is brought for the first time
to the clinic in Jena, it seems to him that—wherever he is—he is being welcomed just as a god *should* be welcomed, and so the great blissful
Yea-sayer, profoundly moved, grandly thanks his astonished psychia-
trists for the "splendid reception." But in Avignon—where, as if in a
total eclipse, "the world" has blotted out God—all Eckhart can do is
use words and his old human faculties in an attempt to begin understanding the dark and inane mechanisms of his defeat. To be conscious,
henceforth, is to be an old man, a would-be philosopher and theologian and knower of God, tracing out the bare outline—it alone is clearly
visible—of his ruin. Must not the constant weight of this contemplation eventually press out of his soul a despairing, a weary, a most un-
Eckhartian and un-Nietzschean and untheological "No"?

---

FOR SOME THE PROPER NOUN 'AVIGNON' evokes the so-called second
Babylonian captivity, the Curia Romana's eighty year domicile "beyond" the Alps; it evokes that curious and spectral politics which collects
on the surface of the mysterious life of soul. But for me Avignon is
Eckhart in Avignon. Perhaps I best honor him —best honor that
mystery I have reduced to "Eckhart," and which Eckhart on his daily
round too often reduces to something known, to "I"—just by acknowl-

edging that I do not know what happens to Eckhart in Avignon. But I honor him as well (and perhaps thereby I will also learn to make my own way through *This* somewhat less unsteadily, and may become more alert, may be enabled, if only slightly, to *see* more) by asking over and over again during the interstices of the day and when I awaken at night, "What happens to Eckhart in Avignon?" Or better, "What does Eckhart experience and do in Avignon?" Or again, "In Avignon Eckhart disappears from view. But into what?"

I have written that from the perspective of reason, common sense, and common experience, the effects of suffering must be: to disrupt the ascetic's way; to deprive soul of that divine contact—the touch—which is the catalyst and food of soul's new life; to clothe consciousness once again in that sensory and verbal world it has abandoned, and within which it now is helpless and out of place. But from another perspective, one outside "the world"—outside all words, reason, and "human" experience—Juan de la Cruz writes, "To arrive at all, desire to be nothing," and Eckhart himself observes that *Abgeschiedenheit* does not desire to be this or that, but "nothing" (*CW*, 67; *Ab*, 540). This means—this seems to mean—that the events of Avignon mesh with and serve "the way." They can do so precisely because they quickly reduce Eckhart to being, from all worldly perspectives, that desirable nothingness.

How in fact can Eckhart, Juan de la Cruz, and Nietzsche—how in fact can you and I—get through suffering? How can we find our way through to its other side, where once again there is strength, that is, the unhindered overflow of inner life and *energeia* into action, and where there is joy, soul's spontaneous delight in and "Yes" to *This*? Reduced to near nothingness, so that we may even have begun to eye curiously that last most sad "No," that final turning-away, we customarily seek to outlast suffering by turning to particular persons, things, conditions, and sentences, to what we can see, touch, hold, name, know, and believe, to "the world." But that loved woman or man, that community of friends, those familiar enjoyments, hopes, and achievings, those intimate, tightly clasped sentences about "me" and about "the world"—aren't they all secondary occasions and vehicles, rather than primary and original *sources* of comfort, strength, and joy? Must not there first of all be something in *us*—the unwavering flame of life burning in its mysterious and nameless stillness deep within—which first impels us to seek comfort and support? And without this occult inner fire, will not those loved ones, attainments, prospects, and sentences be as insignificant, as spectral, as they are for one who—surfeited, mortally weary, and admitting now even to herself that she is tired of these faces, these places, these sights and sounds, these thoughts—calmly and irrevocably turns away? That inner flame, that stubbornly flowing stream of life, comes first, and everything in "the world" is dependent upon it. But upon what does it depend? What is *its* source?

Of the two mysteries we now confront, the first is the mystery of strength, of the capacity to endure, to act, to be. The source from which it flows does not lie within the world, within the realm of things seen, heard, touched, named, and thought. Only those who have fallen out of the world, out of the "mutable and comprehensible," reach it. What is the supreme archetypal manifestation of strength and power? It is that timeless "event" which continually preoccupies Eckhart: the making or arising of all that is: of ourselves, the world, gods, God. It is the mind-breaking coming-to-be, the *being*, of *This*. Whence arises this "matter" and "energy," this "matter" and "spirit," all these material and human and divine worlds? Out of "nothing." And what is the context— the description, the explanation, the logic—of this event? There can be none, for each such description or explanation begs the question by beginning, not with "nothing," but with "something" material or divine. Instead, and finally, everything hinges on—everything can be traced back to—a contextless pure act, an "event" which has no description, explanation, rationale, justification, or "logic," an act which, since it is preceded by "nothing," is not preceded by a cause, or "conditions," or by deliberation or decision, or by the clear perception that the act is justified or unjustified, right or wrong, or by anything that can be said or thought. In the critical moment of pure happening, there are no thoughts or sentences, for that happening is itself the coming to be, among other things, of all thoughts and sentences. That act— that unthinkable crossing—is the pattern of all acts. All our acts, all our manifestations of strength, participate, however feebly, in it. When Eckhart passes outside the world and all contexts, when he reverses the process which produced the creature of space and time "Eckhart," he returns to that source. He is present at the mind-breaking beginning. He is within—he *is*—that "doing," that indescribable *Werk*.

The second mystery, as enigmatic as the first, is the source of joy, of that overflow which spontaneously says "Yes!" rather than "No," and which at once dissolves all thoughts of turning away from *This*. Nothing is more insubstantial and unpredictable than feeling; nothing rules human beings so easily, casually, and inexorably as does "mood"— first master the secrets of conferring immortality and of creating universes and gods, and only then are you ready to attempt the great work: to dissolve desolation, to put joy in a heart in which there is no joy. That airiest of things—mood—rules us, because it is the first manifestation of consciousness as it flows out of nothingness; consequently, consciousness can never get *behind* mood in order to comprehend or control it. Mood, which precedes all acts and "thoughts," is the elusive, all-important, consciousness-pervading taste, aroma, and color of *This*, soul's spontaneous and fateful "Yes!" or "No" to what is.

We customarily seek to manipulate mood by proceeding—again indirectly—through "the world." But here, too: the face or touch of someone we love, an intimately known path or beach, the goldfinch's bounding flight, an unstoppable Bach cadenza, a Borges sentence, walnut's summer smell, and that summer's warm, edgeless nights— none will give us joy if the beginnings of joy are not already within *us*. And here, too: unlike us, Eckhart does not turn towards the carriers and reflectors of joy, but seeks joy's primordial source. Unlike those who still inhabit "the world," he is able to reach it, for the first flowing of joy, just like the coming-to-be of *This*, takes place in that other reality which lies outside "the world" and outside "understanding." This joy, just like the unimaginable great work of creation, precedes all words and comprehendings. If joy depends on words and comprehension, if joy cannot *be* until it has been confirmed that joy is called for, or reasonable, or acceptable, or *understood*, if joy must wait until there is *logic* of joy, joy—just like the world and Bach and the goldfinch and you and I—will never be. The original joy whose arising and first outflow occur in a place outside and more real than "the world" is in fact intimately related to that other event, that pure happening, which has as its context "nothingness," for that first joy is the offspring and reflection of that coming-to-be, of that greatest of all acts, in consciousness. We can picture it as the delight of the gods at what they have made. We can picture it as Shiva and Shakti's shared delight. Insofar as we still are "you" or "I" or "Eckhart," this joy is consciousness' intoxicating inhalation of that coming-to-be, of inexhaustible and uncontained *being*, of Shiva-Shakti, of God. It is the invasion of lesser and sayable reality—of those perceivings we call "the world"—by greater and unsayable reality. Insofar as we no longer *are* "you" and "I," it is the joy of being that coming-to-be, of not being *other* than uncontained and unsayable reality. Soul which has clothed itself in its particular being and name and comprehendings—which has sealed itself off in the little shell we call "the world"—cannot reach that place in the boundlessness outside the world where these two springs flow. But what compels Eckhart in Avignon to clothe himself in this way? What prevents him from finding his way back out of time and place—out of "1328" and "Avignon"—to those remote and uncharted places where both strength and joy are born?

~~~~~~

MIRACLES—THAT HANDFUL OF EVENTS we are alert enough to identify as miracles—are unforeseeable, anomalous, illogical. If there were no miracles, or if there were nothing at all—that is a state of affairs one could understand. Nor can those miracles which actually occur be awaited or desired, for it belongs to the very nature of miracles that we never suspect in advance what any miracle will be. The unexpected and miraculous transformation which now takes place in Avignon— which I see taking place in Avignon—is accomplished quickly, almost as swiftly as Zen's instantaneous enlightenment, for one afternoon the tiny seed appears and already by the next afternoon it has attained perfect fruition. I see (perhaps I see all this now because I now need to marshall Eckhart alongside Irvin and Dad, or because I myself am searching for that aboriginal outflowing of strength and joy whose place is the country on the other side of all human and divine names) that up until the time of Eckhart's miraculous remaking, his consistent endeavor since Virneburg set this nightmare in motion has been to defend and justify himself, and in the end to emerge unscathed and even triumphant as what he has long been: the much loved and admired and celebrated "Meister Eckhart." What is the outcome of this approach? In Avignon its absolute failure has slowly become plain. In the undivided and unrelieved lucidity of Avignon, Eckhart's consciousness is now fixed in—now simply *is*—the intolerable and unchanging syllables "I am lost."

During that twenty-four hour period the unanticipated change, the "miracle," simply *happens*. We can't say—the so-called inner world, like the outer, requires words and distinctions we have not yet dreamed—that he lets "Eckhart" go, or contrarily that "Eckhart" is taken away. All I see is that "Eckhart" is vanishing. But the miracle is not simply the fact that this unforeseen transformation takes place. What overwhelms Eckhart—overwhelms that something which once seemed to be "Eckhart"—is that it takes place exactly as he has described it hundreds of times in his sermons: as soon as soul is emptied of everything that has to do with the "I," God will immediately enter, and in that soul—in the innermost secret depths of that soul, hidden from both words and time— will create the world. The miracle—can it be that in his own "innermost depths" the preacher has not truly believed his own words?—is that he was right, that his descriptions of that paradoxical and even impossible-sounding event were, miraculously, entirely true.

Eckhart's subsequent perceptions, feelings, and actions have little to do with—and may even be said to be contrary to —reason and the obvious facts of his situation. But having taken note of that fact, let us balance it with the following: reason and that ghost called "the obvious" have little to do with reality, and knowing "how things are" and "how to be" in Avignon is the most secure and confining prison in Avignon. As Eckhart moves through the streets of Avignon—as others dream they see "Eckhart" in the streets of "Avignon"—he is not that Eckhart who does and knows and has achieved this or that, who one day is "born" and another "dies," for "he," now, is just that event outside time which is the making, the undivided coming-to-be of *This*. He is the joy and delectation of that event, is the original astonishment and joy of being, of the inexplicable and immeasurable *act* of being. He is that joy which—all theologians want to say—is the true heart of all things. He is the joy which one day appears in "nothing," and which in that very first moment is even more out of place, more adventitious, more singular and unprecedented, more *unheard of* than it would be right now.

After a few days—for even the gods are fascinated by the hazardous and ambiguous dream-concreteness of the particular—the old Eckhart, "little" Eckhart, returns, and begins to move around within the new "big" Eckhart, the "Eckhart" who transcends all pronouns and names. Within big Eckhart—within the supreme event and delight and horizonless lucidity Eckhart has become—little Eckhart moves unhesitatingly through Avignon. He *is* a particular feeling, or phrase, or act, for as long as that feeling or phrase or act lasts, then lets it go and forgets it, as the warm, grainy, sun-filled river of the plains has forgotten the mountain stream. To gauge the metamorphosis which has taken place, Eckhart often recalls the following. Before the miracle, his entire awareness was contained in and molded by the terrible words "I am lost." Now that sentence is a faint silhouette, a bird which now and then passes through remote regions of consciousness. It comes and goes, alone or in a great darting and leaping flock, like any other bird or sentence or fish, like all events, all created and natural "things."

If he chooses, Eckhart can persist in his futile defense —what does that futility matter? He can ask for mercy or menial assignments like those of a novice, join the Beghards, or wander, begging, in or far from Avignon. Whatever that mystery consisting of big and little Eckhart might do, "it" will perform that action as the greatest and most solemn of ceremonies, as the enactment of that event all acts secretly echo and iterate: the making, the miraculous coming-to-be, of *This*. On April 16, 1328, early, Eckhart knows that the sunlit fields, woods, and waysides will be green and wet. He walks past the papal palace with its unimposing twin towers, past the new palace of the curial marshal, where that afternoon the commission will announce its judgment on "Eckhart," past the city gate.

They *are* green and wet. The Eckharts, both cheerful, walk on. The sun still ascends. At a way-crossing far from Avignon stands a single beech. The former student, then teacher, and then twice-called *magister sacrae theologiae* at the Sorbonne recalls the dense beech woods near Paris, their dim, deeply shaded, wonderfully cathedral-like interiors, above all the gracefully undulant silver-gray trunks. Those trunks are free of branches to a great height. It is as if they have been given smooth skin instead of bark, so that they might seem naked just as soul should be naked before God, before that alone which is real. This solitary, open-grown beech ramifies quickly, branching out into a broad, full crown. Its young springtime leaves—and the leaves of beech are always surprisingly small, anyway—could use some encouragement.

At the end of his sermon on the text Matthew 10:28—"And fear not them which kill the body, but are not able to kill the soul"—Eckhart, monk in the Order of Preachers, says that if no one were present, he would have no choice but to preach to the collection-box. At the time, in that convent near Strasbourg, both Eckhart and the nuns are gladdened and uplifted by this expression. Now it, just like that other assertion, turns out to be true. Little Eckhart has not preached for almost two years. Within the unbroken and edgeless quiescence he now is, big Eckhart has never seen or heard little Eckhart preach. The beech is no collection-box, but it will do. Only the first two or three words are difficult. Then Eckhart begins to preach to it of *Abgeschie-denheit*, of Mary and Martha, of the birth of God in the soul, of divine comfort, and of that indefinable and ultimate consanguinity, that shining unbrokenness which is so sadly masked by the superficial dualities "I" and "the world," "I" and "God," "I" and "*This*."

The three mushroom hunters, two women and a young girl, slow down as they approach, then finally stop. It is an open question whether or not the monk has noticed them. The incomprehensible sounds he is making must be the way people speak somewhere else. They have never seen a monk talking, most contentedly or in any other way, to a tree; yet their impression is that he is the very opposite—they have no word for that "opposite"—of crazy.

At one point it occurs to them to sit down, but they remain standing. No sermon they have ever heard has held their attention as does this one. It is possible, and may in fact be the greatest gift given to us, to be aware of something without having words to name or think it. Perhaps just because the scene is so unusual, and also because they cannot enter the passing sense of these particular sounds, all three now are alert as they never have been before or will be again to the mysterious, finally unsayable essence of speech. Once or twice the girl thinks—and from now until *her* dying day she will never forget, or be able to fully explain or comprehend the thought: "As he speaks, that glad monk is making the world." They could not say how long they have listened, but at last the two women move on, and the girl follows. All three turn when the voice unexpectedly stops, and then begin to walk back towards the prone figure. Some time later, a man, fetched by the girl, returns with the ox and cart. All four turn homewards, having lifted onto the cart the Eckhart you can see and hear and lift and remember, the one that just died, the little one.

---

To refresh my memory while writing, I have made use of the biographical information furnished by Baeumler, Kavanaugh, Quint, and Wehr. As extended biographies, Brennan's life of John of the Cross, and *Der ängstliche Adler* (*The Anxious Eagle*), a Nietzsche biography by Werner Ross, are particularly valuable.

# EPILOGUE
# THE TREE

IN THE EARLY MORNING I WALK BEFORE WRIT-
ing, a short meditation-walk that takes me each day along the same
path to the walnut tree where I turn. Its agenda formed quickly ten
years ago when I began writing. During the first half of the walk, I would
take note of my physical surroundings: road, fields, wooded hillsides,
dark winter or illuminated summer sky, the flight, cries, and songs of
the birds. Then, attempting to overcome both time and my own dullness, I tried to be as alertly and intimately aware—as *present* —as I
could possibly be at that unpredictable yet certain future event: my
death. Third and last, I reminded myself of the mystery of existence
and tried to enter into that mystery by asking myself to explain how
the world—how all this—can be. Like other meditators, I soon found
that the conscious mind resists control and reformation. My attention often was diverted or simply strayed, seeming to prefer even the
most gratuitous and banal subjects. At times I was inclined to rebuke
myself for not being able to control my thoughts, or for not being up
to my noble themes. Instead I should have considered the tree.

As Eve knew in the Garden, as Gautama Buddha realized one day
under a pipal tree, as the young Vedāntin Śaṅkara dreamed perfectly
in October's unstirred and infinite heat, there is something primal,
something perhaps even beginningless, about error. Nor is religious

consciousness—consciousness that makes its home in the edgeless mystery which enfolds our delicate and chameleon certainties—immune. I have just pointed toward one example of such error: We often approach practices such as meditation, prayer, or contemplation, and the entire process of inner transformation to which such practices belong, with paradigms, assumptions, and expectations acquired elsewhere. In just one instant I can turn 180 degrees and become a homeowner, husband, or monk. In one moment "everything" can seem to fall apart; within the minuscule spaces of a single moment, someday, I shall die. In that limited realm that is the place, or the dreamed stage, of our sensory and verbal knowings—that is, in "the world"—instantaneous or rapid transformations, many of which we seem to initiate and control, are commonplace. But if there are "instants" and "time" and the "you" and "I" who together make "we" in that other infinitely greater realm, they are of an entirely different kind. In those broader and more unspecifiable, those paradoxically denser and more nourishing spaces, our accustomed paradigms are alien, groundless, easily counterproductive. To contemplate the alchemies that can and do take place in mystical life and awareness, we require different paradigms—images and archetypes of a very particular kind. They will have their source in processes or transformations that occur naturally in "the world," but that seem to have come from somewhere else, so that it is as if they have been placed here just to serve as images or archetypes of that other life which has gone "beyond." What might we take as an example of such archetypal transformation? The slow, unstudied, unperceived, unconscious, silent, unstoppable, tranquil, *hidden* growth of the trunk of a great tree.

In part, all life is life along surfaces. On and among them life is boundless multiplicity turning in mutability's protean swirl. As variable as sea surface forever tuning itself, restlessly, unavailingly, to some eternal unalterable *om,* or the vast foliage that forms the surface of a mature oak that is storm-thrown or rocks gently in the breeze, or in intervals of stillness barely stirs. From dawn to mid-afternoon to midnight the tree's aura changes dramatically, as does its appearance from winter to summer. All this is surface. The tree's enduring reality, its *substance,* is all in the trunk's dense heartwood and in the cool, moist densities of the large sapwood ring that surrounds the heart— the oak's variously ridged and fissured bark hides both from view. The trunk's interior is the focal point of the tree's story and life, *the* place of transformation. Here, unseen and uninstructed, newly made cell is laid down next to cell, summerwood to springwood, ring to annual ring. If we could observe it, we might become exasperated by the unearthly calm suffusing this snaillike proceeding, by the tree's mute, seemingly motionless perfect contentment—these rhythms are not ours. Yet it is here in this quietness and this hiddenness, here in this otherworldly repose remote from all consciousness and even from all "instinct," that genuine transformation—true *happening*—takes place. It is here that the five-inch seedling, almost nothing but leaf, becomes, slowly and unawares, the great tree.

While this transmutation takes place, the tree's surface events remain much the same. The appearance and life story of the seedling's relatively gargantuan leaf and of the anonymous last leaf to fall centuries later from the moribund giant, are perhaps not even distinguishable. Responses to the breezes, storms, and seasons; its annual leafing out; flowering and seed production; the complex processes of photosynthesis; the annual leaf-fall leaving buds to await patiently their one spring—these frequently iterated surface events soon become routine. The surface, in other words, is the site of limited or merely apparent change; the genuine alchemy is elsewhere.

So perhaps it is with soul, with that in us which, unpersuaded by "the world," dwells or seeks to dwell in mystery. It lives among surfaces, but also grows slowly and imperceptibly—let us hope—in untroubled interiors it may not know. I walk and "meditate" and "reflect." At my table in the mornings, I slowly accumulate, test, organize, replace, and join together the words that constitute these essays. You perhaps read them, perhaps ponder them. All these are conscious events on soul's surface. My close attending during my morning walk or my disconcerting failure to attend to the hawk perched at the forest's edge, or to my future death, or to the inexhaustible mystery hidden within the innocuous syllable *is*; the unfolding or branching of one theme and the withering of another; the instantaneous gift of two propositions, and hours straining to create from nothing a third that will connect them; the sudden broad grin of inconsistency; interminable searching, fitting, readjusting, approving, and abandoning of ideas and sentences; the perhaps illusory sense of completion, that what was to be said has been said, and the certainty or fear that it hasn't—more conscious events, more surface. Precisely because they *are* conscious events, erring consciousness spontaneously takes them to be the essence of soul's life. And because, paradoxically, they seem always the same—because, that is, after ten years there remains the same unending flow of sensory and verbal perceptions, the same effort just to attend, the same interminable negotiation with words—it is easy to conclude that "nothing has happened." Now, however, the arboreal comparison makes it possible and perhaps even legitimate to ask: In some remoteness to which consciousness has no direct access might something have happened, something like the imperceptible maturation of a tree?

These essays—products of those surface strivings, processings, and agitations—were written from 1988 to 1996, in a sequence close to the order of their appearance here. In optimistic moments I detect in them hints of transformation, in the following way: The later essays depend on the earlier ones, not as the steps of an argument or as succeeding generations of a family, but as a tree's outer rings, fractionally larger, depend on the previous laying down of those earlier, slightly smaller ones. In varying ways, all have as their theme mystery, that infinite matrix within which we dream "the world." They do not aim to process it or even to describe or name it in the usual way "things" are described or named. Instead they seek only to gesture toward it, to persuade it to allow us a passing glimpse of itself, to coax it to turn and look our way.

At the same time, there are differences, perhaps even growth. The first four essays might be called ways *into* mystery in the sense that they all begin with a particular something—a question, the present moment, the transcribed sermons of a fourteenth-century German monk, and a paradox—which then opens toward and into mystery. The last two might be called more aptly ways *in* mystery—for them mystery is the given, the paradoxically infinite "starting point." The overall movement of the essays toward the interior of mystery is suggested by the fact that the first one takes time as a given, and so portrays Meister Eckhart, for example, as having lived in the past. The final essay assumes the opposite; both it and the Eckhart it perceives inhabit an undivided, ever-present "now." Like the sounds *grain of sand* and the sound *hand*, the two syllables *reading* disguise a heterogeneous profusion—a world—of events and relationships. You alone can discern how this book's growth rings might relate to yours. You can find your particular way around in the book much better than I or anyone else can find it. In relation to you, therefore, these essays can have but one very general aspiration: to stir the foliage of your consciousness and then, instead of vanishing without trace, to be absorbed, processed, and quietly, secretly added—perhaps at the very time when it appears on the surface that they are being "forgotten"—as one or two new atoms, perhaps as one entire new cell, in the wood of the tree, of the mystery, you are.

The likening of soul's transformations to the hidden but certain growth of a tree—in many ways so pleasing, not least because it implies our own potential for growth—is, in another way, deeply troubling. Contemplating these essays, I may happily picture that soul in me has been growing as soul's archetype, the tree, grows. But to compare my arm with the wood in a great log or thick plank of white oak, or to recall that a redwood can lay on ring after broad ring for twenty centuries, is to begin a meditation on fragility and transience. The reflection deepens when we recall that the mystery to which soul seeks to adapt both awareness and life is without limit—to that infinity there can only be an infinite, and unending, awakening. Perhaps nature's best image of this is the bristlecone pine, which lays on microscopically tiny rings annually for 5,000 years, approaching 200 human generations. But it, too, is inadequate, finally, for its growth is limited in space and eventually comes to an end in time. We can only *imagine* the perfection of the soul-tree's uncontained awakening and transformation, as follows: The tree's unthinkable outer ring, inside which are infinitely numerous smaller rings accumulated through unimaginable eternities since the no-beginning, surrounds not just "the world" but also the limitless mystery that encloses the world.

The mystical tree that shows forth the awakening event in its totality will dwarf not just us but all the world's oaks and beeches, all its redwoods and bristlecone pines. It is a tree that has been growing forever, an infinite tree. Considered from these perspectives, we are seedlings or scrawny saplings thatcome into being and vanish again within the same second. We are given one fleeting moment of inchoate awareness during which we are teased from afar by the divine prospect of an eternally acquired, infinite awakening. During our one moment, during the pure irony of our one moment, we may be stirred at our most alert or even intoxicated by a dizzying scent of uncontained, unbroken wholeness; yet, sadly, we ourselves are the quintessence of— we *define*—the fugitive, the divided, the truncated, the incomplete.

Having now stated the comparison's troubling implication, and having also referred in these lines to time, to our transience and fragmentedness, and to that "certain future event: my death," I should add the following. The renowned Buddhist philosopher Nāgārjuna demonstrated that all our notions concerning the persons, things, and events we perceive in time and space are permeated throughout by contradictions, are senseless and consequently "empty." Plato concluded that when we think and talk in our accustomed way about what we see and experience, we are as women and men imprisoned and bound in a cave since infancy. Seeing the shadows of moving puppets cast on the cave wall by a fire, we, who have never seen or experienced anything else, regard those shadows as the world, as reality, as *This.* Śaṅkara held that consciousness's supreme beginningless error is to confuse "the world"—a dream that is finite, changeable, and amenable to verbal formulation—with reality, which is not.

Of course, my reading—my erratic and inefficient absorption—of their irreplaceable writings, like my meditations and reflections and my own daily writing (and for that matter, like all *their* contemplations, ideas, and teachings), is surface event, "foliage." And I have already acknowledged that I cannot look directly within toward that secret, less volatile place where something of genuine mass and substance, where in me some *real wood* might have been laid down. My hope that the essays show signs of growth is mere hope. But now the recollection of Nāgārjunaa, Plato, and Śaṅkara induces me to look one more time at soul's possible treelike growth. It prompts me to review yet again our "transience and fragmentedness," as well as that "certain future event: my death." And I am soon faced by seemingly incontrovertible evidence of real growth, evidence that casts everything in a new light. The source of this evidence is my morning walk.

In the last couple years its contents have been altered, not by deliberate choice but because something inside me—what could it have been other than new wood?—would not let me continue as before. Mesmerized by English sentences such as "I see a hawk," I once spontaneously dreamed the triple dream that the subject "I" performed the act of "seeing" the object "hawk." Now—less naïve, less "mesmerized" —I cannot. Now in my walk's first part there is just the unbroken subjectless/objectless oneness of the seeing event. I once concluded by contemplating the great mystery "is" contains; now, going further, I seek to let awareness pass out through all smelling, touching, seeing, hearing, and tasting events, out of all thinkings and sayings, out even through the verbal opposites "is" and "is not," so that only *This* remains.

In so doing, I have entered or awakened to a place remote from the verbal conception "my death." It is from outside that I then observe that purely linguistic phenomenon: the "certainty" of "my death." Within me a decade ago, consciousness yielded to the sentences "I am in the world" and "I now live, but one day will die" as sentences magically distilling pure reality, as unequivocal "fact." Now that hidden transformation and accumulation—that new wood—makes it impossible for consciousness in me to be captured by those sentences or any other. It allows me to regard them in only one way: as important illustrations of the particular way—one out of an infinite number of possible particular ways—in which English has divided, organized, and veiled *This*.

Within infinite mystery hovers—neither great nor small —the finite Englished world. It is subdivided in turn into "I" and "things," "I" and "the others," the "inner world" and "the world out there." For consciousness contained and organized by English—that is, for consciousness that inhabits "the world"—the perception "my certain future death" is an infallible—a dream-certain—perception. But insofar as awareness has emerged from such containment and organization, insofar as it, having awakened from its particularity and its name, and having itself become "unlimited," dwells in mystery, it is something that was not "born" a few years ago, something that will not "die" a few years or hours hence. Awareness that inhabits and is letting itself become mystery can only be one thing: the *bodhicitta*, that is, the unending "thought of enlightenment" which is the counterpart and remedy to beginningless error. Since here there is neither distinction nor number, awareness—"I"—cannot be anything other than uncontained, unbroken, unchanging, unspecifiable reality—can be only *This*. As certain as the fact that the manifold world's "Luther Askeland" will die is the fact that "I" cannot.

Of course, these very reportings, inferrings, and intimations of immortality—which reason from my walk-meditation's changes to the unseen presence of new wood and beyond—are themselves events in consciousness, surface events, rustlings that pass quickly through the tree's foliage. But in what tree? If I have awakened from being "Luther Askeland," if reality—if *This*—transcends all words and numbers, and if unity, as opposed to the chaotic profusion we usually postulate, has among numbers the flavor most like the taste of that mystical not-one, not-two-ness, then reality is Plotinus' "The One," is Śaṅkara's nameless, undivided, immutable, boundless *brahman*. Then a tree-meditation becomes a meditation on one tree, on "the" tree.

Oblivious without regret to future veilings of *This* as "the universe" or as "atoms in motion," our ancestors sometimes pictured reality in the form of a cosmic tree—that tree is the frame that contains and supports all things, and it is the supreme form or image of *This*. The motif appears in ancient China, in the Arctic, and around the Pacific. The Scandinavians placed particular realms—those of the gods, the giants, the fates, and of hell—in relation to the great tree Yggdrasil; as for earth, water thrown on Yggdrasil to nourish it falls on our plants as honeydew. Odin acquires his wisdom from Mimir's spring, which flows at its root. In the time of Ragnarok, when even the gods perish, it will tremble but not be brought down.

The Upanishads speak of a fig tree as the eternal support of all things. The five elements—earth, wind, fire, water, and space—are its branches. All the worlds rest on it; no one goes "beyond" it. Indeed, all things, mystically, *are* it. It, in turn, is *brahman*—is, as it were, undivided reality made visible to us in one living form. The last specifiable referent of the pronouns "I" and "you"—before they are freed from all limitation and allude to *This*—must be that great tree.

It follows that what we clumsily call "you" and "I" are events—mysteries—within the same being. The seemingly discrete events perceived by us as the writing and reading of these essays also can be known as a single integrated process: as the movement of a few atoms or molecules into or within a cell somewhere in one of the branches, perhaps even in the infinitely divisible densities of the great trunk. Further, since there is neither difference nor number, there obtains a perfect oneness of part and whole. That occult sylvan metabolism we once dreamed —in spite of its ultimate oneness—as the separate writing and reading of these essays is one microscopic event among untold others; at the same time, it contains and *is* the totality of this vast mystery event, of this undivided and boundless *happening*. "We" are the tree. "Ours" is that all-inclusive, that unthinkable because infinite outer ring. About us there is nothing fragmentary or momentary, just an unthinkable wholeness into which time and limitation have vanished. We near an eternal perfect lucidity transcending even the distinction between beginningless error and unending enlightenment. The thing—the trick—is just to awaken to what *This* is, to what "we" are.

# WORKS CITED

Aitken Roshi, Robert. 1987. "The Tail of the Buffalo." In *The Middle Way* 61:4.

*Bhagavad Gita*. 1964. Translated by Franklin Edgerton. New York: Harper & Row.

Brenan, Gerald. 1973. *Saint John of the Cross*. Cambridge: At the University Press.

Chang Chung-yuan. 1969. *Original Teachings of Ch'an Buddhism* (tranlation of selections from *The Transmission of the Lamp*). New York: Random House.

——————. 1975. *Tao: A New Way of Thinking* (translation of the *Tao Te Ching*). New York: Harper & Row.

*The Cloud of Unknowing and Other Works* (includes translation of Dionysius' *Mystical Theology*). 1961. Translated by Clifton Wolters. Hammondsworth, England: Penguin Books.

Conze, Edward. 1967. *Buddhist Thought in India*. Ann Arbor: University of Michigan Press.

——————. 1972. *Buddhist Wisdom Books* (translations of *The Diamond Sutra* and *The Heart Sutra*). New York: Harper & Row.

*The Diamond Sutra and the Sutra of Hui Neng*. 1969. Translated by A. F. Price and Wong Mou-Lam. Boulder: Shambhala.

Dumoulin, S.J., Heinrich. 1976. *Buddhism in the Modern World*. New York: Macmillan.

——————. 1969. *A History of Zen Buddhism*. Translated by Paul Peachey. Paul. Boston: Beacon Press.

Eckhart, Meister. 1979. *Deutsche Predigten und Traktate*. Diogenes.

——————. 1963. "Von Abgeschiedenheit." In *Die deutschen Werke*, vol. 5. Edited by J. Quint. Stuttgart: Die Deutsche Forschungsgemeinschaft.

Hammarskjold, Dag. 1964. *Markings*. Translated by Leif Sjoberg and M.H. Auden. New York: Knopf.

Huang Po. 1958. *The Zen Teaching of Huang Po*. Translated by John Blofeld. New York: Random House.

Hyers, Conrad. 1973. *Zen and the Comic Spirit*. Philadelphia: Westminster Press.

Johannes Scottus Eriugena. 1981. *Periphyseon,* Book III. Translated by I. P. Sheldon-Williams. Dublin: Dublin Institute for Advanced Studies.

John of the Cross, Saint. 1979. *The Collected Works of St. John of the Cross.* Translated by Kieran Kavanaugh, O.C.D. and Otilio Rodriguez, O.C.D. Washington, D.C.: ICS Publications.

——————. 1959. *Dark Night of the Soul.* Translated by E. Allison Peers. New York: Image Books.

Marlin, Lisa Lassell. 1987. "Embodied Truth, the Life and Presence of a Hindu Saint." *Harvard Divinity Bulletin* 17:2, 5-6.

Maurer, Armand A. 1962. *Medieval Philosophy.* New York: Random House.

Merton, Thomas. 1948. *The Seven Storey Mountain.* New York: Harcourt Brace.

Nietzsche, Friedrich. 1956. *Also Sprach Zarathustra.* Stuttgart: Alfred Kröner Verlag.

Pascal, Blaise. 1966. *Pensées.* Translated by A. J. Kreilsheimer. London: Penguin Books.

Plotinus. 1952. *The Six Enneads.* Translated by Stephen MacKenna and B. S. Page. (*Great Books of the Western World,* vol. 17.) Chicago: William Benton.

Reps, Paul. 1957. *Zen Flesh, Zen Bones.* Rutland, Vt.: Charles E. Tuttle Co.

*The Rig Veda: An Anthology.* 1981. Translated by Wendy Doniger O'Flaherty. London: Penguin Books.

Ross, Werner. 1980. *Der ängstliche Adler: Friedrich Nietzsches Leben.* Stuttgart: Deutsche Verlagsansalt.

Ruusbroec, Jan van. 1985. *John Ruusbroec: the Spiritual Espousals and Other Writings.* Translated by James A. Wiseman. New York: Paulist Press.

Scheffler, Johannes [Angelus Silesius]. 1960. *Der Cherubinische Wandersmann.* Munich: Wilhelm Goldmann Verlag.

Schelling, Friedrich Wilhelm Joseph. 1861. *Sämmtliche Werke, Erste Abtheilung,* vol. 8. Stuttgart and Augsburg: J.G. Cotta'scher Verlag.

Schumann, Hans Wolfgang. 1973. *Buddhism: An Outline of its Teachings and Schools.* Wheaton, Ill.: Theosophical Publishing House.

Thomas Aquinas, Saint. 1948. Edited by Anton C. Pegis. *Introduction to Saint Thomas Aquinas* (Selected Writings.) New York: Random House.

Varenne, Jean. 1976. *Yoga and the Hindu Tradition.* Translated by Derek Coltman. Chicago: University of Chicago Press.

Wittgenstein, Ludwig. 1922. *Tractatus Logico-Philosophicus.* London: Routledge & Kegan Paul.

Zimmer, Heinrich. 1969. *Philosophies of India.* Princeton: Princeton University Press.